THE QUICK RESUME AND COVER LETTER BOOK

by J. Michael Farr

JIST the job search people

Other Books by Mike Farr

Mike Farr's books on job seeking and career topics collectively have sold over one million copies. Here are some you are most likely to find in a bookstore or library:

- *The Very Quick Job Search*
- *The Quick Interview and Salary Negotiations Book*
- *America's Fastest Growing Jobs*
- *America's Top Jobs for College Graduates*
- *America's Top Office, Management and Sales Jobs*
- *Job Strategies for Professionals*
- *Getting the Job You Really Want*
- *See the last pages of this book for an order form that includes other books by Mike Farr and other books of interest from JIST.*

Errors and Omissions: We have been careful to provide accurate information in this book but it is possible that errors and omissions have been introduced. Please consider this in making any career plans or other important decisions. Trust your own judtment above all else and in all things.

JIST Works, Inc.
720 North Park Avenue
Indianapolis, IN 46202-3490
(317) 264-3720 or FAX (317) 264-3709

Library of Congress Cataloging-in-Publication Data

Farr, J. Michael.
The quick resume & cover letter book : write and use an effective
resume in only one day / by J. Michael farr.
     p. cm.
     ISBN 1-56370-141-3
     1. Resumes (Employment)   2. Cover Letters.   I. Title.   II. Title:
     The quick resume and cover letter book.
     HF5383.F32   1994
     808'.06665—dc20   94-15776
                                      CIP

ISBN 1-56370-141-3

C O N T E N T S

HOW TO USE THIS BOOK ....**VI**

FOREWORD ....**VII**

SECTION ONE: THE SAME DAY RESUME

This may be the only section of this book that you will need. It presents quick ways to create a good resume, along with tips on how best to use it to get a job in less time.

CHAPTER 1:   QUICK TIPS FOR CREATING AND USING A RESUME **3**

- ■ A resume is…
- ■ Some people say you don't need a resume
- ■ Some good reasons why you should have a resume
- ■ A big problem with resumes is that everyone is an expert
- ■ Resume basics
- ■ Types of resumes
- ■ "Send out your resume to lots of strangers…"

CHAPTER 2:   DO A SIMPLE RESUME IN ABOUT AN HOUR **15**

- ■ Chronological resume samples
- ■ Major sections of a chronological resume
- ■ The final draft

CHAPTER 3:   WRITE A SKILLS RESUME IN LESS THAN ONE DAY **33**

- ■ Sample skills resume
- ■ Constructing a skills resume
- ■ Tips to fine-tune your resume
- ■ Sample skills resumes and JIST cards

SECTION TWO: A MORE THOROUGH APPROACH TO RESUME WRITING (AND CAREER PLANNING)

Several of these chapters go well beyond what you need to know in order to write an acceptable resume. They are quite thorough and some of the activities will take a bit of time to complete. You may not need to review them all, but if you do, you will be much better prepared to do well in an interview than most people. And, of course, you will learn a few more things about producing a superior resume.

CHAPTER 4:   DEVELOP YOUR SKILLS "LANGUAGE" **61**

- The skills triad
- Identifying your skills
- The skills employers want

CHAPTER 5: DOCUMENT YOUR EXPERIENCE **71**
- Work and volunteer history worksheet
- Key accomplishments and skills to tell an employer

CHAPTER 6: BE CLEAR ABOUT YOUR JOB OBJECTIVE **89**
- Consider jobs within clusters of related occupations
- Values, preferences, and other matters to consider in defining your job objective
- writing your resume's job objective
- Job objective worksheet

CHAPTER 7: HOW TO HANDLE "PROBLEMS" ON YOUR RESUME AND OTHER MISCELLANEOUS MATTERS **113**
- Present any "problems" in an interview, not in your resume!
- Some problems are a sensitive subject
- First, some general guidelines for handling "problems"
- Tips for handling some specific problems on a resume

CHAPTER 8: PUTTING IT ALL TOGETHER **133**
- If you aren't good at this, have someone else do as much as possible
- What sort of resume will work best for you?
- Gather information and emphasize accomplishments, skills, and results
- Writing tips
- Tips to design your resume and improve its appearance
- Production tips and getting copies made
- Tips for using a computer to do your resume and other correspondence

• •

SECTION THREE: SAMPLE RESUMES

I've provided dozens of sample resumes in this section, all produced by professional resume writers. It is a wonderful and substantial collection of resumes using a variety of styles and designs. They are divided into these clusters: Education & Human Services; Office Jobs, Including Clerical; Technical, Scientific, & Specialty; Professional, Managerial, & Executive; Recent Graduates & Still in School; Marketing, Sales, Public Relations, & Retail; Career Changers, & Other Special Situations; Creative, Writing, & Media; Military to Civilian Transition.

• •

SECTION FOUR: COVER LETTERS AND OTHER JOB SEARCH CORRESPONDENCE

Presents how to write and, more important, how to use cover letters and other miscellaneous job search correspondence.

CHAPTER 9: WHEN AND HOW TO WRITE A GOOD

COVER LETTER **235**

■ The only two groups of people who will get your cover letters
■ Tips for superior cover letters

CHAPTER 10: OTHER CORRESPONDENCE, INCLUDING THANK-YOU NOTES—A POWERFUL AND OFTEN OVERLOOKED JOB SEARCH TOOL..**259**

■ Some tips on when to send thank-you notes—and why
■ Some tips for writing thank-you notes
■ More sample thank-you notes
■ Other job search correspondence

• •

SECTION FIVE: HOW TO GET A GOOD JOB IN LESS TIME

While this is a resume book, your interest in writing a resume probably exists only because you need or want to find a job. So this may be one of the most important sections of this book, since it presents the basic techniques required to get a good job in less time.

CHAPTER 11: SEVEN STEPS FOR GETTING THE JOB YOU WANT **277**

■ Changing jobs and careers is often healthy
■ Seven steps for a successful job search
■ Step 1: know your skills
■ Step 2: have a clear job objective
■ Step 3: know where and how to look
■ Step 4: spend at least 25 hours a week looking
■ Step 5: get two interviews a day
■ Step 6: you must do well in the interview
■ Step 7: follow up on all contacts

• •

APPENDICES

APPENDIX A: SAMPLE JOB DESCRIPTION FROM THE **OCCUPATIONAL OUTLOOK HANDBOOK** **301**

APPENDIX B: LIST OF CONTRIBUTORS **305**

v

How to Use This Book

I did not write this book for it to be read from cover to cover. Instead, I suggest that you browse, using only those sections that you need most or that interest you.

Since you obviously want to put together a resume, I have to assume that you are also looking for a job, or are thinking about doing so. That being the case, here is what I suggest as the way to best use this book:

1. **Read the table of Contents.** This will introduce you to the content of the book and its chapters.

2. **Read Chapter 1.** This will give you a quick overview of how to write a resume as well as some job search tips.

3. **Complete a basic resume as described in Chapters 2 and 3.** These chapters will show you how to put together a resume that will be just fine for most situations—in a matter of a few hours. You might also want to review the sample resumes in Section 3, to help you do your own.

4. **Begin looking for a job.** Once you have a basic resume together, read Chapter 11 for a review of self-directed job search techniques. These techniques can reduce the time it takes to find a job and there is no reason to delay your search.

5. **Do the activities in Section 2.** Besides being helpful in writing a good resume, this section provides activities and tips that will help you in planning your career, handling interviews, and in helping you get a better job than you might otherwise. You may find some chapters more important (for you) than others so, again, do what you think is best.

6. **If you really need to, and as time permits, write a "dynamite" resume.** While it will take you more time, you may want to revise your resume and create one that is, well, better. This book provides lots of good information and sample resumes that will help you.

There you are. I've written this book to help you over the resume hurdle. It will help you get a resume done quickly and go about the more important task of getting a job. I hope it helps.

FOREWORD

There must be a thousand or more resume books already published, so you might ask just why is there a need for yet another one. The answer is that most resume books misrepresent themselves. They typically argue that the way to get a good job is to:

1. Create an outstanding resume and
2. Put it in front of lots of people who have job openings.

But, if you take that advice (which seems reasonable enough), you will probably be making a big mistake.

The reason is that the logic is flawed. Those authors assume that you should conduct your job search in the traditional way by sending out lots of resumes to personnel offices or employers, in response to an available job opening. And they assume that the resume, if only done well enough, will help you stand out from the pile of resumes they have on their desk. It all seems to make sense from that point of view, *but the problem is that most of the labor market does not work this way anymore!*

The fact is that most jobs are now filled by people the employer knows *before* a job is ever publicly advertised. Even for the relatively few jobs that *are* advertised (and the research indicates that only about 15 percent to 25 percent are), half of *these* jobs are filled by someone who never read the ad. So, if you believe that the way to get a job is to send in your resume for an available job opening, you are missing out on most of the job opportunities that are out there. Most are *never* advertised, so sending in your "dynamite" resume in the conventional way will cause you to miss about 75 percent of the jobs—the ones that are never advertised at all.

You could, of course, send out your dynamite resume to lots of employers and hope for the best—and this has worked for some people. But I think that there is a better way and that is what this book is about. Since you obviously think you need a resume (and you probably do), then the thing to do is to get one together quickly. This approach avoids the all too common problem of taking a week or more to work on your resume before getting started on your job search. Then, as time permits, you can work on writing a better resume.

That is how this book is arranged. I have included in Section 1 directions for creating and using a resume in a matter of several hours. Section 2 provides a much more detailed approach that will help you sort out your skills, job objective, and other matters and provides a form of career counseling. This section will, of course, teach you much more about writing a good resume. Section 3 provides lots of sample resumes, many written by resume-writing professionals from across the country. Section 4 gives you information and examples for other job search correspondence such as cover letters and thank-you notes. And, finally, Section 5 gives you a quick review of job search methods that have been proven to cut the time it takes to get a job.

So this is a real resume book, and it will show you lots of things about resumes. Unlike most resume books, it will show you how to create a resume in stages, beginning with a simple one that you can write in about an hour all the way up to more sophisticated ones. You can decide which approach is right for you. But the real difference in this resume book is that I have spent over 20 years studying, teaching, and writing on job seeking skills, with an emphasis on techniques that work. For this reason, I do something that few resume books do—tell you the facts about what a resume can and can't do:

1. A resume will not get you a job, an interview can.

2. A resume is not a particularly good tool for getting interviews; direct contacts and leads given to you by those you already know—or can come to know—are far more important.

3. A good resume can help you in your job search, but many people get good jobs without using a resume at all.

4. A simple and error-free resume is a far more effective job search tool than an elegant one that you are working on while you should be out there getting interviews.

I hope you like the book and, more importantly, that it helps you get the job you want.

Best of "luck,"

Mike Farr

P.S. Please send me your resume and stories about how you got your job. I'd like to collect them for use in a future book.

However you produce them, it is important that you have plenty of them on hand to use as needed. Important job targets can get an individually typed resume and cover letter as needed.

USE GOOD PAPER

Good quality paper is important. Never use cheap paper like that typically used for photocopies. Most copy machines will copy onto heavy weight paper and you should make sure that you have a good supply. Most print shops have a selection of paper to choose from and you can often get matching envelopes. You can also buy quality paper at many office supply stores. While most resumes are on white paper, I prefer an off-white (ivory) paper. You could use other light pastel colors such as light tan or gray, but I do not recommend red, pink, or green tints.

Papers also come in different qualities and you can see the difference. Ones that include cotton fibers, for example, have a richer texture and feel that is appropriate for a professional-looking resume.

> **"***If you don't communicate what you can do, who will?***"**

USE ACTION WORDS AND STRESS ACCOMPLISHMENTS

Most resumes are boring. Don't simply list what your duties were, emphasize what you got done! Make sure that you mention the specific skills you have to do the job, as well as any accomplishments and credentials. Even a simple resume can include some of these elements, as you will soon see. Look over the list of "Action Words and Phrases" in this chapter for ideas as well as the sample resumes in Chapters 2 and 3 and in Section 3.

DON'T BE HUMBLE

Like an interview, your resume is no place to be humble. If you don't communicate what you can do, who will?

MAKE EVERY WORD COUNT

Write a long rough draft and then edit, edit, edit. If a word or phrase does not support your job objective, consider dropping it.

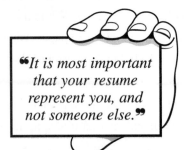

"It is most important that your resume represent you, and not someone else."

Quick Alert

WRITE IT YOURSELF

While I expect you to use ideas and even words or phrases you like from the sample resumes in this book, it is most important that your resume represent *you*, and not someone else. Present your own skills in your resume and support them with your own accomplishments. If you do not have good written communication skills, it is perfectly acceptable to get help from someone who does. Just make sure your resume ends up sounding like you wrote it.

Quick Reminder

BREAK SOME RULES

This will be *your* resume, so you can do whatever makes sense to you. There are few rules that can't be broken in putting together your own resume. In the rest of this and the next two chapters, you will learn about the types of resumes and see a few basic examples. While many additional details will follow throughout this book, remember that it is often far more useful to you to have an acceptable resume as soon as possible—and use it in an active job search—than to delay your job search while working on a better resume. A better resume can come later, after you have created a presentable one that you can use right away.

TYPES OF RESUMES

To keep this simple, I'm going to discuss only three types of resumes. There are other, more specialized types, but these three are generally the most useful:

Quick Reference

THE CHRONOLOGICAL RESUME

The word "chronology" refers to a sequence of events in time, and the primary feature of this resume is the listing of jobs held from the most recent backwards. This is the simplest of resumes and can be a useful format if used properly. Chapter 2 will show you how to create this basic type of resume.

THE SKILLS, OR FUNCTIONAL, RESUME

Rather than listing your experience under each job, this resume style clusters your experiences under major skill areas. For example, if you are strong in "communication skills," under that major heading you could list a variety of supportive experiences from different jobs, school, or volunteer situations. Several other major skill areas would also be presented.

This would make little sense, of course, unless you had a job objective that *required* these skills. For this reason and others, a skills resume is harder to write than a simple chronological resume. If you have limited paid work experience, are changing careers, or have not worked for awhile, a skills resume may be a clearly superior approach to help you present your strengths and avoid displaying your weaknesses.

THE COMBINATION, OR CREATIVE, RESUME

Elements of chronological and skills resumes can be combined in various ways to improve the clarity or presentation of a resume.

There are also creative formats that defy any category but that are clever and have worked for some people. I've seen hand-written resumes (usually *not* a good idea); unusual paper colors, sizes, and shapes; resumes with tasteful drawings and borders; and lots of other ideas. Some were well done and well received; others were not.

"SEND OUT YOUR RESUME TO LOTS OF STRANGERS AND, IF IT IS GOOD ENOUGH, YOU WILL GET LOTS OF JOB OFFERS," AND OTHER FAIRY TALES

Quick Reference

As I will say at various times in this book, your objective should be to get a good job, not to do a great resume. I have written this book to teach you the basics of putting together a useful and effective resume, but any resume will only be as good as you use it. And the **big** problem with resumes is that most people don't understand that a resume really is not a good job search tool at all.

That's right. Contrary to the advice of many people who write resume books, writing a "dynamite" or "perfect" (or whatever) resume will rarely get you the job you want. That will happen only following an interview, with an occasional odd exception. So the task in the job search is to get interviews and to do well in them, and sending out lots of resumes to people you don't know—and other traditional resume advice—is a lot of baloney (or, if you prefer, bologna).

I hope this doesn't upset you. It's simply the truth. That is why I suggest doing a simple resume early in your job search. This approach allows you to get on with getting interviews rather than sitting at home working on a better resume.

While I really can't do a thorough job teaching you all there is to know about getting a job in this book, I have included some information in Section 5 that will surely help. And, for those of you who don't like to read (or are particularly anxious to get on with your job search without delay), the following are some basic tips on getting a good job that I have learned over many years.

The Seven Steps to Getting the Job You Want

Section 5 will provide you with additional information on how to get a good job in less time, but here are the key elements:

▲ **1. Know your skills.** If you don't know what you are good at, how can you expect anyone else to figure it out? One survey of employers found that about 80 percent of those who made it to the interview did not do a good job in presenting the skills they had to do the job. This is a big problem for resumes and throughout the job search.

▲ **2. Have a clear job objective.** If you don't know where you want to go, it will be most difficult to get there. Having a clear job objective is essential for writing most resumes, though you can write one without it. Section 2 will help you with this issue, if you need more help than is provided in Section 1.

▲ **3. Know where and how to look.** Since three out of four jobs are not advertised, you will have to use non-traditional job search techniques to find them. Section 5 provides additional information on the basic techniques that I recommend you use in your search for a job.

▲ **4. Spend at least 25 hours a week looking.** Most job seekers spend far less than this and, as a result, are unemployed longer than they need to be.

▲ **5. Get two interviews a day.** It sounds impossible but this *can* be done once you redefine what an interview is. Section 5 will help you do this and get those two interviews a day. Compare this level of activity to the average of four or five interviews a *month* in the average job search and you can see how it can make a big difference.

▲ **6. Do well in interviews.** You won't get a job offer unless you do well in this critical situation. I've reviewed the research on what it takes to do well in an interview and found, happily, that you can improve your interview performance relatively easily. Knowing what skills you have and being able to support them with examples is a good start. Section 2 provides you with a chapter on identifying your key skills and helps to prepare you for the interview—as well as for writing a superior resume.

▲ **7. Follow up on all contacts.** This one thing can make a big difference in the results you get in your search for a new job. Tips for sending thank-you notes are pro-vided in Section 4 and other tips for following up are provided in Section 5 and elsewhere.

No one should ever say that looking for a job is easy. But I have learned that there are some things you can do to make the process a bit easier and shorter than it typically is. Getting your resume together is something that hangs many people up for entirely too long. The next two chapters should solve that problem.

2

DO A SIMPLE RESUME IN ABOUT AN HOUR

Quick Tip

After reading Chapter 1, I suggest that you go ahead and create the basic resume that is presented there. Doing so will give you the advantage of having a resume without delay and, even if you decide to create a more sophisticated one, will allow you to use it in your job search within 24 hours. The activities in this chapter will also prepare you to take better advantage of the material that follows in other chapters.

Keeping things simple has its advantages. This chapter does just that by presenting information, examples, and an "Instant Resume Worksheet" that you can use to write a basic chronological resume in about an hour. It also includes a few tips for improving your basic resume that would, for most, be worth the extra bit of time.

One big advantage of a chronological resume is that it is easy to do. You can complete a simple one in about an hour. It works best for those who have had several years of experience in the same type of job they are seeking now. This is because a chronological resume will clearly display your recent work experience. If you want to change careers, have been out of the workforce recently, or do not have much paid work experience related to the job you are seeking, a chronological resume may not be the best format for you. (In these instances, you might want to use a skills resume, presented in Chapter 3.)

Most employers will find a chronological resume perfectly acceptable (if not exciting), providing it is neat and has no errors. You can use it early in your job search while you work on a more sophisticated resume. The important point here is to get an acceptable resume together quickly so you won't be sitting at home worrying about your resume instead of out job-hunting.

● ●

CHRONOLOGICAL RESUME SAMPLES

Two sample resumes follow. The first one is a simple one that uses a chronological format. While the information and format are quite basic, it works well enough in this situation since Judith is looking for a job in her present career field and has a good job history. This same resume is then improved in the second example, adding a number of features including a more thorough job objective, a "Special Skills and Abilities" section, and more details regarding her accomplishments and skills in the Education and Experience sections. While this improved resume would take most people longer than an hour to create, it still uses the basic chronological approach and could be completed by most people in one day or less.

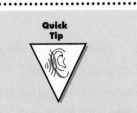

Quick Tip

The sample resumes throughout this book include job objectives that you can look at to see how others have phrased them. Jot down a draft job objective and refine it until it "feels good." Then rewrite it on the Instant Resume Worksheet following this section.

is *not* a good objective at all. Who cares? This objective, a real one that someone actually wrote, displays a self-centered, "gimme" approach that will turn off most employers.

Refer to the following examples of simple but useful job objectives. Most provide some information on the type of job that is sought as well as the skills that person offers. The best ones avoid a narrow job title and keep their options open to a wide variety of possibilities within a range of appropriate jobs.

EDUCATION AND TRAINING

Recent graduates can put their educational credentials towards the top of their resume since they represent a more important part of their experience. But, for

---

SAMPLE JOB OBJECTIVES

▲ A responsible, general office position in a busy, medium-sized organization.

▲ A management position in the warehousing industry. Position should require supervisory, problem-solving, and organizational skills.

▲ Computer programming and/or systems analysis. Prefer an accounting-oriented emphasis and a solution-oriented organization.

▲ Medical assistant or secretary in a physician's office, hospital, or other health services environment.

▲ Responsible position requiring skills in public relations, writing, and reporting.

▲ An aggressive and success-oriented professional, seeking a sales position offering both challenge and growth.

▲ Desire position in the office management, secretarial, or clerical area. Position should require flexibility, good organizational skills, and an ability to handle people.

more experienced workers, your education typically is placed towards the end of your resume.

The education and training section can also be dropped if it doesn't help support your job objective or if you don't have the educational credentials that are typically required by those seeking the same type of position. This is particularly true if you have lots of work experience in your career area. Usually, though, you should emphasize the most recent and/or highest level of education or training that relates to the job.

Drop or downplay details that don't support your objective! If you are a recent graduate, and if your education was not job related, but you have paid work experience in your career area, this may be the most important part of your resume. Look at the sample resumes in this chapter for ideas. Then, on a separate piece of paper, rough out your section on education and training. After you edit it to its final form, write it on the Instant Resume Worksheet following this section.

Quick Reminder

USE ACTION WORDS AND PHRASES

Use active rather than passive words and phrases, such as those in this list, throughout your resume. Also look at the sample resumes in this chapter and in Section 3 for additional ideas.

• •

ACTION WORDS AND PHRASES

Administered	Established priorities	Organized
Analyzed	Expanded	Planned
Controlled	Implemented	Presented
Coordinated	Improved	Promoted
Created	Increased productivity	Reduced expenses
Designed	(profits)	Researched
Developed	Initiated	Scheduled
Diagnosed	Innovated	Solved
Directed	Instructed	Supervised
Established policy	Modified	Trained
	Negotiated	

• •

WORK AND VOLUNTEER HISTORY

This section of your resume provides the details of your work history, starting with the most recent job. If you have had significant work history, list each job along with details of what you accomplished and any special skills you used. Emphasize any skills that directly relate to the job objective you have stated on your resume. Any significant volunteer or military experience can be treated in the same way as job experience.

 PREVIOUS JOB TITLES

Remember that you can modify the title you had to more accurately reflect your responsibilities. For example, if your title was "Sales Clerk" but you frequently opened and closed the store and were often left in charge, you might use the more descriptive title of "Night Sales Manager." Check with your previous supervisor if you are worried about this and ask if they would object.

If you were promoted, you can handle the promotion as a separate job and, if so, make sure that you mention that you were promoted.

 PREVIOUS EMPLOYERS

Provide the organization's name and city, state, or province in which it was located. A street address or supervisor's name is not necessary—you can provide those details on a separate sheet of references.

 EMPLOYMENT DATES

If you have large gaps in your employment history that are not easily explained, just use full years as a way to avoid displaying them. Additional information on handling this and other problems are covered in Chapter 7 of this book, should you want additional details. If you do have a significant period of time where you did not work, did you do anything else during that time that could explain it in a positive way? School? Travel? Raise a family? Self-employment? Even if you mowed lawns and painted houses for money while you were unemployed, that could count as self-employment. It's much better than saying you were unemployed.

In writing about your work experience, be sure to use action words and

emphasize what you accomplished. Quantify what you did and provide evidence you did it well. Take particular care to mention skills that would directly relate to doing well in the job you want.

Use separate sheets of paper to write rough drafts of what you will use in your resume. Edit it so every word contributes something and, when done, transfer your statements to the Instant Resume Worksheet.

PROFESSIONAL ORGANIZATIONS

If you belong to job-related professional groups, it may be worth mentioning, particularly if you were an officer or were active in some other way. Mention any accomplishments or awards.

RECOGNITION AND AWARDS

If you have received any formal recognition or awards that support your job objective, consider mentioning them. You might create a separate section, or they can be put in the work experience, skills, education, or personal sections.

PERSONAL INFORMATION

Traditionally, somewhere on a resume things like height, weight, marital status, hobbies, leisure activities, and other trivia are mentioned. My advice is to not include this sort of information. Earlier I advised you to make every word count—if it does not support your job objective, delete it. Same here. There are situations

Quick Tip

Emphasize accomplishments! Think about the things you accomplished in jobs, school, military, and other settings. Make sure that you emphasize these things, even if it seems arrogant or unconventional to do so. Many of the sample resumes include statements about accomplishments to show you how this can be done.

where these characteristics or activities do help you and, if so, go ahead and use them. Look at the sample resumes later in this chapter and in Section 3 for ideas and decide for yourself.

While a personal section is optional, I sometimes like to end a resume on a personal note. Some of the sample resumes throughout this book provide a touch of humor or playfulness as well as selected positives from outside school and work lives. This is also a good place to list significant community involvements, a willingness to relocate, or personal characteristics an employer might like. Keep it short. Turn now to the Instant Resume Worksheet and list any personal information you feel is appropriate.

Quick Reminder

REFERENCES

It is not necessary to include the names of your references on a resume. There are better things to do with the precious space. It's not even necessary to state "references available upon request" at the bottom of your resume, since that is obvious. If an employer wants them, they know they can ask you for them.

It *is* helpful to line up your references in advance. Pick people who know your work as an employee, volunteer, or student. Make sure they will say nice things about you by asking them just what they would say. Push for any negatives and don't feel hurt if you get some. Nobody is perfect, and it gives you a chance to get them off your list before they do you any damage. Once you know who to include, type up a clean list on a separate sheet. Include name, address, phone number, and details of why they are on your list.

Be aware that due to company policy, some supervisors are not allowed to give references over the phone. I have refused to hire people who probably had good references but about whom I could not get information. If this is the case with a previous employer, ask them to write a letter of reference for you to photocopy as needed. This is a good idea in general, so you may want to ask them for one even if they have no rules against phone references.

Keep organized copies of the list and any letters of recommendation and be able to provide them when asked. Do not attach them to your resume unless you are asked to do so.

THE FINAL DRAFT

At this point, you should have completed the Instant Resume Worksheet at the end of this chapter. Carefully review dates, addresses, phone numbers, spelling, and other details of the information it contains. The worksheet can now be used as a guide for preparing a better-than-average chronological resume.

" The lack of a resume should not become a barrier for your job search."

Use the examples of simple chronological resumes in this chapter as the basis for creating your own chronological resume. Additional examples of skills resumes follow in Chapter 3 and in Section 3. You should look them over for ideas for writing and formatting your own. The sample resumes in Chapter 3 tend to be simpler and easier to write and format than some found in Section 3 and will provide better models for creating a resume quickly.

Remember that your initial objective is not to do a wonderful, powerful, or creative resume at all. That can come later. You first need to have an acceptable resume, one that can be used tomorrow, to begin an active job search. So keep it simple and set a tight deadline so that the lack of a resume does not become a barrier for your job search.

Once you have completed the Instant Resume Worksheet, you have the information you need for a basic resume. If you have access to your own computer, go ahead and put the information you have collected into the form of a resume. Make sure that you edit each section carefully and that the resume has no errors at all.

Quick Reminder

If you do not have a computer or are not a good typist, I suggest that you have someone else type or word process your resume for you. But whether you do it yourself or have it done, *carefully review it once more* for typographical or other errors that may have slipped in. Then, when you are certain that everything is correct, have the final version prepared.

"INSTANT RESUME" WORKSHEET

••

Identification

Name _____

Home address _____

_____ **Zip** _____

Phone number, description (if any) _____ ( ) _____

Alternate phone number, description _____ ( ) _____

Job Objective _____

_____

_____

_____

Experience
Most Recent Position

Dates: from _____ **to** _____

Title _____

Organization name _____

City, State/Province _____

Duties & Accomplishments _____

_____

_____

_____

_____

_____

_____

_____

_____

_____

_____

_____

Next Most Recent Position

Dates: from _____ **to** _____

Title _____

Organization name _____

City, State/Province _____

Duties & Accomplishments _____

_____

_____

_____

_____

_____

_____

_____

_____

_____

_____

_____

_____

Next Most Recent Position

Dates: from _____ **to** _____

Title _____

Organization name _____

City, State/Province _____

Duties & Accomplishments _____

_____

_____

_____

_____

_____

_____

_____

_____

_____

_____

Next Most Recent Position

Dates: from _____ **to** _____

Title _____

Organization name _____

City, State/Province _____

Duties & Accomplishments _____

_____

_____

_____

_____

_____

_____

_____

_____

_____

_____

_____

Education & Training
Highest Level/Most Recent

Institution name _____

City, State/Province (optional) _____

Relevant awards, achievements, & experiences _____

_____

_____

_____

_____

College/Post High School

Institution name _____

City, State/Province (optional) _____

Relevant awards, achievements, & experiences _____

_____

_____

_____

_____

High School
(Optional if Attended College)

Institution name _____

City, State/Province (optional) _____

Relevant awards, achievements, & experiences _____

_____

_____

_____

_____

Armed Services Training and Other Training or Certification

_____

_____

_____

_____

Professional Organizations

_____

_____

_____

_____

Personal Information

_____

_____

_____

_____

3

WRITE A SKILLS RESUME IN LESS THAN ONE DAY

Quick Tip

While it does take a bit longer to do a skills resume, you should consider writing one for a variety of reasons. This chapter will show you how, as well as explain why a skills resume may be a good thing to consider. But you should first read Chapters 1 and 2 and do the activities (particularly the Instant Resume Worksheet in Chapter 2) before completing the skills resume described in this chapter.

This chapter shows you how to write a resume that is organized around the key skills you have that are relate to the job you want. While this type of resume takes a bit longer to write, it has some advantages that may make it worthwhile to consider.

In its simplest form, a chronological resume is little more than a list of job titles and other details. If you want to change your career or increase your level of responsibility, the chronological style of resume can often be an obituary because many employers look for candidates with a successful history in a job similar to the available position. If you are a recent graduate or have little prior experience in the career you now want, you will find that a simple chronological resume emphasizes your lack of related experience rather than your ability to do the job.

A skills resume avoids these problems by highlighting what you have done under the heading of your specific skills rather than jobs you have held. If you hitchhiked across the country for two years, a skills resume won't necessarily display this as a gap in your employment record. Instead, you could now say "Traveled extensively throughout the country and am familiar with most major market areas." That could be a very useful experience for certain positions.

Because it is a tool that can hide your problem areas, some employers do not like a skills resume. But many do and we've already discussed how you can't please everyone. Besides, if you do have a problem that a traditional chronological resume highlights, a skills resume may help get you the opportunity to meet with a prospective employer (who doesn't like your resume) rather than get screened out. Who wins?

Even if you don't have anything to hide, a skills resume can let you emphasize key skills and experiences more clearly. And you can always include a chronological listing of jobs as one part of your skills resume, as in some of the examples in this book. So a skills resume should be considered by everyone, though a good one does take a bit more work to create.

● ●

SAMPLE SKILLS RESUME

On the next page is an example of a basic skills resume. The example is for a recent high school graduate whose only experience has been in a hamburger place. A skills resume is a good choice here since it allows her to emphasize her strengths without emphasizing that her work experience is limited. While the sample format is simple, it presents her in a positive way. Since her employment will be at the entry level in a non-technical area, an employer will be more interested in the skills she has garnered in her past, rather than her job-specific experiences. What work experience she has is a plus. And notice how she presented her gymnastics experience under "Hardworking."

Look in Section 3 of this book for additional examples of skills resumes used by those with considerable work experience. The skills format can work well for a variety of situations and may be right for you.

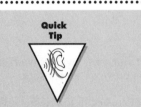

Quick Tip

It is essential that your resume emphasize the skills you have that directly support the job you want. While Chapter 2 includes a list of action words to use in your resume, you might benefit greatly from doing the skills identification activities in Chapter 4. These include several lists of skills that you might find of particular value in writing a skills resume.

CONSTRUCTING A SKILLS RESUME

The skills resume uses a number of sections that are similar to those in a chronological resume. Here I will discuss only those sections that are substantially different—the job objective and skills sections. Refer back to comments related to the chronological resume for information on sections that are common to both. Tips on combination and creative resume formats are provided later in this chapter, followed by sample resumes. These samples will give you ideas on resume language, organization, layout, and how special problems are handled.

Don't be afraid to use a little creativity in writing your own skills resume, since you are allowed to break some rules in this format if it makes sense to do so.

FIGURE 3-1 Example of a Skills Resume.

Lisa M. Rhodes
813 Evergreen Drive
Littleton, Colorado 81613
Home: (413) 643-2173   Message: (413) 442-1659

Position
Sales-oriented position in a retail sales or distribution business.

Skills and Abilities

Communications: Good written and verbal presentation skills. Use proper grammar and have a good speaking voice.

Interpersonal: Able to accept supervision and get along well with co-workers. Received positive evaluations from previous supervisors.

Flexible: Willing to try new things and am interested in improving efficiency on assigned tasks.

Attention to Detail: Like to see assigned areas of responsibility completed correctly. Am concerned with quality and my work is typically orderly and attractive.

Hard Working: Have previously worked long hours in strenuous activities while attending school full-time. During this time, maintained above average grades. At times, I was handling as many as 65 hours a week in school and other structured activities.

Customer Contacts: Have had as many as 500 customer contacts a day (10,000 per month) in a busy retail outlet. Averaged lower than a .001% rate of complaints and was given the "Employee of the Month" award in my second month of employment

Cash Sales: Handled over $2,000 a day ($40,000 a month) in cash sales. Balanced register and prepared daily sales summary and deposits.

Education

Franklin Township High School. Took advanced English and other classes. Member of award-winning band. Excellent attendance record. Superior communication skills. Graduated in top 30% of class.

Other

Active gymnastics competitor for four years—taught me discipline, team work, and following instructions. I am ambitious, outgoing, and willing to work.

THE JOB OBJECTIVE

While a simple chronological resume does not absolutely require a career objective, a skills resume does. Without a reasonably clear job objective, it is not possible to select and organize the key skills you have to support that job objective. It may be that the job objective you wrote for the chronological resume is good just as it is, but for a skills resume, your job objective statement should answer the following questions:

1. **What sort of position, title, or area of specialization do you seek?** By now, you should know how to present what sort of job you are seeking. Is it too narrow and specific? Is it so broad or vague as to be meaningless? If necessary, turn to Chapter 5 to identify more clearly your job objective.

2. **What level of responsibility interests you?** Job objectives often indicate a level of responsibility, particularly for supervisory or management roles. If in doubt, always try to keep open the possibility of getting a job with a higher level of responsibility (and salary) than your previous one. Write your job objective to include this possibility.

3. **What are your most important skills?** What are the two or three most important skills or personal characteristics needed to succeed on the job you've targeted? These are often mentioned in a job objective.
Review the "Sample Job Objectives" in the previous chapter and look over the sample resumes later in this chapter and in Section 3. Notice that some of these resumes use headings such as "position desired" or "career objective" to introduce the job objective section. Many people think that these headings sound more professional than "Job Objective" and I leave it to you to decide how best to handle this on your own resume.

Quick Tip

If you have ready access to a **computer** *and* **are familiar with word processing software, go ahead and write your draft on a computer. But, if computers are new to you, this is probably not the time to learn. It might be far better to take your handwritten resume to a professional typist or word processor and have them polish it for you.*

THE SKILLS SECTION

This section can also be headed as "Areas of Accomplishment" or "Summary of Qualifications" or "Areas of Expertise and Ability" or by other terms as used in various sample resumes. Whatever you choose to call it, this section is what makes a skills resume. To construct it, you must carefully consider which skills you want to emphasize. You should feature those skills that are essential to success on the job you want *and* those skills that are your particular strengths. You probably have a good idea of which skills meet both criteria, but you may find it helpful to review Chapter 4, as needed.

Note that many of the skills resumes in this book emphasize skills that are not specific to a particular job. For example, the skill of being "well organized" is important in *many* jobs. In your resume, you will provide specific examples of situations or accomplishments that show that you do have that skill, and this is where you can often bring in examples from previous work or other experiences.

KEY SKILLS LIST

Here is a short list of skills that I consider to be key skills for success on most jobs. If you have to emphasize some skills over others, these are ones to consider (if you have them, of course). This list is expanded in several skills lists that appear in Chapter 4, should you want to see more.

TABLE 3-1

The Basics:	Key Transferable Skills *(can be used in a variety of jobs):*
can accept supervision	can instruct others
can get along with co-workers	can manage money and budgets
can get things done on time	can manage people
good attendance	can meet deadlines
hard worker	can meet the public
honest	can negotiate
on time	can organize/manage projects
productive	public speaking
	written communication skills

In addition to these types of skills, most jobs require skills specific to that particular job. For example, an accountant would need to know how to set up a general ledger, use accounting software, develop income and expense reports, and do other tasks typically required in this type of job. These skills are called job content skills and can also be quite important in qualifying for a job.

IDENTIFYING YOUR KEY SKILLS

Look over the key skills list above and include any skills that you have *and* that are particularly important for the job you want. Also include any other skills you have that you feel you must communicate to an employer regarding the job you want. Write at least three, but no more than six, of these most important skills below:

1. _____
2. _____
3. _____
4. _____
5. _____
6. _____

PROVING YOUR KEY SKILLS

Now, write down each of the skills you wrote above on a separate piece of paper. For each one, write any particularly good examples of when you used that skill. If possible, you should use work situations, but you can also use other situations such as volunteer work, school activities, or any other life experience. Whenever possible, quantify the example by including numbers such as money saved, increased sales, or other measures to support those skills. Emphasize results you achieved and accomplishments.

An example of what one person wrote for one of their key skills follows and may give you an idea of how you can document your own skills.

AN EXAMPLE OF A KEY SKILL

KEY SKILL: MEETING DEADLINES

I volunteered to help my social organization raise money. I found out about special government funds, but the proposal deadline was only 24 hours away. I stayed up all night and submitted it on time. We were one of only three whose proposals were approved and we were awarded over $100,000!

Quick Reminder

EDITING YOUR KEY SKILLS PROOFS

Go over each "proof sheet" from the previous exercise and select those proofs that you feel are particularly valuable in supporting your job objective. You should have at least two proofs for each skills area. Once you have selected your proofs, rewrite them using action words and short sentences. Delete anything that is not essential. For example, here is a rewrite of the example I provided earlier. Do a similar editing job on each of your own proofs until they are clear, short, and powerful. You can then use these statements in your resume, modifying them as needed to fit that format.

KEY SKILL REWRITE

KEY SKILL: MEETING DEADLINES

On 24 hours notice, submitted a complex proposal that successfully obtained over $100,000 in funding.

TIPS TO FINE-TUNE YOUR RESUME

Quick Reference

Before you make a final draft of your skills resume, look over the following sample resumes for ideas on content and format. Several of them use interesting techniques that may be useful for your particular situation.

For example, if you have a good work history, providing a very brief chronological listing of jobs can be a helpful addition to your skills resume. If you have substantial work history, beginning the resume with a summary of total experience can provide the basis for details that follow. Remember that this is your resume, so do with it what you think is best. Trust your own good judgment and be willing to break a few rules if you think it will help you.

Write out the draft resume contents on separate sheets of paper or on a computer, if you have access to one. Rewrite and edit until the resume communicates what you really want to say about yourself.

If you are doing your resume on a computer, print out the "final" copy and ask someone else to *very carefully* review it for typographical and other errors. Even if you are having someone else prepare your resume, have their "final" copy reviewed by someone other than yourself for any errors you have overlooked. Only after you are certain that your resume contains no errors, should you have the final version prepared.

SAMPLE SKILLS RESUMES AND JIST CARDS

Quick Reference

Look over the sample resumes that follow to see how others have adapted the basic skills format to fit their own situation. These examples are based on real resumes (though their names and other details are not real) and I have included comments to help you understand details that may not be apparent.

The formats and designs of the sample resumes in this chapter are intentionally basic and can be done by virtually any word processor or, even, a good typewriter. Many additional examples of skills resumes can be found in Section 3, including some with fancier designs. Remember that it is better to have a simple resume and be out there using it than to be home working on a "fancier" one.

I have also included examples of a job search tool that I developed many years ago called a JIST Card. These are a type of mini-resume that you can use in a variety of ways in your job search. They can be attached to applications or resumes; given to people in your network of contacts; enclosed in thank-you notes before or after an interview; put under the windshields of cars (really, this has been done and with good results) and in many other ways. While they are not the focus of this book, I present them here as an idea for you to consider using in your job search. The more you have in circulation, the better. They do work. If you want to learn more about JIST Cards, several of my books in the bibliography present them in more detail.

FIGURE 3-3 Thomas' Resume.

THOMAS P. MARRIN
80 Harrison Avenue
Baldwin L.I., New York 11563
Answering Service: (716) 223-4705

OBJECTIVE:
A middle/upper level management position with responsibilities including problem solving, planning, organizing, and budget management.

EDUCATION:
University of Notre Dame, BS in Business Administration. Course emphasis on accounting, supervision, and marketing. Upper 25% of class. Additional training: Advanced training in time management, organization behavior, and cost control.

MILITARY:
US Army — 2nd Infantry Division, 1984 to 1987. 1st Lieutenant and platoon leader —stationed in Korea and Ft. Knox, Kentucky. Supervised an annual budget of nearly $4 million and equipment valued at over $40 million. Responsible for training, scheduling, and activities of as many as 40 people. Received several commendations. Honorable discharge.

BUSINESS EXPERIENCE:

Wills Express Transit Co., Inc. — Mineola, New York

Promoted to Vice President, Corporate Equipment — 1992 to Present
Controlled purchase, maintenance and disposal of 1100 trailers and 65 company cars with $6.7 MM operating and $8.0 MM Capital expense responsibilities

- Scheduled trailer purchases, 6 divisions
- Operated 2.3% under planned maintenance budget in Company's second best profit year while operating revenues declined 2.5%.
- Originated schedule to correlate drivers' needs with available trailers.
- Developed systematic Purchase and Disposal Plan for company car fleet.
- Restructured Company Car Policy, saving 15% on per car cost.

Promoted to Asst. Vice President, Corporate Operations — 1991 to 1992
Coordinated activities of six sections of Corporate Operations with an operating budget over $10 million.

- Directed implementation of zero base budgeting.
- Developed and prepared Executive Officer analyses detailing achievable cost reduction measures. Resulted in cost reduction of over $600,000 in first two years.
- Designed policy and procedure for special equipment leasing program during peak seasons. Cut capital purchases by over $1 million.

Promoted to Manager of Communications — 1989 to 1991
Directed and Managed $1.4 MM communication network involving 650 phones, 150 WATS lines, 3 switchboards, 1 teletype machine, 5 employees.

- Installed computerized WATS Control System. Optimized utilization of WATS lines and pinpointed personal abuse. Achieved payback earlier than originally projected.
- Devised procedures that allowed simultaneous 20% increase in WATS calls and a $75,000/year savings.

Hayfield Publishing Company, Hempstead, New York.

Communications Administrator — 1987 to 1989

Managed daily operations of a large Communications Center. Reduced costs and improved services.

47

PETER NEELY'S RESUME AND JIST CARD

Comments on Peter's Resume

Peter lost his factory job when the plant closed in the early 1990s. He had picked up a survival job as a truck driver and now wants to make this his career because it allows him to earn good money and he likes the work.

Notice how his resume emphasizes skills from previous experiences that are essential for success as a truck driver. This resume uses a "combined" format since it includes elements from both the skills and chronological resume formats. The skills approach allows him to emphasize specific skills that support his job objective and the chronological listing of jobs allows him to display his stable work history.

The miscellaneous jobs he had before 1977 are simply clustered together under one grouping, since they are not as important as more recent experience—and because doing this does not display his age. For the same reasons, he does not include dates for his military experience or high school graduation, nor does he separate them into different categories such as "Military Experience" or "Education." They just aren't as important in supporting his current job objective as they might be for a younger person. An unusual element here is his adding comments about his not smoking or drinking, although it does work, as do his comments about a stable family life.

Peter also has another version of this resume that simply changed his job objective to include supervision and management of trucking operations and added a few details to support this. When it made sense, he used the other version.

He got a job in a smaller long distance trucking company driving a regular trip and now supervises other drivers.

PETER'S JIST CARD

Peter Neely

Messages: (237) 649-1234
Beeper: (237) 765-9876

Position: Truck Driver

Background and Skills: Over twenty years of stable work history including no traffic citations or accidents. Formal training in diesel mechanics and electrical systems. Am familiar with most major destinations and have excellent map-reading and problem-solving abilities. I can handle responsibility and have a track record of getting things done.

Excellent health, good work history, dependable

FIGURE 3-4 Peter's Resume.

Peter Neely
203 Evergreen Road
Houston, Texas 39127
Messages:(237) 649-1234   Beeper:(237) 765-9876

POSITION DESIRED: Truck Driver

Summary of Work Experience: Over twenty years of stable work history, including substantial experience with diesel engines, electrical systems, and truck driving.

SKILLS

Driving Record/ Licenses: Chauffeur's license, qualified and able to drive anything that rolls. No traffic citations or accidents for over 20 years.

Vehicle Maintenance: I maintain correct maintenance schedules and avoid most breakdowns as a result. Substantial mechanical and electrical systems training and experience permits many breakdowns to be repaired immediately and avoid towing.

Record Keeping: Excellent attention to detail. Familiar with recording procedures and submit required records in on a timely basis.

Routing: Knowledge of many states. Good map reading and route planning skills.

Other: Not afraid of hard work, flexible, get along well with others, meet deadlines, responsible.

WORK EXPERIENCE

1993 - Present — CAPITAL TRUCK CENTER, Houston, Texas
Pick up and deliver all types of commercial vehicles from across the United States. Am trusted with handling large sums of money and handling complex truck purchasing transactions.

1983 - 1993 — QUALITY PLATING CO., Houston, Texas
Promoted from production to Quality Control. Developed numerous production improvements resulting in substantial cost savings.

1981 - 1983 — BLUE CROSS MANUFACTURING, Houston, Texas
Received several increases in salary and responsibility before leaving for a more challenging position.

1977 - 1981 — Truck delivery of food products to destinations throughout the south. Also responsible for up to 12 drivers and equipment maintenance personnel.

Prior to 1977 — Operated large diesel-powered electrical plants. Responsible for monitoring and maintenance on a rigid schedule.

OTHER

Four years experience in the U.S. Air Force operating power plants. Stationed in Alaska, California, Wyoming, and other states. Honorable discharge. High school graduate plus training in diesel engines and electrical systems. Excellent health, love the outdoors, stable family life, non-smoker and non-drinker.

ANDREA ATWOOD'S RESUME AND JIST CARD

Comments on Andrea's Resume

This resume uses few words and lots of white space. It looks better, I think, than more crowded resumes. I would like to see more numbers used to indicate performance or accomplishments. For example, what was the result of the more efficient record-keeping system she developed? And why did she receive the Employee-of-the-Month awards?

Andrea does not have substantial experience in her field, having had only one job. For this reason, this skills format allows her to present her strengths better than a chronological resume. Since she has formal training in retail sales and is a recent graduate, she could have given more details about specific courses she took or other school-related activities that would support her job objective. Even so, her resume does a good job of presenting her basic skills to an employer in an attractive format.

ANDREA'S JIST CARD

Andrea Atwood

Home: (303) 447-2111

Message: (303) 547-8201

Position Desired: Copywriter or Account Executive in Advertising or Public Relations Agency

Skills: Two years of retail sales training including accounting, promotional writing, and advertising design. Computer skills in desktop publishing, graphics design, accounting, and word processing. Good written and verbal communication skills. Experienced in dealing with customers, direct sales, and in solving problems.

Punctual, honest, reliable, and hard-working

FIGURE 3-5 Andrea's Resume.

ANDREA ATWOOD
3231 East Harbor Road
Grand Rapids, Michigan 41103

Home: (303) 447-2111   Message: (303) 547-8201

Objective: A responsible position in retail sales.

**Areas of
Accomplishment:**

Customer Service
- Communicates well with all age groups.
- Able to interpret customer concerns to help them find the items they want.
- Received six Employee of the Month awards in 3 years.

Merchandise Display
- Developed display skills via in-house training and experience.
- Received Outstanding Trainee award for Christmas Toy Display
- Dress mannequins, arrange table displays, and organize sale merchandise.

Stock Control and Marking
- Maintained and marked stock during department manager's 6-week illness.
- Developed more efficient record-keeping procedures.

Additional Skills
- Operate cash register and computerized accounting systems,
- Willing to work evenings and weekends.
- Punctual, honest, reliable and hard-working

Experience:

Harper's Department Store
Grand Rapids, Michigan
1992 to present

Education:

Central High School
Grand Rapids, Michigan
3.6/4.0 grade point average
Honor Graduate in Distributive Education

Two years retail sales training in Distributive Education. Also courses in Business Writing, Computerized Accounting and Word Processing.

LINDA MARSALA-WINSTON'S RESUME AND JIST CARD

Linda's resume is based on one included in a book by David Swanson titled *The Resume Solution*, and it shows the type of resume style that he prefers. It uses lots of white space, short sentences, and brief but carefully edited narrative.

The format for this resume is based on a resume template provided with a popular word processing program. That program offers several pre-determined design options that include various typefaces and the use of other simple but effective format and design elements. Other resumes in Section 3 also have used similar templates as a basis for their designs, and this approach makes formatting a resume much easier.

Linda's resume is short but does present good information to support her job objective. I have included other examples of resumes from *The Resume Solution* in Section 3 and they all share the same principles of less being more. Of course, they are being used with Dave's permission.

LINDA'S JIST CARD

Linda Marsala-Winston   Messages: (415) 555-6755

Career Objective: Copywriter, account executive in advertising or public relations agency

Over seven years of experience in promoting various products and services. Advanced education and training in journalism, advertising, writing, design, psychology, and communications. Excellent written communication skills and have won several awards for excellence. Am creative in solving problems and in getting results.

Persuasive, innovative, meet deadlines

FIGURE 3-6 Linda's Resume.

Linda Marsala-Winston
6673 East Avenue
Lakeland, California, 94544
(415) 555-1519 (leave message)

Objective: Copywriter, Account Executive in Advertising or Public Relations Agency
Professional Experience

Copywriter
Developed copy for direct mail catalogs featuring collectible items, for real estate developments and for agricultural machinery and equipment.

Writer
Wrote for Habitat magazine. Specialized in architecture, contemporary lifestyles and interior design.

Sales Promotion
Fullmerís Department Store, Detroit. Developed theme and copy for grand opening of new store in San Francisco Bay area.

Fabric Designer
Award-winning textile designer and importer of African and South American textiles.

Other Writing and Promotion
News bureau chief and feature writer for college newspaper, contributor to literary magazine. Script writer for fashion shows. Won creative writing fellowship to study in Mexico. Did public relations for International Cotton Conference. Summer graduate fellow in public information, United Nations, New York City.

Education
University of California, Berkeley
Bachelor of Arts Degree in English. Graduate study, 30 credits competed in Journalism.

California State University, Fresno
Master of Arts Degree in Guidance and Counseling
professional membership
San Francisco Women in Advertising

SUSAN SMITH'S RESUME AND JIST CARD

Comments on Susan's Resume

This is a two page resume that is based on one included in a book by Richard Lathrop titled *Who's Hiring Who*. It originally was squeezed onto one page. While he calls it a "Qualifications Brief," it is a pure form example of a skills resume.

This resume is unconventional in a variety of ways. It clearly takes advantage of the skills format by avoiding all mention of a chronology of past jobs. There are no references to specific employers, to employment dates, or even to job titles. If you read it carefully, you may figure out that Susan's job history has been as a housewife. This is a clever example of how a well-done skills resume can present a person effectively in spite of a lack of formal paid work experience—or to cover other problems. Students, career changers, and others can benefit in similar ways.

SUSAN'S JIST CARD

Susan Smith   (416) 486-3874

Job Objective: Program development, coordination, and administration

Skills: B.A. degree plus over 15 years of experience in management, budgeting, and problem solving. Good financial management skills including cost control, purchasing, and disbursement. Able to organize and manage multiple tasks at one time and to meet deadlines. Excellent communication skills.

Well organized, efficient, can give and accept responsiblily

FIGURE 3-7 Susan's Resume.

SUSAN SMITH
1516 Sierra Way
Piedmont, California 97435
Telephone: (416) 486-3874

OBJECTIVE

Program Development, Coordination, and Administration

...especially in a people-oriented organization where there is a need to assure broad coop-
erative effort through the use of sound planning and strong administrative and persuasive
skills to achieve community goals.

MAJOR AREAS OF EXPERIENCE AND ABILITY

Budgeting and Management For Sound Program Development

With partner, established new association devoted to maximum personal development and
self-realization for each of its members. Over a period of time, administered budget
totalling $285,000. Jointly planned growth of group and related expenditures, investments,
programs, and development of property holdings to realize current and long-term goals. As
a result, holdings increased twenty-fold over the period, reserves invested increased 1200%
and all major goals for members have been achieved or exceeded

Purchasing to Assure Smooth Flow of Needed Supplies and Services

Made purchasing decisions to assure maximum production from available funds.
Determined on-going inventory needs, selected suppliers, and maintained a strong continuing line of credit while minimizing financing costs. No significant project was ever
adversely affected by lack of necessary supplies, equipment, or services on time.

Personnel Development and Motivation

Developed resources to assure maximum progress in achieving potential for development
among all members of our group. Frequently engaged in intensive personnel counseling to
achieve this. Sparked new community progress to help accomplish such results. Although
arrangements with my partner gave me no say in selecting new members (I took them as
they came), the results produced by this effort are a source of strong and continuing satisfaction to me. (See "specific results.")

FIGURE 3-7B Susan's Resume *(continued)*.

Susan Smith   Page Two

Transportation Management

Determined transportation needs of our group and, in consultation with members, assured specific transportation equipment acquisitions over a broad range of types (including seagoing). Contracted for additional transportation when necessary. Assured maximum utilization of limited motor pool to meet often-conflicting requirements demanding arrival of the same vehicle at widely divergent points at the same moment. Negotiated resolution of such conflicts in the best interest of all concerned. In addition, arranged four major moves of all facilities, furnishings, and equipment to new locations.

Other Functions Performed

Duties periodically require my action in the following additional functional areas: Crisis management; proposal preparation; political analysis; nutrition; recreation planning and administration; stock market operations; taxes; building and grounds maintenance; community organization; social affairs administration (including VIP entertaining); catering; landscaping; (two awards for excellence); contract negotiations; teaching and more.

Some Specific Results

Above experience gained in 10 years devoted to family development and household management in partnership with my husband, Harvey Smith, who is equally responsible for results produced. *Primary achievements:* Daughter Sue, 12, leading candidate for the U.S. Junior Olympics team in gymnastics. A lovely home in Piedmont (social center for area teenagers). *Secondary achievements:* Vacation home at Newport, Oregon (on the beach) and a cabin in Big Sur. President of Piedmont High School PTA two years. Organized successful citizen protest to stop incursion of Oakland commercialism on Piedmont area. Appointed by Robert F. Kennedy as coordinator for this campaign in Oakland.

PERSONAL DATA AND OTHER FACTS

Often complimented on appearance. Bachelor of Arts (Business Administration), Cody College, Cody, California. Highly active in community affairs. Have learned that there is a spark of genius in almost everyone which, when nurtured, can flare into dramatic achievement.

A MORE THOROUGH APPROACH TO RESUME WRITING (AND CAREER PLANNING)

Introduction

This section does not *have* to be read or completed at all. As I said in Section 1, all you may really need is a simple resume that allows you to get started on an active job search—and there is enough information in Section 1 to help you do a respectable resume. But, if you are motivated to do a better resume, there are some advantages to doing so.

You should know that this section is more than it may appear to be at first. It is:

- **A Series of Chapters That Will Build the Contents of a Superior Resume.** Each of the chapters in this section will help you build specific content that you can use in creating a powerful resume. For example, Chapter 4 will show you how to identify the wide array of skills you possess and to select those that are most important to include in a resume.

- **A Process to Help Your Career and Life Planning.** While you are working on the activities needed to write a superior resume, you will also learn things that can be quite important to you in your career and life planning. For example, what *are* you really good at? What sorts of things do you *enjoy* doing? What *values* are important to include in your next job? And what sort of job will you be looking for, *specifically*? These are just some of the things that the chapters in this section will explore and they all can be very important indeed—far more important to you than "just" putting together a resume.

- **A Series of Activities That Will Help You Tremendously Throughout Your Job Search—and Beyond.** One of the big questions you will have to answer in an interview is "Why should I hire you?"—though it is rarely asked that clearly. In doing the activities in this section, you will be able to better handle this essential interview question. This is but one of the many examples of how the process of writing a superior resume can benefit you in many other ways. I have included a number of activities and tips that will help you write a resume as well as help you in other, and surely more important, ways.

ADAPTIVE SKILLS / PERSONALITY TRAITS

These are skills you use every day to survive and get along. They are called adaptive or self-management skills because they allow you to adapt or adjust to a variety of situations. Some of them also could be considered part of your basic personality. Examples of adaptive skills valued by employers include getting to work on time, honesty, enthusiasm, and being able to get along with others.

TRANSFERABLE SKILLS

These are general skills that can be useful in a variety of jobs. For example, writing clearly, good language skills, or the ability to organize and prioritize tasks would be desirable skills in many jobs. These are called transferable skills because they can be transferred from one job—or even one career—to another.

JOB-RELATED SKILLS

These are the skills people typically first think of when asked, "Do you have any skills?" They are related to a particular job or type of job. An auto mechanic, for example, needs to know how to tune engines and repair brakes. Typing or being able to read a micrometer are other examples of job-related skills.

This system of dividing skills into three categories is not perfect. Some things, such as being trustworthy, dependable, or well-organized are really not skills as much as they are personality traits. There is also some overlap between the three skills categories. For example, a skill such as being organized can be considered either adaptive or transferable. For our purposes, however, the Skills Triad is a very useful system for identifying skills that are important in the job search.

IDENTIFYING YOUR SKILLS

Since it is so important to know your skills, I have included a series of checklists and other activities in this chapter to help you identify the skills that will be most important to consider in completing your resume. Doing this will help you develop a skills language that can also be very helpful to you during interviews and throughout your job search.

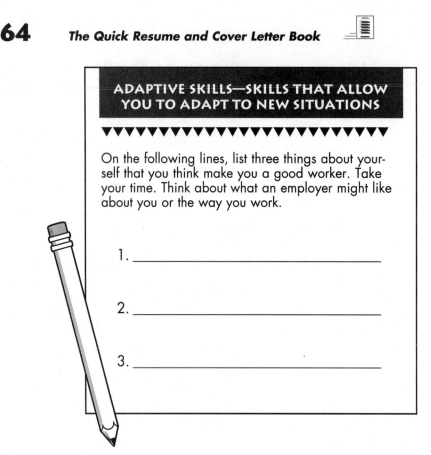

ADAPTIVE SKILLS—SKILLS THAT ALLOW YOU TO ADAPT TO NEW SITUATIONS

▼▼▼▼▼▼▼▼▼▼▼▼▼▼▼▼▼▼▼▼▼▼▼▼▼▼▼

On the following lines, list three things about yourself that you think make you a good worker. Take your time. Think about what an employer might like about you or the way you work.

1. _____

2. _____

3. _____

The skills you just wrote may be among the most important things that an employer will want to know about you. Most (but not all) people write adaptive skills when asked this question. Whatever you wrote, these are important things to mention in the interview. In fact, presenting these skills well will often allow a less experienced job seeker to get the job over someone with better credentials.

ADAPTIVE SKILLS/PERSONALITY TRAITS CHECKLIST

I have created a list of adaptive skills that tend to be important to employers. The ones listed as "The Minimum" are those that most employers consider essential. They will typically not hire someone who has problems in these areas.

Look over the list and put a checkmark next to each adaptive skill on the list that you have. Put a second checkmark next to those skills that are particularly important to you to use or include in your next job.

● ●

ADAPTIVE SKILLS CHECKLIST

The Minimum
- ❏ Good attendance
- ❏ Honesty
- ❏ Arrive on time
- ❏ Follow instructions
- ❏ Meet deadlines
- ❏ Get along with supervisor
- ❏ Get along with co-workers
- ❏ Hardworking, productive

Other Adaptive Skills
- ❏ Able to coordinate
- ❏ Friendly
- ❏ Ambitious
- ❏ Good-natured
- ❏ Assertive
- ❏ Helpful
- ❏ Capable
- ❏ Humble
- ❏ Cheerful
- ❏ Imaginative
- ❏ Competent
- ❏ Independent
- ❏ Complete assignments
- ❏ Industrious
- ❏ Conscientious
- ❏ Informal
- ❏ Creative
- ❏ Intelligent

- ❏ Dependable
- ❏ Intuitive
- ❏ Discreet
- ❏ Learn quickly
- ❏ Eager
- ❏ Loyal
- ❏ Efficient
- ❏ Mature
- ❏ Energetic
- ❏ Methodical
- ❏ Enthusiastic
- ❏ Modest
- ❏ Expressive
- ❏ Motivated
- ❏ Flexible
- ❏ Natural
- ❏ Formal
- ❏ Open-minded
- ❏ Optimistic
- ❏ Sincere
- ❏ Original
- ❏ Solve problems
- ❏ Patient
- ❏ Spontaneous
- ❏ Persistent
- ❏ Steady
- ❏ Physically strong
- ❏ Tactful
- ❏ Practice new skills
- ❏ Take pride in work
- ❏ Reliable
- ❏ Tenacious
- ❏ Resourceful
- ❏ Thrifty

- ❏ Responsible
- ❏ Trustworthy
- ❏ Self-confident
- ❏ Versatile
- ❏ Sense of humor
- ❏ Well-organized

Add any adaptive skills to the list above that were not listed but that you think are important to include.

- ❏ _____
- ❏ _____
- ❏ _____
- ❏ _____
- ❏ _____
- ❏ _____
- ❏ _____
- ❏ _____
- ❏ _____
- ❏ _____
- ❏ _____

● ●

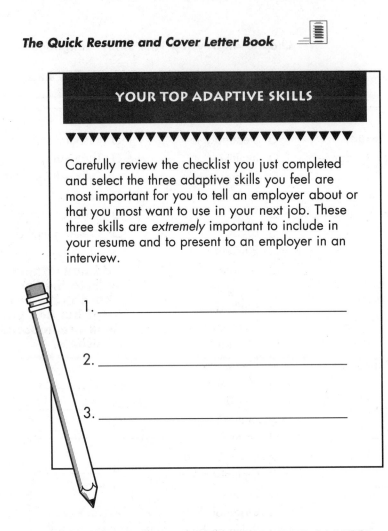

YOUR TOP ADAPTIVE SKILLS

▼▼▼▼▼▼▼▼▼▼▼▼▼▼▼▼▼▼▼▼▼▼▼▼▼▼▼

Carefully review the checklist you just completed and select the three adaptive skills you feel are most important for you to tell an employer about or that you most want to use in your next job. These three skills are *extremely* important to include in your resume and to present to an employer in an interview.

1. _____

2. _____

3. _____

TRANSFERABLE SKILLS—SKILLS THAT TRANSFER TO MANY JOBS

Over the years, I have assembled a list of transferable skills that are important in a wide variety of jobs. In the checklist that follows, the skills listed as "Key Transferable Skills" are those that I consider to be most important to many employers. The key skills are also those that are often required in jobs with more responsibility and higher pay, so it pays to emphasize these skills if you have them.

The remaining transferable skills are grouped into categories that may be helpful to you. Go ahead and check each skill you are strong in, then double check the skills you want to use in your next job. When you are finished, you should have checked 10 to 20 skills at least once.

Key Transferable Skills

- ❏ Meet deadlines
- ❏ Plan
- ❏ Speak in public
- ❏ Control budgets
- ❏ Supervise others
- ❏ Increase sales or efficiency
- ❏ Accept responsibility
- ❏ Instruct others
- ❏ Solve problems
- ❏ Manage money or budgets
- ❏ Manage people
- ❏ Meet the public
- ❏ Negotiate
- ❏ Organize/manage projects
- ❏ Written communications

Other Transferable Skills

Dealing with Things

- ❏ Use my hands
- ❏ Assemble or make things
- ❏ Build, observe, inspect things
- ❏ Construct or repair buildings
- ❏ Operate tools and machinery
- ❏ Drive or operate vehicles
- ❏ Repair things
- ❏ Good with my hands
- ❏ Use complex equipment

Dealing with Data

- ❏ Analyze data or facts
- ❏ Investigate
- ❏ Audit records
- ❏ Keep financial records
- ❏ Budget
- ❏ Locate answers or information

- ❏ Calculate, compute
- ❏ Manage money
- ❏ Classify data
- ❏ Negotiate
- ❏ Compare, inspect, or record facts
- ❏ Count, observe, compile
- ❏ Research
- ❏ Detail-oriented
- ❏ Synthesize
- ❏ Evaluate
- ❏ Take inventory

Working with People

- ❏ Administer
- ❏ Patient
- ❏ Care for
- ❏ Persuade
- ❏ Confront others
- ❏ Pleasant
- ❏ Counsel people
- ❏ Sensitive
- ❏ Demonstrate
- ❏ Sociable
- ❏ Diplomatic
- ❏ Supervise
- ❏ Help others
- ❏ Tactful
- ❏ Insightful
- ❏ Teach
- ❏ Interview others
- ❏ Tolerant
- ❏ Kind
- ❏ Tough
- ❏ Listen
- ❏ Trust
- ❏ Negotiate
- ❏ Understand
- ❏ Outgoing

Using Words, Ideas

- ❏ Articulate
- ❏ Inventive
- ❏ Communicate verbally
- ❏ Logical
- ❏ Correspond with others
- ❏ Remember information

- ❏ Research
- ❏ Create new ideas
- ❏ Design
- ❏ Speak in public
- ❏ Edit
- ❏ Write clearly

Leadership

- ❏ Arrange social functions
- ❏ Motivate people
- ❏ Competitive
- ❏ Negotiate agreements
- ❏ Decisive
- ❏ Plan
- ❏ Delegate
- ❏ Run meetings
- ❏ Direct others
- ❏ Self-controlled
- ❏ Explain things to others
- ❏ Self-motivated
- ❏ Get results
- ❏ Solve problems
- ❏ Mediate problems
- ❏ Take risks

Creative, Artistic

- ❏ Artistic
- ❏ Music appreciation
- ❏ Dance, body movement
- ❏ Perform, act
- ❏ Draw, sketch, render
- ❏ Play instruments
- ❏ Expressive
- ❏ Present artistic ideas

Add Any Other Transferable Skills That You Think Are Important

- ❏ _____
- ❏ _____
- ❏ _____
- ❏ _____
- ❏ _____

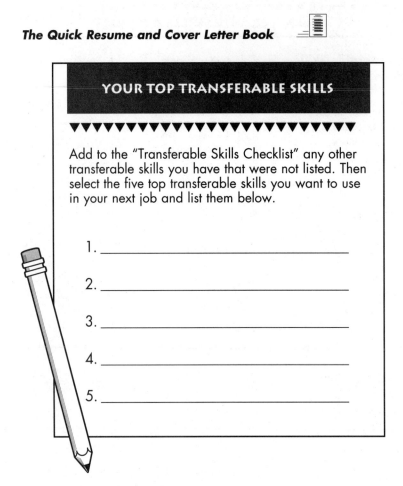

YOUR TOP TRANSFERABLE SKILLS

▼▼▼▼▼▼▼▼▼▼▼▼▼▼▼▼▼▼▼▼▼▼▼▼▼▼▼

Add to the "Transferable Skills Checklist" any other transferable skills you have that were not listed. Then select the five top transferable skills you want to use in your next job and list them below.

1. _____

2. _____

3. _____

4. _____

5. _____

Quick Fact

IDENTIFYING YOUR JOB-RELATED SKILLS

Many jobs require skills that are specific to that occupation. An airline pilot will obviously need to know how to fly an airplane and, thankfully, having good adaptive and transferable skills would not be enough to be considered for that job.

Job-related skills may have been gained in a variety of ways including education, training, work, hobbies, or other life experiences. The next chapter in this book will review your education, work, and other experiences and use this as a basis for identifying your key job-related skills which can then be presented in your resume and interviews.

THE SKILLS EMPLOYERS WANT

As a way to illustrate that employers value adaptive and transferable skills very highly, I have included the top skills that employers want in the people they hire. This information comes from a study of employers conducted jointly by the U.S. Department of Labor and the American Association of Counseling and Development. Note that all are either adaptive or transferable skills. (I rest my case.)

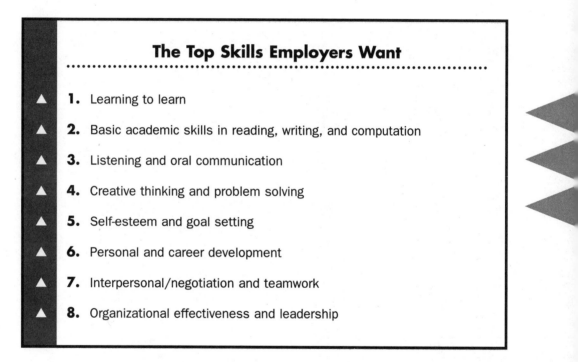

The Top Skills Employers Want

- **1.** Learning to learn
- **2.** Basic academic skills in reading, writing, and computation
- **3.** Listening and oral communication
- **4.** Creative thinking and problem solving
- **5.** Self-esteem and goal setting
- **6.** Personal and career development
- **7.** Interpersonal/negotiation and teamwork
- **8.** Organizational effectiveness and leadership

5

DOCUMENT YOUR EXPERIENCE

Quick Tip

I admit that this is a tedious chapter, with lots of forms to complete. And, for that reason, you would be forgiven for not wanting to complete them all. But the details this chapter asks for will help you recollect skills, accomplishments, competencies, and results that can later help you in developing a superior resume and, more importantly, in the interview. All the information will give you a chance to reflect on your varied experiences and gather up those that best support what you want to do next.

All resumes require you to provide information about what you have done in the past. This chapter will help you collect the basic information needed to complete a resume, but it will also encourage you to consider your accomplishments, identify additional skills, and develop specific examples of when and where you used those skills. These additions to the dry facts can make your resume a much more powerful tool in presenting yourself well. This thorough review of your history also will prepare you to better answer questions in the interview.

A series of forms will ask you for information on your education, training, work and volunteer history, and other life experiences. While you may have already completed some of this information in Section 1 of this book, the forms that follow are considerably more detailed.

When completing the forms in this chapter, emphasize the key skills you have identified from the previous chapter. Those skills, as well as your accomplishments and results, are of particular interest to most employers.

Pay particular attention to those experiences and accomplishments that you really enjoyed—these often demonstrate skills that you should try to use in your next job. When possible, include numbers to describe your activities or their results. For example, saying "spoke to groups as large as 200 people" has more impact than "did presentations."

In some cases, you may want to write a draft on a separate sheet of paper before completing the form in this book. Use an erasable pen or pencil on the worksheets to allow for changes. In all sections, emphasize the skills and accomplishments that best support your ability to do the job you are seeking.

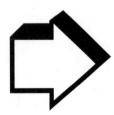

EDUCATION WORKSHEET

. . . .

High School Worksheet

Unless you are a recent high school graduate, most employers won't
be interested in too many details related to your work in high school.
Still, it can be worthwhile to emphasize highlights, particularly if you
are a recent graduate.

Name of school(s)/years attended: _____

_____

Subjects you did well in or might relate to the job you want: _____

_____

_____

_____

_____

_____

Extracurricular activities/hobbies/leisure activities: _____

_____

_____

_____

_____

_____

Accomplishments/things you did well (in or out of school): _____

_____

_____

_____

_____

_____

College Worksheet

If you graduated from college or took college classes, this is often of interest to an employer. If you are a new graduate, these experiences can be particularly important. Consider those things that directly support your ability to do the job. For example, working your way through school supports your being hardworking. If you took courses that specifically support your job, you can include details on these as well.

Name of school(s)/years attended: _____

_____

Courses related to job objective: _____

_____

_____

_____

_____

Extracurricular activities/hobbies/leisure activities: _____

_____

_____

_____

_____

_____

Accomplishments/things you did well (in or out of school): _____

_____

_____

_____

_____

Specific things you learned or can do that relate to the job you want:

_____

_____

_____

_____

_____

Post-High School Training

List any training that might relate to the job you want. Include military and on-the-job training, workshops, or informal training (such as from a hobby).

Training/dates/certificates: _____

_____

_____

_____

_____

_____

_____

Specific things you can do as a result: _____

_____

_____

_____

_____

_____

_____

_____

Specific things you learned or can do that relate to the job you want:

_____

_____

_____

_____

_____

_____

_____

_____

_____

WORK AND VOLUNTEER HISTORY WORKSHEET

**Quick
Fact**

Virtually all resumes include information on work you have done in
the past. Use this worksheet to list each major job you have held and
the information related to each. Begin with your most recent job first,
followed by previous ones.

Include military experience and unpaid work here too. Both are work
and are particularly important if you do not have much paid civilian
work experience. Create additional sheets to cover *all* of your significant jobs or unpaid experiences as needed. If you have been promoted, consider handling that as a separate job.

Whenever possible, provide numbers to support what you did: number of people served over one or more years; number of transactions
processed; percent sales increase; total inventory value you were
responsible for; payroll of the staff you supervised; total budget you
were responsible for; and other data. As much as possible, mention
results using numbers too.

I have provided four of the worksheets but, if you need more, please
feel free to photocopy extras for each of the jobs you need
to document.

● ●

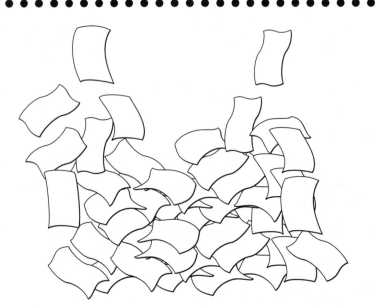

JOB / VOLUNTEER WORKSHEET

....

Job #1

Name of organization: _____

Address: _____

_____

Employed from: _____ **to:** _____

Job title(s): _____

Supervisor's name: _____

Phone number: ( ) _____

Machinery or equipment you used: _____

_____

_____

_____

Data, information, or reports you created or used: _____

_____

_____

_____

People-oriented duties or responsibilities to co-workers, customers, others:

_____

_____

_____

_____

_____

Services you provided or goods you produced: _____

_____

_____

_____

_____

_____

Promotions or salary increases, if any: _____

_____

_____

Details on anything you did to help the organization, such as increase productivity, simplify or reorganize job duties, decrease costs, increase profits, improve working conditions, reduce turnover, or other improvements. Qualify results when possible—for example, "Increased order processing by 50 percent, with no increase in staff costs."

_____

_____

_____

_____

_____

_____

Specific things you learned or can do that relate to the job you want:

_____

_____

_____

_____

_____

_____

What would your supervisor say about you? _____

_____

_____

_____

_____

_____

JOB / VOLUNTEER WORKSHEET

....

Job #2

Name of organization: _____

Address: _____

_____

Employed from: _____ **to:** _____

Job title(s): _____

Supervisor's name: _____

Phone number: (   ) _____

Machinery or equipment you used: _____

_____

_____

_____

Data, information, or reports you created or used: _____

_____

_____

_____

People-oriented duties or responsibilities to co-workers, customers, others:

_____

_____

_____

_____

_____

Services you provided or goods you produced: _____

_____

_____

_____

_____

_____

_____

Promotions or salary increases, if any: _____

_____

_____

Details on anything you did to help the organization, such as increase productivity, simplify or reorganize job duties, decrease costs, increase profits, improve working conditions, reduce turnover, or other improvements. Qualify results when possible—for example, "Increased order processing by 50 percent, with no increase in staff costs."

_____

_____

_____

_____

_____

_____

Specific things you learned or can do that relate to the job you want:

_____

_____

_____

_____

_____

_____

What would your supervisor say about you? _____

_____

_____

_____

_____

_____

JOB / VOLUNTEER WORKSHEET

••

Job #3

Name of organization: _____

Address: _____

_____

Employed from: _____ **to:** _____

Job title(s): _____

Supervisor's name: _____

Phone number: (___ **)** _____

Machinery or equipment you used: _____

_____

_____

_____

Data, information, or reports you created or used: _____

_____

_____

_____

People-oriented duties or responsibilities to co-workers, customers, others:

_____

_____

_____

_____

_____

Services you provided or goods you produced: _____

_____

_____

_____

_____

_____

_____

Promotions or salary increases, if any: _____

_____

_____

Details on anything you did to help the organization, such as increase productivity, simplify or reorganize job duties, decrease costs, increase profits, improve working conditions, reduce turnover, or other improvements. Qualify results when possible—for example, "Increased order processing by 50 percent, with no increase in staff costs."

_____

_____

_____

_____

_____

_____

Specific things you learned or can do that relate to the job you want:

_____

_____

_____

_____

_____

_____

What would your supervisor say about you? _____

_____

_____

_____

_____

_____

_____

JOB / VOLUNTEER WORKSHEET

• •

Job #4

Name of organization: _____

Address: _____

_____

Employed from: _____ **to:** _____

Job title(s): _____

Supervisor's name: _____

Phone number: (   ) _____

Machinery or equipment you used: _____

_____

_____

_____

Data, information, or reports you created or used: _____

_____

_____

_____

People-oriented duties or responsibilities to co-workers, customers, others:

_____

_____

_____

_____

_____

Services you provided or goods you produced: _____

_____

_____

_____

_____

_____

_____

Promotions or salary increases, if any: _____

_____

_____

Details on anything you did to help the organization, such as increase productivity, simplify or reorganize job duties, decrease costs, increase profits, improve working conditions, reduce turnover, or other improvements. Qualify results when possible—for example, "Increased order processing by 50 percent, with no increase in staff costs."

_____

_____

_____

_____

_____

_____

Specific things you learned or can do that relate to the job you want:

_____

_____

_____

_____

_____

_____

What would your supervisor say about you? _____

_____

_____

_____

_____

_____

OTHER LIFE EXPERIENCES WORKSHEET

Use the worksheet that follows to include accomplishments or other significant information from hobbies, family responsibilities, recreational activities, travel, or any other experiences in your life. Write any that seem particularly meaningful to you below and name the key skills you think were involved in doing them.

SITUATION 1: _____

_____

_____

_____

_____

_____

Details and skills used: _____

_____

_____

_____

_____

Specific things you learned or can do that relate to the job you want:

_____

_____

_____

_____

_____

SITUATION 2: _____

_____

_____

_____

_____

_____

Details and skills used: _____

_____

_____

_____

_____

Specific things you learned or can do that relate to the job you want:

_____

_____

_____

_____

SITUATION 3: _____

_____

_____

_____

_____

Details and skills used: _____

_____

_____

_____

_____

Specific things you learned or can do that relate to the job you want:

_____

_____

_____

_____

KEY ACCOMPLISHMENTS AND SKILLS TO TELL AN EMPLOYER

Here are a few questions that can help you consider which of the things from your history are most important to include in your resume or to mention in an interview.

▼▼

1. **What are the most important accomplishments and skills you can tell an employer regarding your education and training?**

_____

_____

_____

_____

_____

_____

2. **What are the most important accomplishments and skills you can present to an employer regarding your paid and unpaid work experiences?**

_____

_____

_____

_____

_____

_____

_____

3. **What are the most important accomplishments and skills you can present to an employer regarding your other life experiences?**

_____

_____

_____

_____

_____

_____

▲▲

The above skills are the ones to emphasize in your resume and in interviews!

C H A P T E R

• •

6

BE CLEAR ABOUT
YOUR JOB OBJECTIVE

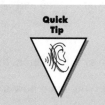

Quick Tip

I think that a resume should have a job objective. Even if your objective is general, it allows you to select those details for your resume that best support what you want to do next. But whether you do or do not have a clear job objective, this chapter will help show you how to explore career and job alternatives that you might not have considered. It pays to be both well-informed and flexible..

This chapter will help you in a number of ways:

1. It will help you more clearly identify the range of jobs that you can include in your job search.

2. It will show you how to obtain more information related to jobs that interest you.

3. It will assist you in writing your resume's job objective statement and in supporting it via skills and other details.

4. It will assist you in making good career decisions.

One of the worst things you can do with your resume is to try to make it work for "any" job. While it is acceptable for you to consider a broad range of jobs, few employers are impressed by someone who doesn't seem to know what they want to do. This means that all but the simplest of resumes deserve to have a job objective.

Another mistake made on many resumes is the failure to target your skills to closely match the job that you say you want. Of course, if you are not clear about what sort of job you *do* want, it will be most difficult to present the skills you have to do the job, won't it?

As you may already know, deciding on a job objective can be quite complicated. There are over 12,000 job titles that are defined by the U.S. Department of Labor and it would be most impractical to try to consider all possible alternatives. But it is likely that you already have some idea of the sorts of jobs that either interest you or that you are most likely to consider. But even if you don't have any idea at all about what you want to do, you need to settle the matter (or at least make it appear as if you have settled it) as you write your resume and begin your search for a job.

While this book is not designed to provide comprehensive career information, this chapter can help you learn more about the options available to you—and how to use career information sources in constructing your resume.

● ●

CONSIDER JOBS WITHIN CLUSTERS OF RELATED OCCUPATIONS

Most people overlook too many job opportunities. They often do this simply because they don't know about all the occupations that could use a person with their skills, interests, and experience. As I've mentioned, there are over 12,000 jobs that are defined by the U.S. Department of Labor. This is entirely too large a number for anyone to comprehend in any meaningful way.

Most people simply go about their lives and careers with very little information about the universe of career and job possibilities that might suit them. They often end up in an educational program and, later, find jobs in a haphazard way. That is how it happened for me during my early years and it was probably that way for you. Things simply happened.

But I think that most of us can do better. While I am not suggesting that the process of career planning is a simple one, I do think that there are a few simple things that we can do to help us make better decisions. And, in this chapter, I will present to you a few things that I think can be particularly helpful.

One of those things is to introduce you to several of the ways that labor market experts have organized jobs and information about jobs. Fortunately, the over 12,000 job titles that exist are not arranged in random order. Someone else has spent a lot of time arranging them into clusters of related jobs. Knowing these arrangements can help you in a variety of ways. For example, you might identify possible job targets, prepare for interviews, consider long-term career plans and, of course, write a better resume.

Quick Tip

I've included one job description from the current OOH in Appendix A for you to ponder. Even though that particular job may not interest you, reading the description will help you understand how useful the OOH job descriptions can be. Read it soon while my comments on the OOH are fresh in your mind...

THE 250 JOBS IN THE OCCUPATIONAL OUTLOOK HANDBOOK (OOH)

I consider the *Occupational Outlook Handbook* to be one of the most helpful books on career information available. I urge you either to buy one or arrange for frequent access to it throughout your job search because it is so useful in a variety of ways.

The *OOH* provides descriptions for about 250 of the most popular jobs in our work-force. While that may not sound like many—compared to the over 12,000 job titles that exist—these 250 jobs are the ones that about 85 percent of the workforce actually work in.

Updated every two years by the U.S. Department of Labor, the *OOH* provides the latest information on salaries, projections for growth, related jobs, skills required, education or training needed, working conditions, and many other details. Each job is described in a readable and interesting format.

SOME WAYS TO USE THE OOH

▼▼

To identify the skills needed in the job you want: You can look up a job that interests you and the *OOH* will tell you the transferable and job-related skills it requires. Assuming that you have these skills, you can then emphasize them in your resume and interviews.

To find skills from previous jobs to support your present objective: Look up *OOH* descriptions for jobs you have had in the past. A careful read will help you identify skills you used there that can be transferred and used in the new job. Even "minor" jobs can be used in this way. For example, if you waited on tables while going to school, you would discover that doing this requires the ability to work under pressure, good communications skills, the ability to deal with customers, work quickly, and many other skills. If, for example, you were now looking for a job as an accountant, you can see how transferable skills used in an apparently unrelated past job (such as waiting on tables) really can be used to support your ability to do another job.

To identify related job targets: Each of the major jobs described in the *OOH* includes a listing of other jobs that are closely related. The listing also includes information on positions that the job might lead to through promotion or experience. And, since the jobs are listed within clusters of similar jobs, you can easily browse descriptions of similar jobs that you may have overlooked. All of this information gives you options to consider in your job search as well as information to include in the job objective section of your resume.

To find out the typical salary range, trends, and other details: While you should *never* (well, almost never) list your salary requirements in a resume or cover letter, the *OOH* will help you to know what pay range to expect as well as many other details about the job and trends that are affecting it. But note that your local pay and other details can differ significantly from the national information provided in the *OOH*.

▲▲

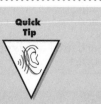

Quick Tip

Most libraries will have the Occupational Outlook Handbook *but you probably won't be able to take it home. There is another book titled* America's Top 300 Jobs *which provides the very same information and may be available for circulation. You can also order either of these books through most bookstores, something I sincerely recommend based on how often they should be used as a reference tool during your job search and after. Either book costs less than $20 and you can order them by using the order form in the back of this very book.*

LIST OF JOBS IN THE
OCCUPATIONAL OUTLOOK HANDBOOK

The following is a list of jobs in the current edition of the *OOH*. The jobs are arranged in clusters of related jobs and the listing will give you an idea of other jobs you might want to consider when writing your resume and conducting your job search.

One way to use this list is to check those jobs that you have held in the past as well as those that interest you now. Later, you can look these jobs up in the *OOH* and obtain additional information related to each.

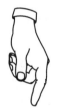

DETAILED TABLE OF OCCUPATIONS BY CLUSTER

EXECUTIVE, ADMINISTRATIVE, AND MANAGERIAL OCCUPATIONS

Accountants and auditors
Administrative services managers
Budget analysts
Construction and building inspectors
Construction contractors and managers
Cost estimators
Education administrators
Employment interviewers
Engineering, science, and data processing managers

Financial managers
General managers and top executives
Government chief executives and legislators
Health services managers
Hotel managers and assistants
Industrial production managers
Inspectors and compliance officers, except construction
Management analysts and consultants

Marketing, advertising, and public relations managers

Personnel, training, and labor relations specialists and managers

Property and real estate managers

Purchasing agents and managers

Restaurant and food service managers

Underwriters

Wholesale and retail buyers and merchandise managers

PROFESSIONAL SPECIALTY OCCUPATIONS

Engineers
Aerospace engineers
Chemical engineers
Civil engineers
Electrical and electronics engineers
Industrial engineers
Mechanical engineers
Metallurgical, ceramic, and materials engineers
Mining engineers
Nuclear engineers
Petroleum engineers
Architects and surveyors
Architects
Landscape architects
Surveyors
Computer, mathematical, and operations research occupations
Actuaries
Computer systems analysts
Mathematicians
Operations research analysts
Statisticians
Life scientists
Agricultural scientists
Biological scientists
Foresters and conservation scientists
Physical scientists
Chemists
Geologists and geophysicists
Meteorologists
Physicists and astronomers
Lawyers and judges
Social scientists and urban planners
Economists and market research analysts
Psychologists
Sociologists
Urban and regional planners
Social and recreation workers
Human services workers
Social workers
Recreation workers
Religious workers
Protestant ministers

Rabbis
Roman Catholic priests
Teachers, librarians, and counselors
Adult education teachers
Archivists and curators
College and university faculty
Counselors
Kindergarten and elementary school teachers
Librarians
Secondary school teachers
Health diagnosing practitioners
Chiropractors
Dentists
Optometrists
Physicians
Podiatrists
Veterinarians
Health assessment and treating occupations
Dietitians and nutritionists
Occupational therapists
Pharmacists
Physical therapists
Physician assistants
Recreational therapists
Registered nurses
Respiratory therapists
Speech-language pathologists and audiologists
Communications occupations
Public relations specialists
Radio and television announcers and newscasters
Reporters and correspondents
Writers and editors
Visual arts occupations
Designers
Photographers and camera operators
Visual artists
Performing arts occupations
Actors, directors, and producers
Dancers and choreographers
Musicians

TECHNICIANS AND RELATED SUPPORT OCCUPATIONS

Health technologists and technicians
Clinical laboratory technologists and technicians
Dental hygienists
Dispensing opticians
EEG technologists
EKG technicians
Emergency medical technicians
Licensed practical nurses
Medical record technicians
Nuclear medicine technologists
Radiologic technologists

Surgical technicians
Technologists, except health
Aircraft pilots
Air traffic controllers
Broadcast technicians
Computer programmers
Drafters
Engineering technicians
Library technicians
Paralegals
Science technicians
Tool programmers, numerical control

MARKETING AND SALES OCCUPATIONS

Cashiers
Counter and rental clerks
Insurance agents and brokers
Manufacturers' and wholesale
  sales representatives
Real estate agents, brokers, and appraisers

Retail sales workers
Securities and financial service
  sales representatives
Services sales representatives
Travel agents

ADMINISTRATIVE SUPPORT OCCUPATIONS, INCLUDING CLERICAL

Adjusters, investigators, and collectors
Bank tellers
Clerical supervisors and managers
Computer and peripheral equipment operators
Credit clerks and authorizers
General office clerks
Information clerks
Hotel and motel clerks
Interviewing and new accounts clerks
Receptionists
Reservation and transportation ticket
  agents and travel clerks
Mail clerks and messengers
Material recording, scheduling, dispatching, and distributing occupations
Dispatchers
Stock clerks
Traffic, shipping, and receiving clerks

Postal clerks and mail carriers
Record clerks
Billing clerks
Bookkeeping, accounting, and
  auditing clerks
Brokerage clerks and statement clerks
File clerks
Library assistants and bookmobile drivers
Order clerks
Payroll and timekeeping clerks
Personnel clerks
Secretaries
Stenographers and court reporters
Teacher aids
Telephone, telegraph, and teletype operators
Typists, word processors, and data entry
  keyers

SERVICE OCCUPATIONS

Protective service occupations
Correction officers
Firefighting occupations
Guards
Police, detectives, and special agents
Food and beverage preparation and service occupations
Chefs, cooks, and other kitchen workers
Food and beverage service occupations
Health service occupations
Dental assistants
Medical assistants

Nursing aides and psychiatric aides
Personal services and building and grounds service occupations
Animal caretakers, except farm
Barbers and cosmetologists
Flight attendants
Gardeners and groundskeepers
Homemaker-home health aides
Janitors and cleaners
Preschool workers
Private household workers

AGRICULTURE, FORESTRY, FISHING, AND RELATED OCCUPATIONS

Farm operators and managers
Fishers, hunters, and trappers

Timber cutting and logging workers

MECHANICS, INSTALLERS, AND REPAIRERS

Aircraft mechanics and engine specialists
Automotive body repairers
Automotive mechanics
Diesel mechanics
Electronic equipment repairers
Commercial and industrial electronic equipment repairers
Communications equipment mechanics
Computer and office machine repairers
Electronic home entertainment equipment repairers
Telephone installers and repairers
Elevator installers and repairers

Farm equipment mechanics
General maintenance mechanics
Heating, air-conditioning, and refrigeration technicians
Home appliance and power tool repairers
Industrial machinery repairers
Line installers and cable splicers
Millwrights
Mobile heavy equipment mechanics
Motorcycle, boat, and small-engine mechanics
Musical instrument repairers and tuners
Vending machine servicers and repairers

CONSTRUCTION TRADES AND EXTRACTIVE OCCUPATIONS

Bricklayers and stonemasons
Carpenters
Carpet installers
Concrete masons and terrazzo workers
Drywall workers and lathers
Electricians
Glaziers
Insulation workers

Painters and paperhangers
Plasterers
Plumbers and pipefitters
Roofers
Roustabouts
Sheet-metal workers
Structural and reinforcing ironworkers
Tilesetters

PRODUCTION OCCUPATIONS

Assemblers
Precision assemblers
Blue-collar worker supervisors

Food processing occupations
Butcher and meat, poultry, and fish cutters
Inspectors, testers, and graders

METALWORKING AND PLASTICS-WORKING OCCUPATIONS

Boilermakers
Jewelers
Machinists
Metalworking and plastics-working
   machine operators
Numerical-control machine-tool operators
Tool and die makers
Welders, cutters, and welding machine
   operators
Plant and systems operators
Electric power generating plant
operators and power distributors
   and dispatchers
Stationary engineers
Water and wastewater treatment plant
   operators

Printing occupations
Prepress workers
Printing press operators
Bindery workers
**Textile, apparel, and furnishings
occupations**
Apparel workers
Shoe and leather workers and repairers
Textile machinery operators
Upholsterers
Woodworking occupations
Miscellaneous production occupations
Dental laboratory technicians
Ophthalmic laboratory technicians
Painting and coating machine operators
Photographic process workers

TRANSPORTATION AND MATERIAL MOVING OCCUPATIONS

Busdrivers
Material moving equipment operators
Rail transportation occupations

Truckdrivers
Water transportation occupations

HANDLERS, EQUIPMENT CLEANERS, HELPERS, AND LABORERS

JOB OPPORTUNITIES IN THE ARMED FORCES

THE 12,000 JOBS IN THE COMPLETE GUIDE FOR OCCUPATIONAL EXPLORATION (CGOE)

The *Occupational Outlook Handbook* provides excellent descriptions of the major jobs but does not cover more specialized ones. This can be a limitation if you have experience, education, or interest in a specific area and want to know the variety of jobs that area offers. In some cases, you may also want to know the variety of jobs you might consider in making a career change or in searching for a new job.

"*All along the way, helpful information is provided related to each group of jobs.***"**

ALL JOBS ARE ORGANIZED INTO JUST TWELVE INTEREST AREAS

Unlike the *OOH*, the *CGOE* does not provide descriptions of jobs. What it does do is arrange virtually every known job—over 12,000 of them—in a very useful way.

All jobs are first organized within just twelve major interest areas. These areas are then divided into 64 groupings of related jobs and 348 additional subgroups of even more closely related jobs. Each of these groupings and subgroupings is described in an easy-to-understand way, including the types of training, skills required, and many other details. If you are looking for other jobs to consider as job targets, the *CGOE*'s arrangement will allow you to quickly identify groupings of jobs that are most closely related to what you want to do. All along the way, from major interest area to the various subgroupings, helpful information is provided related to each group of jobs. So, even if some of the jobs themselves are not familiar to you, there is enough information provided to help you understand the jobs within that grouping and what they require. In a quick and logical way, you can narrow down the thousands of job possibilities to the dozen or so that most closely match what you want to do and are good at.

The *CGOE*'s twelve major interest areas, along with brief definitions of each, follow. Typically, most of the careers that interest you are within one or two of these major clusters.

The CGOE's **Twelve Major Interest Areas**

▲ **1. Artistic:** An interest in creative expression of feelings or ideas.

▲ **2. Scientific:** An interest in discovering, collecting, and analyzing information about the natural world, and in applying scientific research findings to problems in medicine, the life sciences, and the natural sciences.

▲ **3. Plants and Animals:** An interest in working with plants and animals, usually outdoors.

▲ **4. Protective:** An interest in using authority to protect people and property.

▲ **5. Mechanical:** An interest in applying mechanical principles to practical situations by use of machines or hand tools.

▲ **6. Industrial:** An interest in repetitive, concrete, organized activities done in a factory setting.

▲ **7. Business Detail:** An interest in organized, clearly defined activities requiring accuracy and attention to details, primarily in an office setting.

▲ **8. Selling:** An interest in bringing others to a particular point of view by personal persuasion, using sales and promotional techniques.

▲ **9. Accommodating:** An interest in catering to the wishes and needs of others, usually in a one-on-one basis.

▲ **10. Humanitarian:** An interest in helping others with their mental, spiritual, social, physical, or vocational needs.

▲ **11. Leading and Influencing:** An interest in leading and influencing others by using high-level verbal or numerical abilities.

▲ **12. Physical Performing:** An interest in physical activities performed before an audience.

SUBGROUPINGS OF RELATED JOBS

As mentioned earlier, each of the twelve interest areas is further broken down into more specific groupings of related jobs. Each one of these subgroups include information related to that grouping as well as specific job titles that fit into each.

The chart below shows you how the Artistic interest area is broken down into its subgroups. The most specific groupings provide lists of jobs as well as some information regarding each job within the group.

This arrangement makes it easy to locate the types of jobs you want to explore by simply turning to the appropriate section of the *CGOE*. Once there, you can quickly see the specific jobs that are within that grouping and identify other jobs that may be suitable for job targets based on skills you already have.

Look over the sample listing of subgroups for the Artistic interest area that follows. If you are interested in jobs involving artistic skills, this arrangement would allow you to quickly identify major groupings in the *CGOE* that you were most qualified to do or most interested in learning more about.

● ●

SUBGROUPINGS WITHIN THE ARTISTIC INTEREST AREA

Literary Arts
Editing
Creative Writing
Critiquing

Visual Arts
Instructing and
   Appraising
Studio Art
Commercial Art

Performing Arts: Drama
Instructing and
   Directing
Performing
Narrating and
   Announcing

Performing Arts: Music
Instructing and
   Directing
Composing and
   Arranging
Vocal Performing
Instrumental
   Performing

Performing Arts: Dance
Instructing and
   Choreography
Performing

Craft Arts
Graphic Arts and
   Related Crafts
Arts and Crafts
Hand Lettering,
   Painting, and
   Decorating

Elemental Arts
Psychic Science
Announcing
Entertaining

Modeling
Personal Appearance

● ●

Quick Tip

While the CGOE *is a big book, it is quite easy to use. The subgroupings of related jobs allow you to find quickly jobs of interest. There is also a useful self-assessment section at the beginning.*

"*While the* CGOE *can be helpful, it does not include descriptions of the over 12,000 jobs it cross-references.***"**

USING THE CGOE

While the *CGOE* is almost 1,000 pages long, it is very easy to use and will quickly help you identify the many specialized jobs that are related to the skills, education, and experiences you already have. There are also a variety of cross-referencing systems in the *CGOE* that allow you to look up jobs based on education, hobbies and leisure interests, military experience, and many other factors.

DICTIONARY OF OCCUPATIONAL TITLES

While the *CGOE* can be very helpful in exploring career and job alternatives, it does not include descriptions of the over 12,000 jobs it cross-references (doing so would require the *CGOE* to be almost 2,500 pages long). So, once you locate a job that interests you, the *CGOE* points you to a description for that job in another book, the *Dictionary of Occupational Titles*, also published by our friends at the U.S. Department of Labor. The *DOT* provides brief descriptions for each of the over 12,000 jobs listed in the *CGOE*, as

Quick Tip

Look up the OOH *and/or* DOT *description of a job you will interview for and include details of that job in your resume, cover letter, and interview. You will be much better prepared to target your presentation and give the specific strengths you have that are needed for that job.*

well as additional cross-referencing systems that you may find useful—including a way to find occupations that are related to a specific industry.

Both the *CGOE* and *DOT* are valuable resources for finding job targets that would be overlooked otherwise. The information they provide can also help you identify skills and other information to include in your resume or cover letter such as the key skills needed in the jobs that interest you.

Quick Tip

The CGOE, DOT, *and* EGOE *are all relatively expensive books to own for personal use, costing about $100 for the set of three. But you can find them at most good libraries and, if they are not there, ask the librarian to order them for you. They are all published by or available from JIST. You can also use the order form in the back of this book, should you want your own copies.*

ENHANCED GUIDE FOR OCCUPATIONAL EXPLORATION

There is one other book that might interest you, titled the *Enhanced Guide for Occupational Exploration* (the *EGOE*, of course). This book uses the same organizational structure as the *CGOE* and includes *DOT* descriptions for about 2,500 jobs. These descriptions cover over 95 percent of the workforce, including all but the most obscure of jobs. Unless you are interested in highly specialized jobs, the *EGOE* will also help you locate a wide variety of jobs related to your interests.

VALUES, PREFERENCES, AND OTHER MATTERS TO CONSIDER IN DEFINING YOUR JOB OBJECTIVE

As you probably know, figuring out your career or job objective can be quite complicated. As if choosing from over 12,000 job titles isn't enough to deal with, there are many other considerations to be made.

I present here a brief review of some of the things that others have found important in making their career plans. While this certainly won't replace a good career planning process, you may find it helpful in considering a variety of issues that relate to deciding on a job objective, working on your resume, and in making career plans.

DEFINING YOUR IDEAL JOB

If you were to develop a profile of your ideal job, just what would it include? As you probably realize, there is more to this than simply picking out a job title. I have selected a series of questions that you should consider in defining what your ideal job might be. Of course, there is a bit of reality you will have to deal with in doing this (and I have included some of these elements), but dreams can never come true if you don't have them. So, I present the following very important but sometimes overlooked issues for you to consider in planning your job objective.

WHAT SKILLS DO YOU HAVE THAT YOU WANT TO USE IN YOUR NEXT JOB?

Review the skills lists that you worked on in Chapter 4 and the key skills you identified at the end of Chapter 5. Think about those skills that you enjoy using *and* are good at. Then list the five that you would most like to use in your next job.

1. _____

2. _____

3. _____

4. _____

5. _____

WHAT TYPE OF SPECIAL KNOWLEDGE DO YOU HAVE THAT YOU MIGHT USE IN YOUR NEXT JOB?

Perhaps you know how to fix radios, keep accounting records, or cook food. You don't have to have used these skills in a previous job to include them. Write down the things you have learned from schooling, training, hobbies, family experiences, and other sources. Perhaps one or more of them could make you a very special applicant in the right setting. For example, an accountant who knows a lot about fashion would be a very special candidate if she just happened to be interviewing for a job with an organization that sells clothing.

1. _____

2. _____

3. _____

4. _____

5. _____

WHAT TYPES OF PEOPLE DO YOU PREFER TO WORK WITH?

It is unlikely that you will be happy in any job if you are surrounded by people that you don't like. One way to approach this is to think about characteristics of people that you *would not* want to work with. The opposite characteristics are those that you probably would enjoy.

1. _____

2. _____

3. _____

4. _____

5. _____

WHAT TYPE OF WORK ENVIRONMENT DO YOU PREFER?

Do you want to work inside, outside, in a quiet place, a busy place, a clean place, or have a window with a nice view—or what? For example, I like to have variety in what I do as I am easily bored and so I want a work environment with lots of action and variety (and a window). Once again, you can review what you have disliked about your past work environments to give you clues for what you would most appreciate. Write those things that are most important to have on your next job on the lines below.

1. _____

2. _____

3. _____

4. _____

5. _____

WHERE DO YOU WANT YOUR NEXT JOB TO BE LOCATED—IN WHAT CITY OR REGION?

This could be as simple as finding a job that allows you to live where you are now (because you want to live near your relatives, for example). But, if so, would you prefer to work in a particular area, close to a child care center? If you are able to live or work anywhere, what would your ideal community be like?

1. _____

2. _____

3. _____

4. _____

5. _____

HOW MUCH MONEY DO YOU HOPE TO MAKE IN YOUR NEXT JOB?

Many people will take less money if the job is great in other ways—or to survive. Think about the minimum you would take as well as what you would eventually like to earn. Realistically, your next job will probably be somewhere between your minimum and maximum amounts.

1. _____

2. _____

HOW MUCH RESPONSIBILITY ARE YOU WILLING TO ACCEPT?

In most organizations, those who are willing to accept more responsibility are also typically paid more. There *is* typically a relationship between the two. Higher levels of responsibility often require you to supervise others or to make decisions that affect the organization. Some people are willing to accept this responsibility and others, understandably, would prefer not to. Decide how much responsibility you are willing to accept and write that below.

You should also ask yourself if you prefer to work by yourself, be part of a group, or be in charge. If so, at what level? Jot down where you see yourself, in terms of accepting responsibility for others, and in other ways within an organization.

1. _____

2. _____

3. _____

4. _____

5. _____

WHAT THINGS ARE IMPORTANT OR HAVE MEANING TO YOU?

What are your values? I once had a job where the sole reason for the existence of the organization was to make money. Not that this is necessarily wrong, it's just that I wanted to be involved in things that I could believe in. For example, some people work to help others, some to clean up our environment, and others to build things, make machines work, gain power or prestige, care for animals or plants—or something else. I believe that all work is worthwhile if done well, so the issue here is just what sorts of things are important to you. Write these values below.

1. _____

2. _____

3. _____

4. _____

5. _____

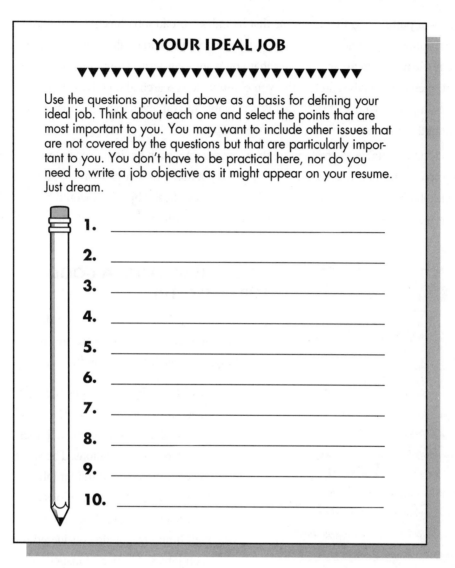

YOUR IDEAL JOB

▼▼▼▼▼▼▼▼▼▼▼▼▼▼▼▼▼▼▼▼▼▼▼▼▼

Use the questions provided above as a basis for defining your ideal job. Think about each one and select the points that are most important to you. You may want to include other issues that are not covered by the questions but that are particularly important to you. You don't have to be practical here, nor do you need to write a job objective as it might appear on your resume. Just dream.

1. _____

2. _____

3. _____

4. _____

5. _____

6. _____

7. _____

8. _____

9. _____

10. _____

WRITING YOUR RESUME'S JOB OBJECTIVE

Once you have a relatively good idea of the type of job you want, you need to write the job objective you will use in your resume. For many, this can be more difficult to do than it might seem. It assumes, for example, that you have a good idea of the type of job or jobs that you want.

You may need to spend more time researching various career alternatives before you settle on one that you can use in your resume. If that is the case with you, consider putting together a resume that includes a broad job objective that makes the resume acceptable for a variety of jobs that you would qualify for, even if you are not sure that these are the ones that you want long-term. Doing this will allow you to conduct a job search while you continue to research alternatives. In some cases, a job may present itself that is acceptable to you, even though it may be in a field that you were not sure of. It does happen.

It is also acceptable to create more than one resume, each having a separate job objective. This approach allows you to write your resume's content to support each job objective in a specific way. In most cases, these objectives would be related in some way—though this is certainly not required.

Quick Tip

If you don't know what type of job you want, concentrate on what you want to do NEXT. That might be working towards a long-term objective such as going back to school or starting your own business. In the meantime, you may also need to earn a living, so decide on a short-term job goal that you are qualified for and go after it. That short-term job goal would become the job objective that you would state on your resume.

TIPS FOR WRITING A GOOD JOB OBJECTIVE

While the job objective you write should meet your specific needs, here are some things to consider in writing it:

1. **Avoid job titles.** Job titles such as "Secretary" or "Marketing Analyst" can involve very different activities in different organizations. The same job can often have different job titles in different organizations and your using such a title may very well limit your being considered for such jobs as "Office Manager" or "Marketing Assistant." It is best to use broad categories of jobs rather than specific titles, so that you can be considered for a wide variety of

jobs related to the skills you have. For example, instead of "Secretary" you could say "Responsible Office Management or Clerical Position" if that is what you would really consider—and qualify for.

2.   **Define a "Bracket of Responsibility" to include the possibility of upward mobility.** While you may be willing to accept a variety of jobs related to your skills, you should include those that require higher levels of responsibility and pay. In the example above, it keeps open the option to be considered for an office management position as well as clerical jobs. In effect, you should define a "bracket of responsibility" in your objective that includes the range of jobs that you are willing to accept. This bracket should include the lower range of jobs that you would consider as well as those requiring higher levels of responsibility, up to and including those that you think you could handle. Even if you have not handled those higher levels of responsibility in the past, many employers may consider you for them if you have the skills to support the objective.

3.   **Include your most important skills.** What are the most important skills needed for the job you want? Consider including one or more of these as being required in the job that you seek. The implication here is that if you are looking for a job that requires "Organizational Skills," then you have those skills. Of course, your resume content should support those skills with specific examples.

4.   **Include specifics if these are important to you.** If you have substantial experience in a particular industry (such as "Computer Controlled Machine Tools") or have a narrow and specific objective that you *really* want (such as "Art Therapist with the Mentally Handicapped"), then it is OK to state this. But, in so doing, realize that by narrowing your alternatives down you will often not be considered for other jobs for which you might qualify. Still, if that is what you want, it just may be worth pursuing (though I would still encourage you to have a second, more general resume just in case...).

JOB OBJECTIVE WORKSHEET

Use this worksheet to create a draft of your resume's job objective. It includes a variety of questions and activities that you can use to decide what to include.

1. **What sort of position, title, and area of specialization do you seek?** Write out the type of job you want just as you might explain it to someone you know.

    _____

    _____

    _____

2. **Define your "Bracket of Responsibility."** Describe the range of jobs that you would accept at a minimum as well as those that you might be able to handle if given the chance.

    _____

    _____

    _____

3. **Name the key skills that you have that are important in this job.** Describe the two or three key skills that are particularly important for success in the job that you seek. Select one or more of these that you are strong in and that you enjoy using and write it (or them) below.

    _____

    _____

    _____

4. **Name any specific areas of expertise or strong interests that you want to utilize in your next job.** If you have substantial interest, experience, or training in a specific area *and* want to include it in your job objective (knowing that it may limit your options), what might it be?

_____

_____

_____

5.   **Is there anything else that is important to you?** Is there anything
     else that you want to include in your job objective? This could include
     a value that is particularly important to you (such as "A position that
     allows me to affect families" or "Employment in an aggressive and
     results-oriented organization"); a preference for the size or type of organ-
     ization ("A small to mid-size business"); or some other thing.

_____

_____

_____

**Quick
Reference**

FINALIZING YOUR JOB OBJECTIVE STATEMENT

Look over the job objectives in the various sample resumes in
Sections 1 and 3 to see how others have written their job objectives.
Most do not include all the elements that are presented in the Job
Objective Worksheet and that is perfectly acceptable. Some are very
brief, providing just a job title or category of jobs, others are quite
long and detailed.

JOB OBJECTIVE STATEMENT FOR YOUR RESUME

There are no rigid rules for writing your resume's job objective. You should only include information that is essential for an employer to know in considering you and this means that the objective should be brief. Each and every word should be important in some way. Go ahead and write your job objective below just as you want it to appear on your resume. Edit it so that each word counts and make certain that each word creates a positive impression.

_____

_____

_____

_____

_____

_____

7

HOW TO HANDLE "PROBLEMS" ON YOUR RESUME AND OTHER MISCELLANEOUS MATTERS

Quick Tip

In a perfect world, we would be considered solely on our ability to do the job. But the reality is that employers are subjective and "feelings" about someone do enter into the hiring decision. In this chapter, I present common concerns I have heard from job seekers over the years and try to give you a positive way to present them to employers. Employers are people too, and most are more understanding than you might think. I hope that this information helps.

While it may not be apparent in many of the resumes used as examples in this book, a well-written resume often covers a job seeker's weaknesses or flaws. All of of the resumes used in Section 3 and other sections of this book are based on actual resumes written for and by real people. They follow a primary rule of writing a resume: *never highlight a negative.* Since everyone has less-than-perfect credentials for a given job, all resumes hide one thing or another to some degree. In some cases, I have provided notes on the sample resume that point out how that resume has handled certain problems the job seeker has. Use these as an example of how similar problems might be handled in your own resume.

While the review of problems that follows is not exhaustive, it will help you to handle various problems that many people have to deal with during their job search.

Note also that these are often not just resume problems—they are also problems to resolve when completing applications or in interviews. While the solutions offered relate primarily to handling them on a resume, you should gain some insight on how to approach the same problem in other situations as well.

• •

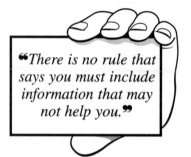

> **"***There is no rule that says you must include information that may not help you.***"**

PRESENT ANY "PROBLEMS" IN AN INTERVIEW, NOT IN YOUR RESUME!

A resume should present your strengths, so only present things that an employer can interpret as positive. In writing your resume, try to think like an employer and exclude anything that you might interpret as a negative. If something does not support your job objective, you should probably eliminate it.

There is no rule that says you must include information in a resume that may not help you. While this does not mean that you should be dishonest, neither should you present negative information. In many cases, things that concern or worry you may not be a problem to an employer at all. And, if you feel strongly that an employer needs to know something potentially negative about you, this can be presented in the interview. (Better yet, don't bring it up at all until after you are offered a job!)

SOME PROBLEMS ARE A SENSITIVE SUBJECT

Quick Fact

Even mentioning that some of the things covered in this chapter might be "problems" will make some people angry. For example, some would object to any mention that someone over 50 might experience discrimination in the labor market—although anyone over 50 *knows* that their age makes it harder to get a good job. Others will resent the implication that employers would even consider such things as race, religion, national origin, childcare arrangements and other "politically sensitive" matters in evaluating people for employment.

So, with the risk of offending someone, I have included information in this section that is a bit sensitive for some. But I think that you, as a job seeker, need to accept reality and look for ways to overcome problems. It can be done. I and many others *know* that some employers are unfair. Some *do* consider things in making hiring decisions that should not be a factor. Older people *do* have a harder time getting jobs than younger ones. Many employers *are* interested in whether or not a young woman has children (or is planning to in the near future).

And that is why I have listed some of the problems that follow, along with some suggestions for handling them.

FIRST, SOME GENERAL GUIDELINES FOR HANDLING "PROBLEMS"

Quick Reference

You could argue that employers should not consider issues such as age in a hiring decision, and I would agree. Some employers, like all other categories of people, are not fair. But most employers are simply good people trying to do their jobs. They want to select people who will stay on the job, be reliable, and do well. That is often the reason why an employer, male or female, wants to know as much as they can about you. Why, for example, are you new to this area? Do you plan on staying and, if so, why? If you are "overqualified," are you likely to be unhappy and leave after a short period of time?

Many times an employer wants to determine whether or not they can depend on you and to find out, they want to know more about you.

**Quick
Reference**

They want to understand your true motivations and this can often involve understanding things such as how likely you are to stay in the area and other issues that are not work-related. In the process of completing a resume, some of these issues might be presented, though they are often far more of an issue in an interview. In many cases, a cover letter provides additional details, but an interview is where most "problems" can be best addressed. In that context, I suggest that you consider your situation in advance and be able to present to the employer that, in your case, the issue is simply not a problem at all, but an advantage.

In any case, an interview is where you deal with problems, not a resume. A resume is simply a preliminary piece of paper and it should *never* present a problem of any kind. If yours does, it should be redone until that problem is not evident.

In the interview, learn to be candid and present your problem as a potential advantage, should it come up. In that context, I hope that the tips that follow help you to see that there are two sides to almost every problem.

TIPS FOR HANDLING SOME SPECIFIC PROBLEMS ON A RESUME

☑ GAPS IN WORK HISTORY

Many people have gaps in their work history. If you have a legitimate reason for major gaps, such as going to school or having a child, you can simply state this on your resume. You could, in some situations, handle one of these gaps by putting the alternative activity on the resume, with dates, just as you would handle any other job.

Minor gaps, such as being out of work for several months, do not need an explanation at all. You can often simply exclude any mention of months on your resume. Instead, just refer to the years you were employed such as "1993 to 1994" and any gap of several months is not apparent at all.

☑ BEING OUT OF WORK

Some of the most accomplished people I know have been out of work at one time or another and one out of five people in the workforce experiences some unemployment each year. It's really not a sin and many people who are bosses have experienced it themselves, as have I. But the tradition is to try to hide this on the resume. One technique is to put something like "19xx to Present" on your resume when referring to your most recent job. This approach makes it look like you are still employed. While this might be an acceptable approach in some cases, it may also require you to have to explain yourself early on in an interview. This soft deception can start you off on a negative note and may not end up helping

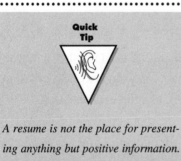

Quick Tip

A resume is not the place for presenting anything but positive information. If something might be interpreted as negative, do not include it. Use your judgment on this and, if in doubt, cut it out.

you at all. If you are currently out of work, your other alternatives are to write the actual month that you left your last job or to write in some interim activity such as being self-employed. Even if that means that you are working at a temporary agency or doing odd jobs, it may be better than being deceitful. Remember that many employers have experienced being out of work themselves and may have more understanding of your situation than you realize.

☑ BEING FIRED AND OTHER NEGATIVES IN YOUR WORK HISTORY

There is no reason for a resume to include any details related to why you have left previous jobs—unless, of course, they were positive. For example, leaving to accept a more responsible job is to your credit. If you have been fired, analyze why. In most cases, it is for reasons that do not have to do with your performance. Most often, people are fired as a result of interpersonal conflicts. These are quite common and do not indicate that you will necessarily have the same problem in a different situation. If your performance was the reason, you may have to explain why that would not be the case in a new job.

The resume itself should present what you did well in previous situations. Leave the discussion of problems for the interview, and take time in advance to practice what you will say, if asked.

☑ JOB HISTORY UNRELATED TO YOUR CURRENT JOB OBJECTIVE

If your previous work experience is in jobs that don't relate to what you want to do next, your best bet is to use a skills resume. This resume format was presented in Chapter 3 and you can see examples of it there and in Section 3. In this situation, using a traditional chronological resume will simply display an apparent lack of preparation for the job you want now.

The advantage of the skills resume in this situation is that it allows you to emphasize those transferable skills that you have developed and used in other settings. If you carefully select skills that are needed in the job you want next, you can draw from work and life experiences to demonstrate that you have the needed skills. And, of course, you would emphasize any education, training, or other experiences that directly prepared you for the job you now seek.

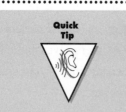

Quick Tip

Interview skills, including how to answer problem questions, is a topic of another book in the "JIST Quick" series. If you need more information on handling a problem that may come up in an interview, consider The Quick Interview and Salary Negotiations Book. *I humbly suggest that this book will help you handle most interview situations well.*

☑ CHANGING CAREERS

This is a situation related to the one described above and would also be handled through the use of a skills resume. A change in careers does require some justification on your part, so that it makes sense to an employer. This should mean that you should present experiences where you have demonstrated an ability in or preparation for success in a different occupational area. For example, a teacher who wants to become a real estate sales agent could point to his hobby of investing in and fixing up old houses. He could point to his superior communications skills and his ability to get students to do what he wanted in a classroom. And he could point to the many after-hours activities he has been involved in as a sign of a high energy level and a willingness to work the nights and weekends needed to sell real estate.

☑ RECENT GRADUATE

If you have recently graduated, you probably are competing against those with similar levels of education *and* more work experience. If you don't have a lot of work experience related to the job you want, you will obviously want to emphasize your recent education or training. This might include specific mention of courses you took and other activities that most directly relate to the job you now seek.

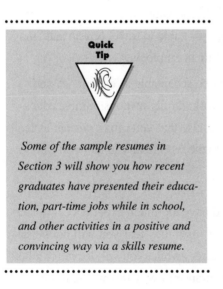

Quick Tip

Some of the sample resumes in Section 3 will show you how recent graduates have presented their education, part-time jobs while in school, and other activities in a positive and convincing way via a skills resume.

New graduates need to look at their school work as the equivalent of work. Indeed, it *is* work in that it required self-discipline, completion of a variety of tasks, and other activities that are similar to those required in many jobs. You also may have learned a variety of things that are directly related to doing the job you want and you should present these in a skills resume in the same way you might present work experiences in a chronological resume.

You should also play up the fact, if you can, that you are familiar with the latest trends and techniques in your field and can apply these skills right away to the new job. And, since you are experienced in studying and learning new things, you will be better able to quickly learn the new job.

A skills resume will also allow you to more effectively present skills you used in other jobs (such as waiting on tables) that don't seem to directly relate to the job you now want. These jobs were also work experiences and can provide a wealth of adaptive and transferable skills that you can use, with some thought, to support your resume's job objective.

✓ TOO LITTLE EXPERIENCE

Young people, including recent graduates, often have difficulty in getting the jobs they want since employers will often hire someone with more experience. In this case, you may want to emphasize your adaptive skills (see Chapter 5) that would tend to overcome a lack of experience. Once again, a skills resume would allow you to present yourself in the best light. For example, emphasizing skills such as "hardworking" and "learn new things quickly" may impress an employer enough to consider you over more experienced workers.

You should also consider expressing a willingness to accept difficult or less desirable conditions as one way to break into a field and gain experience. For example, "willing to work weekends and evenings" or "able to travel or relocate" may open up some possibilities that might appeal to an employer.

You should also look for anything that might be acceptable as experience and emphasize it. This might include volunteer work, family responsibilities, education, training, military experience, or anything else that you might present as legitimate activities that support your ability to do the work that you feel you can do.

✓ OVERQUALIFIED

It doesn't seem to make sense that you could have too much experience, but some employers may think so. This is in a situation when they fear you will not be satisfied with the job that is available and that, after awhile, you will leave for a better one. So what they really need is some assurance of why this would *not* be the case for you. If, in fact, you are looking for a job with higher pay—and if you communicate this in some way to an employer—it is quite likely that they will not offer you a job for fear that they will soon lose you. And they may be right. After a period of unemployment, most people become more willing to settle for less than they had hoped for. If you are willing to accept jobs where you may be defined as overqualified, consider not including some of your educational or work-related credentials on your resume—though I do not necessarily recommend doing this. And be prepared to explain, in the interview, why you *do* want this particular job and how your wealth of experience is a positive and not a negative.

☑ RACE, RELIGION, OR NATIONAL ORIGIN

There is simply no need to make this an issue on your resume at all. In some situations, being a minority can help you be considered and it would be foolish not to take advantage of this. But the more important issue is whether you can do the job well. For this reason, I discourage people from including in their resume details that refer to these issues.

☑ NOT SURE OF JOB OBJECTIVE

As I have mentioned on several occasions, including a job objective on your resume is highly desirable but not required. If you really can't settle on a long-term job objective, consider on settling on a short-term one, and use that on your resume. In some cases, you can also do several resumes, each with its own job objective. This can make sense in some situations and will allow you to select information that will support your various options to best effect.

☑ RECENTLY MOVED

Employers are often concerned that someone who has recently moved to an area may soon leave. If you have recently moved to a new area, you should consider explaining this on your resume. A simple statement such as "Relocated to _____ to be closer to my family,"—or any other reasonable explanation will often be enough to present yourself as stable so as not to be of concern to an employer.

☑ NO DEGREE OR LESS EDUCATION THAN TYPICALLY REQUIRED

If you have the previous experience and skills to do a job that is often filled by someone with more education, you should take special care in preparing the education and experience sections of your resume.

For those with substantial work experience, you can simply not include a section on education at all. While this does have the advantage of not presenting your lack of formal credentials in an obvious way, a better approach might be to present the education and training that you do have without indicating that you do or do not have a degree. For example, mention that you attended such and such a college or program but don't mention that you did not complete it. Several of the sample resumes in Section 3 do just that. This approach avoids your being screened out unnecessarily and provides you with a chance at an interview that you might not otherwise get.

Note that I do not suggest that you misrepresent yourself here by overstating your qualifications or claiming a degree you do not have. That would result in your later being fired and is clearly not a good idea. But again, there is no law that says you need to display your weaknesses on your resume. As I said earlier, the interview is where you can bring up any problems or explain any weaknesses.

❝*Consider what aspects of your youth are advantageous.***❞**

☑ TOO YOUNG

Young people need to present their youth as an advantage rather than a disadvantage. So consider just what aspects of your youth might be seen as advantages. For example, perhaps you are willing to work for less money, accept less desirable tasks, work longer or less convenient hours, or do other things that a more experienced worker might not. If so, say so.

You do need to realize that many employers prefer to hire workers with experience and demonstrated ability in jobs related to those they have available. Still, young people who present themselves effectively *can* be considered over those with better credentials.

"To avoid sounding too old, exclude any dates that can be used to indicate your age."

☑ TOO OLD

Older workers need to present their wealth of experience and maturity as an advantage rather than a disadvantage. If that sounds similar to the advice I offered for being "too young," you're right. In all cases, each of us need to look for ways to turn what someone might consider a negative into a positive. Older workers often have some things going for them that younger workers do not. On a resume, stress your years of experience as a plus, emphasize your loyalty to previous employers, and list accomplishments that occurred over a period of time.

If you have over 15 years or so of work experience, emphasize your more recent work experience. Select activites that best support you ability to do the job you are now seeking and emphasize them on your resume. Unless it is clearly to your advantage, you don't need to provide many details on your work or other history from earlier times.

To avoid sounding "too old," you might also consider not including dates that you graduated from school or other dates from many years ago that can be used to indicate your age. You can also cluster earlier jobs into one statement that covers them by saying something like "Various jobs requiring skills in engineering," or whatever. In most cases, your more recent experiences will be more important to an employer. Do emphasize any recent training, accomplishments, or responsibilities in your resume and include dates on these items as appropriate.

☑ FAMILY STATUS AND CHILDREN

There is absolutely no need for your resume to mention your marital status or whether or not you have children. It simply should not be relevant. In some cases, resumes do provide some family information that the writer thinks will help them, for example "Children all grown and am now able to concentrate on my career." You can be the judge on this matter but it is certainly not necessary.

> **"**Disability is not
> supposed to be
> a limitation to
> being considered
> for a job.**"**

✓ PHYSICAL LIMITATIONS AND DISABILITIES

I assume that you will not seek a job that you can't or should not do. That, of course, would be foolish. So that means that you are looking for a job that you are capable of doing, right? And, that being the case, you don't have a disability related to doing this job at all. For this reason, I see no need to mention any handicaps on your resume. New laws require employers to consider all applicants based on the requirements of the job and the *ability* of the applicant to do that job. This means that any disability you have is not supposed to be a limitation to being considered for a job that you are able to do. Of course, employers will still be able to use their judgment in selecting the best person for the job and that will mean that people with disabilities will have to compete for jobs along with everyone else. That is fair, so you will need to present to a prospective employer a convincing argument for why the employer should hire you over someone else. But on your resume, you should *never* mention a disability. Instead, focus on your *ability* to do the job.

✓ NEGATIVE REFERENCES

Most employers will not contact your previous employers unless you are being seriously considered as a candidate for the job. If you fear that one of your previous employers may not give you a positive reference, here are some things you can do:

1. List someone other than your supervisor as a reference from that employer, someone who knew your work there and who will give you a positive reference.

2. Discuss the issue in advance with your previous employer and negotiate what they will say. Even if not good, at least you know what they are likely to say and can prepare potential employers in advance.

3. Get a written letter of reference. In many cases, employers will not give references over the phone—or negative references at all—for fear of being sued. Having a letter in advance allows you to give a copy to a prospective employer and this may help them in making a decision.

Quick
Fact

CRIMINAL RECORD

A resume should *never* include any negative information about yourself. So if you have ever been "in trouble"with the law, you would certainly not mention this in your resume. Newer laws even limit an employer from including such general questions on an application as "Have you ever been arrested?" and limit formal inquiries to "Have you ever been convicted of a felony?"

In most cases, your criminal record would never be an issue on a resume at all, since you would not mention it. In this country, we are technically innocent until proven guilty (thank goodness) and that is why employers are no longer allowed to consider an arrest record in a hiring decision. Being arrested and being guilty are two different things. And arrests for minor offenses are also not supposed to be considered in a hiring decision.

A felony conviction is a different matter. These crimes are more serious and current employment laws do allow an employer to ask for and get this information—and to use it in making certain hiring decisions. For example, few employers would want to hire an accountant who had been convicted for stealing money from a previous employer. Certain types of arrest records, such as those for child molesting, are also allowed to be considered by an employer in making certain

Quick
Fact

hiring decisions. For example, few would want to have a person with this kind of record in charge of childrens' programs.

If you have an arrest or conviction record that an employer has a legal right to inquire about, my advice is to avoid looking for jobs where your record would be a big negative. The accountant in the above example should consider changing careers. I would advise people in this situation to avoid jobs where they could easily commit the same crime, since few employers would even consider hiring them for that reason. Even if they did get such a job because they concealed their criminal history, they could be fired at any time in the future. Instead, I might suggest they consider selling accounting software, starting their own business, or getting into a career completely unrelated to accounting.

As always, your resume should reflect what you *can* do rather than what you can't. If you chose your career direction wisely and present a convincing argument that you can do the job well, many employers will, ultimately, overlook previous mistakes. As you prove yourself and gain good work experience, your distant past becomes less important.

So a criminal history really isn't an issue for a resume at all. Instead, it is a career planning, job search, and interview issue. If you have ever done hard time in jail or been convicted of a felony (usually, of course, one is related to the other), there are a series of special things that you can do in the job search to help minimize the damage to your chances of getting a job. This is not the focus of this book, however, and space does not permit me to go into those techniques here.

OTHER THINGS TO INCLUDE—OR NOT INCLUDE—IN YOUR RESUME

A HEADING SUCH AS "RESUME"

Really, few people would confuse a resume with something else, so using a header is not necessary. Even so, some people do include a heading of some type and several of the sample resumes in this book include them. In some cases, this is done to make the resume appear more formal or, at times, just because the writer wanted it that way. As I said earlier, this is your resume, so a header is up to you.

A WAY TO REACH YOU BY PHONE

I had mentioned in Section 1 that you should *always* include a phone number on your resume. This is because employers are most likely to try to reach you by phone. For this reason, it is *essential* that you include a phone number with the following criteria:

1. **The telephone must always be answered.** In most cases, an employer will try to call you during their regular business hours. If you are using your home as the base of your job search, you may be gone too often to reliably receive phone calls there yourself. The solution is to get an answering machine, if you don't already have one. These are quite inexpensive and the cost of missing an important call is worth far more than any inconvenience that an answering machine may cause.

    Another solution is to hire an answering service or a voice-mail system. These are listed in the *Yellow Pages* of the phone book under "Telephone Answering Services" and are often quite reasonable. Some computers also include a voice-mail system that can be used at home, should you have such a system. While some people don't like leaving messages on machines, most businesspeople are used to it and are likely to leave a message asking you to return their call. This is far better than their not being able to reach you at all.

2. **The phone must be answered appropriately and reliably.** First impressions count, so make sure that your phone is answered appropriately. If you are using your home phone, instruct *anyone* answering the phone during the day (when employers are most likely to call) to conduct themselves in a professional way. You should also make certain that any person who answers the phone knows how to take reliable messages, including the name and organization of the caller and their phone number. If there is any question about this, train anyone

Quick Alert

involved until you are certain that they can do what is needed. If you are using an answering machine, make sure that the outgoing message is appropriate and professional. Howling wolves and silly greetings should not greet a prospective employer.

3. **Your telephone number must include an area code.** Always include the correct area code for your phone number, even if you don't want to move to another area. Resumes have a way of getting circulated widely and in ways that you might not expect. In some cases, this may mean that you will get a call from an employer who lives out of your area (at a corporate office, for example) but who has the authority to offer you a job where you are.

4. **The number must remain the same throughout your job search.** Resumes can be filed for quite some time, which can result in an employer trying to reach you long after your resume was first put into circulatation, so include a long-term phone number. If you are in the process of moving, for example, you might consider using an answering service until you no longer need it. You can even arrange for a local phone number to be used in a distant location by obtaining an answering service there. This will avoid creating the impression that you are not readily available.

IF THERE IS ANY QUESTION, INCLUDE AN ALTERNATE PHONE NUMBER!

In many situations, it is wise to include more than one phone number on your resume and many of the resume examples include two numbers for this reason. This allows you to use your home number (for example) as the primary place to reach you as well as an alternate number, should the first one be unavailable, busy, or no longer in service. As you can see in the various sample resumes in this book, you can simply indicate the status of each phone number with words such as:

Daytime

Messages

Home

Office

Evenings

Answering Service

Voice Mail

FAX Messages

or whatever...

> *"Be sure to include your complete address and zip code to allow any mail to reach you."*

ALTERNATE ADDRESSES

While an address is not an absolutely essential element of a resume, it is typically included. I say it is not essential for the same reason that I say a phone number *is*—an employer is far more likely to call than to write.

In most cases, simply including your home address is enough. Just be sure to include your complete address and ZIP code to allow any mail to reach you. There are rare situations where you might want to include either no address at all or to include an alternate one. For example, perhaps you don't consider your home address to be a positive because it is in a "bad area," you live out of the area, or for some other reason. Before you exclude an address at all, consider asking someone else to accept your mail at their address and to forward it to you. If you are moving and know what the new address will be, you may include both, along with a statement like "Moving, please mail all correspondence to new address below after (such and such date)." This is not the best of solutions but it can work.

PERSONAL INFORMATION

Older resume books often advise the inclusion of personal information on your resume such as height, weight, health, and marital status. I still see this sort of thing on resumes, though there is little advantage to including it. Newer laws require employers to base hiring decisions only on a person's ability to do the job rather than personal characteristics and, for this reason, details such as these are no longer appropriate.

SOME PERSONAL INFORMATION MAY BE OK

While some personal information is neither required nor desired on a resume,

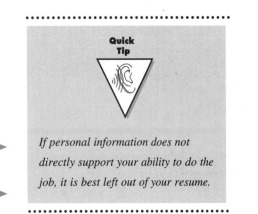

Quick Tip

If personal information does not directly support your ability to do the job, it is best left out of your resume.

some resumes do effectively include personal information that is not directly related to doing the job. Some of the sample resumes at the end of Chapter 3 as well as some in Section 3 do include such information. This information can be included when it reinforces the ability to do the job or provides some positive reflection of your personality and style.

In some cases, providing information on such things as leisure pursuits, hobbies, and volunteer activities can be included. But beware, most of these activities are of little interest to an employer and some may even hurt you. I've seen some silly things such as someone saying that they are a fan of a specific sports team or member of a fraternal organization that is not universally understood or admired. In these cases, if the reader is not enthusiastic about your information, mentioning it may hurt you.

Quick Alert

PHOTOGRAPHS

There is some controversy about including your photograph on your resume. I personally do not like to include them for a variety of reasons. The biggest problem is that a photograph can give an indication of your age, race, and other characteristics that an employer may later be accused of using in screening applicants. For this reason, many larger employers request that photographs not be included on or with your resume and they will not consider resumes that include them.

Also, believe it or not, many people may (consciously or unconsciously) form first impressions about others simply by seeing a picture of them. Although you might feel that your photo exudes brilliance, warmth, and competence, there's no telling what someone else's impression might be. As I've said before, I think we should all be considered on our merit to do the job and I do not recommend the use of photographs.

REFERENCES

Some resumes include a statement such as "References Available Upon Request" at the bottom. Older resume books typically advise you to do this but it is not necessary. I say this because employers know that they can ask for references if they want to check them out.

In some cases, if you feel that you have particularly good references, you may add a statement such as "Excellent References Available" to indicate that you have a good work history and nothing to hide. Several of the sample resumes in Section 3 have such statements, sometimes incorporated as a narrative statement in another section rather than listed at the bottom of the resume.

A FINAL FEW WORDS ON HANDLING PROBLEMS

Thankfully, there are a variety of laws and regulations that require employers to con-

Quick Tip

Get letters of reference from previous employers. Many employers will not give out information on your performance after you leave, so get previous supervisors to write you a letter of reference that you can copy and give to prospective employers who ask for references. You might consider writing a draft of the letter yourself and then having it approved and signed by your supervisor. Some previous employers might appreciate this, as it saves them time, but others may take offense. Use your judgment. While I don't suggest that you list your references on your resume itself, I do suggest that you create a separate list of references. A sample of such a sheet can be found in Section 4, "Other Job Search Correspondence." Having your references available in advance allows you to get them quickly to those employers who ask for them— and conserves valuable space on your resume for use in documenting more important information.

sider each applicant on their ability to do a job rather than such personal attributes as race, religion, age, disability, gender, etc. Most employers are wise enough to avoid making decisions based on things that should not matter. They are often just like you are. They *will* try to hire someone who convinces them that they can do the job well.

For this reason, it is *your* responsibility to present them with a convincing argument as to why they should hire you over somone else. Even if your "problem" does not come up in the interview, it may be to your advantage to bring it up and deal with it. This is particularly true if you think that an employer might wonder about this issue or that it might hurt you if you don't answer it. However you handle the interview, the ultimate question you have to answer is "Why should I hire you?"—so provide a good answer, even if the question is not asked quite so obviously.

8

PUTTING IT ALL TOGETHER

One of the decisions I made in writing this book was to put all the basic information on how to do a resume in the first section. And I did say there that, for most people, that section would be all they would need to know in order to write their resume—with the exception of looking at the sample resumes in Section 3, if desired. So, should you now be reading this, you need to know that this chapter assumes that you have read and done the activities in Chapters 1, 2, and 3. I also assume that you have already done a basic resume as outlined in those chapters, and I hope you have taken my advice to use it right away while you worked on creating a "better" resume as time permits.

If that information is not fresh in your mind, then what follows won't make much sense since it is primarily supplemental to the information presented earlier, in the first three chapters. So, with that caveat, I present you with additional and sometimes redundant information on writing an improved resume.

IF YOU AREN'T GOOD AT THIS, HAVE SOMEONE ELSE DO AS MUCH AS POSSIBLE

Quick Alert

I begin this chapter with some advice—if writing and designing a resume are not skills that you are particularly good at, consider having someone help you with various elements. There are several sources of this kind of help and I will provide some information on each one.

RESUME WRITING SERVICES

The fees that some resume writers charge are a bargain while others charge entirely too much for what you actually get. There are few regulations or requirements to set up a business as a resume writer and the quality and pricing of their services vary widely. Many resume writers work out of their homes, while others work out of more conventional offices.

In reviewing their capabilities, you need to have a good idea of the kinds of services you want and be willing to buy only those that you need. For example, some resume writers have substantial experience and skills in career counseling and can help you clarify what you want to do with your career. Helping you write your resume may only be the end result of more expensive and time-consuming career counseling services. In other cases, the writer is essentially a typist who takes the information that you provide and puts it into a simple format without asking you any questions. These services do not have the same types of value and obviously should cost less.

Some services will print out a number of finished resumes and matching envelopes and offer other services. Obviously, you should be willing to pay more if you need or expect to get more. Counseling of any kind takes time and, if the person is helpful and good, their time is worth money.

I said early in this book that writing a good resume creates the structure for considering a variety of issues that will help you clarify just what you want to do in a career sense. That process is not a simple

**Quick
Alert**

one and you just might benefit greatly from the help of a true career counseling professional who also happens to be a resume writer.

On the other hand, you can also get ripped off, so do ask for prices and know exactly what is included before you commit to any resume writing services. There is a group called the Professional Association of Resume Writers and someone who belongs to this group offers better assurance of legitimate services. Note that many of the sample resumes presented in Section 3 were written by members of this association. This affiliation is often included in *Yellow Pages* advertisements. That same group also determines who may be listed as a "Certified Professional Resume Writer" and that or the "CPRW" designation may also be found in some phone book ads.

In any situation, ask for the credentials of the person who will provide the service and see examples of their work before you agree to anything.

CAREER OR JOB SEARCH COUNSELORS AND COUNSELING SERVICES

Buyer beware! There are good, legitimate job search and career professionals out there and they are worth every bit of their reasonable fees. But there are also busi-

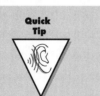

**Quick
Tip**

You can locate resume writers through the Yellow Pages *under "Resume Service" or similar headings. Also, you can often find their ads in the help wanted section of the newspaper. But the best source is through a referral by someone who has used the agency, so ask around.*

nesses that prey on unsuspecting and vulnerable souls who are unemployed. Some service "packages" can cost thousands of dollars and are not worth the price. In fact, I have said for years that many job seekers would gain more from reading a few good job search books than they might get from some of the less legitimate businesses offering these services.

But how do you tell the legitimate from the illegitimate? One clue is high pressure sales and high fees—fees over $1,000 are clearly out of line for most situations. If this is the case, your best bet is to walk out quickly. Call the agency first and get some information on what services are offered and what they cost. If the agency requires that you come in to discuss this, assume that this is a high pressure sales outfit and avoid them.

Quick Tip

There is a group called the National Association of Job Search Trainers that you might use as a source of career counseling. They have a code of ethics and their membership, while small, consists of people who have good credentials and experience. While many work in agencies and do not provide career counseling and related services to individuals, some do. You can get a list of members by sending a self-addressed stamped envelope to me via the publisher.

There are often low cost services available from local colleges or other organizations. These may consist of workshops and access to reading materials, assessment tests, and other services at a modest or even no cost. Consider these as an alternative to higher priced services and be sure to compare and contrast services and rates.

PRINT SHOPS

Some print shops now offer substantial services including resume typing and design on desktop publishing systems, resume copying and printing services, a selection of good paper and matching envelopes, and related services. Their prices are often quite reasonable, though few are capable of providing significant help in the writing of your resume.

Some print shops are listed in the Resume Service section of the *Yellow Pages* but most are listed under "Printers," as you might expect. Read their ads and call a few; you may be surprised at what they offer.

WHAT SORT OF RESUME WILL WORK BEST FOR YOU?

As you know, there are just a few basic resume types but there are many variations that could make sense for your particular situation. Since there are no firm rules for most resumes, you will have to use your judgment about how to structure and write your own.

I covered the basic resume types in Section 1 of this book but here is a review, along with some additional information.

Quick Reminder

A BRIEF REVIEW OF RESUME TYPES

☑ THE SIMPLE CHRONOLOGICAL RESUME

Chapter 2 provides examples of a simple chronological resume. As you know, this resume arranges your history in chronological order, beginning with your most recent work experience. Education and training may come before or after your work history, depending on your situation.

BEST FOR THESE SITUATIONS

Since a chronological resume organizes information by your work experience, it highlights previous job titles, locations, dates employed, and tasks. This is fine if you are looking for the same type of job that you have held in the past or are looking to move up in a related field.

For employers, this resume type has the advantage of clearly presenting a progression of career moves and allows them to quickly screen out those applicants whose backgrounds are not conventional or do not fit the preferred profile.

This format is not a good one for those who have limited work experience (such as recent graduates), want to do something different from what they have done in the past, or who have less-than-ideal work histories such as job gaps.

☑ CONSIDER A MODIFIED CHRONOLOGICAL RESUME

While a basic and traditional chronological resume has limitations, you can add some information and modify its style in such a way that will help you. Here are some of the things you can do, depending on your situation:

ADD A JOB OBJECTIVE

While a basic chronological resume may not include a job objective, yours certainly can. While this does have the disadvantage of limiting your resume to certain types of jobs, you should be focusing your job search in this way for other reasons.

EMPHASIZE SKILLS AND ACCOMPLISHMENTS

Most chronological resumes simply provide a listing of tasks, duties, and responsibilities, but once you have included a job objective, you should clearly emphasize skills, accomplishments, and results that support your job objective.

EXPAND YOUR SECTION ON EDUCATION AND TRAINING

Let's say that you are a recent graduate who worked your way through school, got decent grades (while working full time), and got involved in a variety of extracurricular activities. The standard listing of your education would not do you justice, so consider expanding that section to include statements about your accomplishments while going to school.

ADD NEW SECTIONS TO HIGHLIGHT YOUR STRENGTHS

There is no reason that you can't add one or more sections to your resume to highlight something you think will help you. For example, let's say that you do have excellent references from previous employers. You might add a statement to that effect and even include one or more positive quotes. Or, maybe you got exceptional performance reviews, wrote some articles, edited a newsletter, traveled extensively, or did something else that might support your job objective. If so, there is nothing to prevent your creating a special section or heading to highlight these activities.

Some of the sample resumes in Section 3 break the "rules" and include features that make sense for the person who created that resume. And that is one of the few rules that really matters—that your resume communicates your strengths in an effective way.

☑ THE SKILLS OR FUNCTIONAL RESUME

Chapter 3 reviews the basics of writing a skills resume. This style of resume arranges content under major skills rather than jobs previously held. A well done skills resume emphasizes several skills that are most important to succeed in the job that is stated in the job objective. Of course, these should also be the same skills that you possess. These resumes are sometimes called "functional" resumes because they use a functional design that is based on the skills needed for the job being sought.

BEST FOR THESE SITUATIONS

A skills resume is often used in situations where the writer wants to avoid displaying obvious weaknesses that appear highlighted on a chronological resume. For example, someone who has been a "secretary" in the past but who now wants to be an "Office Manager" could clearly benefit from a skills resume—so could a teacher who now wants to have a career in sales.

A skills resume can help hide a variety of other weaknesses as well, such as limited work experience, gaps in job history, lack of educational credentials, and other flaws. This is one reason why some employers don't like them—they make it harder for them to quickly screen out applicants. Personally, I like skills resumes. Assuming that you honestly present what you can do, this resume often gives you the best opportunity to present your strengths in their best light. And, if a chronological format presents you well, you can also include elements of this. Several of the sample resumes in Section 3 have successfully merged the skills resume and chronological resume formats.

☑ COMBINATION FORMATS

In a combination format, you might highlight your key skills related to your job objective *and* include a separate section that presents your work history in a conventionally chronological way. Again, you will find examples of this format in Section 3. Consider using this approach if it can present you well.

☑ CREATIVE RESUMES

There is one other type of resume that defies easy description: These resumes use innovative formats and styles. Some use dramatic graphics, colors, and shapes. Graphic artists, for example, may use their resumes as examples of their work and include various graphic elements. An advertising or marketing person might use a writing style that approximates copy writing and a resume design that looks more like a polished magazine ad.

I've seen all sorts of special resumes over the years; some are well done and create a good impression and some do not. I haven't included many examples of these resumes in this book since they do not lend themselves to the format of a conventional book (black ink on white paper). How, for example, could I do justice to the resume I once saw that had been written on a watermelon?

So use your judgment on this. In some cases, creative resumes can make sense. Good design can certainly help, particularly in professions where good design *is* the profession.

☑ RESUME REPLACEMENTS AND ENCLOSURES

Some occupations typically require a portfolio of your work or some other concrete example of what you have done. Artists, copy writers, advertising people, clothing designers, architects, radio and TV personalities, and many others know this and should take care to provide good examples of what they do.

I've also seen many gimmicks such as a dollar bill attached to a resume and a statement that this person would help his employer make lots of money. Some of these gimmicks do work for some people and you can certainly try them but I encourage you to stick to the basics: write a resume that shows you deserve the interview, rather than relying on gimmicks to get it for you.

☑ SPECIAL FORMATS

Attorneys, college professors, physicians, scientists, and various other occupations have their own rules or guidelines for preparing a "Professional Vita" or some other special format. If you are looking for a job in one of these specialized areas, you should certainly learn how to prepare a resume to those specifications. These types of specialized and occupation-specific resumes are not in the scope of this book and examples are not included.

GATHER INFORMATION AND EMPHASIZE ACCOMPLISHMENTS, SKILLS, AND RESULTS

Quick Reminder

Chapters 2 and 3 included worksheets and activities that were designed to help you gather essential information for your resume. And many of the chapters in Section 2 provided more detailed information and activities to help you gather information about yourself, identify key skills and other details, and to consider alternative ways to present what you want to include in your resume.

Of course, much of the information in Section 2 does more than simply help you write a resume. It was also designed to help you in your career planning. But, assuming that you did some or all of those activities, you now have to select those key elements to be included in your resume.

I have provided an expanded worksheet in this chapter to help you gather the information that is most important to include in a resume. Some of the information is the same as that called for in the "Instant Resume Worksheet" in Chapter 2 but the new worksheet is considerably more thorough and complete. If carefully completed, it will prepare you for the final step of writing your resume.

THE COMPREHENSIVE RESUME WORKSHEET

General Instructions

Use this worksheet to write a draft of the material you will include in your resume. Use a writing style similar to that of your resume, emphasizing skills, accomplishments, and keeping your narrative as brief as possible.

Use a pencil or erasable pen to allow for changes as needed. You may find it helpful to use a separate sheet of paper for drafting the information in some of the worksheet sections that follow. Once you have done that, *then* go ahead and complete the worksheet in the book. The information you write on the worksheet should be pretty close to the information you will later use to write your resume, so do write it carefully. For some sections, you will probably need to refer back to the appropriate section of this book to find previously recorded information.

Identification

Name _____

Home address _____

_____ **Zip** _____

City/State or Province/ZIP or Postal Code: _____

_____

Primary Phone #: _____ **Comment:** _____

Alternate Phone #: _____ **Comment:** _____

Job Objective

Write your job objective here, as you would like it to appear on your resume. Writing a good job objective is a tricky business and requires you to have a good sense of what you want to do as well as the skills you have to offer. You may want to refer to the work you did in Chapter 6 and review sample resumes in Section 3 before completing this.

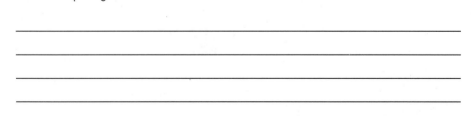

In Just a Few Words, Why Should Someone Hire You?

A good resume will answer this question in some way. So, to clarify the essential reasons why someone should hire you over others, write a brief answer to the question in the space below. Then, in some way, make sure that your resume gets this across.

_____

_____

_____

_____

_____

Key Adaptive Skills to Emphasize in Your Resume

What key adaptive skills do you have that support your stated job objective? Review Chapter 4 to identify your top adaptive skills and list those that best support your job objective in the spaces below. Next to each, write any accomplishments or experiences that best support those skills. Be brief and emphasize numbers and results when possible.

Adaptive Skill: _____

Proof of this skill: _____

_____

_____

_____

_____

_____

Adaptive Skill: _____

Proof of this skill: _____

_____

_____

_____

_____

_____

Adaptive Skill: _____

Proof of this skill: _____

_____

_____

_____

_____

_____

Key Transferable Skills to Emphasize in Your Resume

Once again, select your transferable skills that best support your stated job objective. Refer to Chapter 4 as needed to help identify these skills and list them below, along with examples of when you used or demonstrated these skills.

Transferable Skill: _____

Proof of this skill: _____

_____

_____

_____

_____

_____

Transferable Skill: _____

Proof of this skill: _____

_____

_____

_____

_____

_____

Transferable Skill: _____

Proof of this skill: _____

_____

_____

_____

_____

_____

Transferable Skill: _____

Proof of this skill: _____

_____

_____

_____

_____

_____

Transferable Skill: _____

Proof of this skill: _____

_____

_____

_____

_____

_____

What Are the Key Job-Related Skills Needed in the Job You Want?

If you don't know, you need to refer to Chapter 5 to learn how to identify the key skills needed in the job you want. If you have selected an appropriate job objective, you should have those very skills. Write at least four or five job-related skills below (more if you know them) along with examples to support these skills.

Job-Related Skill: _____

Proof of this skill: _____

_____

_____

_____

_____

_____

Job-Related Skill: _____

Proof of this skill: _____

_____

_____

_____

_____

_____

Job-Related Skill: _____

Proof of this skill: _____

_____

_____

_____

_____

_____

Job-Related Skill: _____

Proof of this skill: _____

_____

_____

_____

_____

_____

Job-Related Skill: _____

Proof of this skill: _____

_____

_____

_____

_____

_____

What Specific Work or Other Experience
Do You Have That Supports Your Doing This Job?

If you completed the worksheets in Chapter 5, you have plenty of information to draw upon in completing this section. If you are doing a chronological resume, you should organize the information below in order of the jobs that you have held. If you are doing a skills resume, you would organize the information within major skill areas. Space has been provided for both of these arrangements and I suggest that you complete both sections. In doing so, write the content as if you were writing it for inclusion on your resume. You can, of course, further edit what you write here into its final form but try to approximate the writing style you will use in your resume. Use short sentences. Include action words. Emphasize key skills. Include numbers to support your skills and emphasize accomplishments and results rather than simply listing your duties.

In previous jobs that don't relate well to what you want to do next, emphasize adaptive and transferable skills (and accomplishments) that relate to the job you want. Mention any promotions, raises, or positive evaluations as appropriate. If you did more than your title suggests, consider a title that is more descriptive (but not misleading) such as "Head Waiter and Assistant Manager," if that is what you were, instead of "Waiter." If you have had a number of short-term jobs, consider combining them all under one heading such as "Various Jobs While Attending College."

You may need to complete several drafts of this information before it begins to "feel good" so please use additional sheets of paper if necessary.

Experiences by Chronology

Most Recent or Present Job Title: _____

Dates (month/year) From: _____   **To:** _____

Organization Name: _____

City/State or Province/ZIP or Postal Code: _____

_____

Duties, Responsibilities, Accomplishments: _____

_____

_____

_____

_____

_____

_____

_____

_____

Next Most Recent Job Title:

Dates (month/year) From: _____ **To:** _____

Organization Name: _____

City/State or Province/ZIP or Postal Code: _____

Duties, Responsibilities, Accomplishments: _____

_____

_____

_____

_____

_____

_____

_____

_____

_____

_____

Next Most Recent Job Title:

Dates (month/year) From: _____ **To:** _____

Organization Name: _____

City/State or Province/ZIP or Postal Code: _____

Duties, Responsibilities, Accomplishments: _____

_____

_____

_____

_____

_____

_____

_____

_____

_____

_____

Next Most Recent Job Title:

Dates (month/year) From: _____ **To:** _____

Organization Name: _____

City/State or Province/ZIP or Postal Code: _____

Duties, Responsibilities, Accomplishments: _____

_____

_____

_____

_____

_____

_____

_____

_____

_____

Experience Organized by Skills

Look at the sample resumes in Section 3 and you will see how many of them organize their experience under key skills needed for the job. These resumes often include statements regarding accomplishments and results as well as duties. They also often mention other skills that are related to or support the key skill as well as specific examples. These can be work-related experiences or can come from other life experiences.

If you completed the activities in Chapter 5, you already have quite a bit of information available to you that you can use in the worksheet that follows. Review that information as needed. Begin by listing the key skills you want to present on your resume. Your key adaptive and transferable skills were listed earlier in the Chapter 5 worksheet along with the key job-related skills required by your job objective. These skills are the same ones you should emphasize on your resume, along with any key job-related skills that you think are particularly important to include.

I have included space to list six key skills below. Select those to be included in your resume, then write statements to support each. Remember to use the writing style that you will use in the resume itself.

Key Resume Skill #1: _____

Resume statement to support this skill: _____

_____

_____

_____

_____

_____

_____

_____

_____

Key Resume Skill #2: _____

Resume statement to support this skill: _____

_____

_____

_____

_____

_____

_____

_____

Key Resume Skill #3: _____

Resume statement to support this skill: _____

_____

_____

_____

_____

_____

_____

_____

Key Resume Skill #4: _____

Resume statement to support this skill: _____

_____

_____

_____

_____

_____

_____

_____

Key Resume Skill #5: _____

Resume statement to support this skill: _____

_____

_____

_____

_____

_____

_____

_____

_____

Key Resume Skill #6: _____

Resume statement to support this skill: _____

_____

_____

_____

_____

_____

_____

_____

_____

What Education or Training Do You Have That Supports Your Job Objective?

Once again, Chapter 5 provides a worksheet that organizes your education and training in a thorough way. Go back and review that information before completing the section that follows.

In writing the education and training section, be sure to include any additional information that supports your being qualified for your job objective. New graduates will need to emphasize their education and training more than experienced workers and should consider including more details in this section.

Use the space that follows to write what you want to include on your resume under the education and/or training heading.

School Attended: _____

Dates attended or graduated: _____

Degree or certification obtained: _____

Anything else that should be mentioned: _____

_____

_____

_____

School Attended: _____

Dates attended or graduated: _____

Degree or certification obtained: _____

Anything else that should be mentioned: _____

_____

_____

_____

Related Training: _____

_____

_____

_____

Other Resume Sections

If you want to include other sections on your resume, go ahead and write their headings below and write out whatever you want to include. Examples might be "Summary of Experience," or "Special Accomplishments," or others. See the headings of this kind among the sample resumes in Section 3 for inspiration.

_____

_____

_____

_____

_____

_____

_____

_____

_____

_____

_____

WRITING TIPS

While I covered the basics of writing a resume in Section 1, here are some additional tips and information that you may find helpful in writing your resume.

> **"**Though you may
> borrow ideas from
> this book, your resume
> must end up being
> yours.**"**

AS MUCH AS POSSIBLE, WRITE YOUR RESUME YOURSELF

I have come to realize that some people, even very smart people who are good writers, can't write a good resume. They just can't. And there really is not a good reason to force them to write one from start to finish. If you are one of these people, just decide that your skills are in other areas and don't go looking for a job as a resume writer.

But, even if you resist writing your own resume, you should do as much as possible yourself. The reason is that if you don't, your resume may not be yours. Your resume may present you well, but it won't be *you*. Not only will your resume misrepresent you to at least some extent, you also will not have learned what you need to learn by going through the process of writing your own resume. You would not have struggled with your job objective statement in the same way—and may not have as clear a sense of what you want to do as a result. You would not have the same understanding of the skills you have to support your job objective. And, as a result, you probably won't do as well in an interview.

So, while I realize that you will "borrow" ideas from the various sample resumes in this book, your resume must end up being yours. You have to be able to defend its content and prove each and every statement you've made.

Even if you end up hiring someone to help you with your resume, you must provide them with what to say and let them help you with how to say it. If you don't agree with something they do (and assuming that you have ascertained why they did it that way but still do not agree), ask them to change it to your specifications. However you do it, make sure that your resume is *your* resume and that it represents you accurately.

Quick
Alert

DON'T LIE AND DON'T EXAGGERATE

Many applicants for jobs misrepresent themselves. They lie about where they went to school or say that they have a degree that they do not have. They state previous salaries that are higher than they really were. They present themselves as having responsibilities and titles that were not even close to the truth.

I do not recommend this practice. For one reason, it is simply not the right thing to do, and that is reason enough. It is similar in nature to how I feel about those who cut in front of lines that I am waiting in. But there are also practical reasons for not doing so. The first is that you just might get a job that you can't handle. If that were to happen, and you fail, it would serve you right. Another reason is that some employers do check references and backgrounds more thoroughly than you might realize. Sometimes, this can occur years after you are employed and, if caught, you could lose your job.

So, my advice is this: honesty is the best policy.

Quick
Reminder

NEVER INCLUDE A NEGATIVE

Telling the truth does not mean you have to tell *everything* and some things are better left unsaid. A resume should present your strengths and not your weaknesses. So, in writing your resume, you should *never* include anything that an employer might interpret as a negative. For example, if many of those who compete for similar jobs have a degree that you don't have, it is better to not mention your education (or, in this case, lack of it) at all. Instead, emphasize your skills and accomplishments. If you can do the job, it really shouldn't matter anyway, and some employers will hire based on what you can do, rather than what you don't have.

THIS IS NO PLACE TO BE HUMBLE

Being honest on your resume also does not mean that you can't present the facts in the most positive way. A resume is not a place to be humble. So work on *what* you say and *how* you say it, so that you present your experiences and skills as positively as possible.

USE SHORT SENTENCES AND SIMPLE WORDS

Short sentences are easier to read. They communicate better than long ones. Simple words also communicate more clearly than long ones. So use short sentences and easy-to-understand words in your resume (like I've done in this paragraph).

Many people like to throw in words and phrases that are related to their field but are used little elsewhere. Some of this may be necessary but too often I see language that is too specialized, which will turn off many employers. So be careful in your use of jargon. Good writing is easy to read and understand. It is harder to do but it is worth it.

IF IT DOESN'T SUPPORT YOUR JOB OBJECTIVE, YOU SHOULD PROBABLY CUT IT OUT

A resume is only one or two pages long, so you have to be careful in what you do and do not include. One way to do this is to review each and every thing you include and ask yourself: "Does this support my ability to do the job in some clear way?" If that item does not support your job objective, then it should go.

INCLUDE NUMBERS

Many of the sample resumes in Section 3 include some numbers. They could refer to the speed at which someone types, the number of transactions processed per month, percentage of increased sales, number of people or orders processed, or some other numerical measure of their performance. Numbers communicate in a special way and you should try to include some that support key skills you have or that reflect your accomplishments or results.

EMPHASIZE SKILLS

It should seem obvious by now that you should emphasize skills in your resume. Besides listing the key skills in a skills resume, you should also include a variety of skill statements in all narrative sections of your resume. In each case, select skills you have that support your job objective.

HIGHLIGHT ACCOMPLISHMENTS AND RESULTS

Anyone can go through the motions of doing a job but employers want to know how *well* you have done things in the past. Did you accomplish anything out of the ordinary? What were the results you achieved? Chapter 4 includes many activities that will help you emphasize accomplishments and results from a variety of work and life situations.

LOOK AT SAMPLE RESUMES FOR IDEAS

Before you actually write your resume, look at the sample resumes in Section 3. As you find things that you like or can use, jot them down on a separate piece of paper or use some other system for including those ideas in your resume (for example, storing the ideas on index cards may work for you).

THE IMPORTANCE OF DOING DRAFTS

It will probably take you several rewrites before you begin to be satisfied with the content of your resume. And it will take even more before you are finished. Writing, modifying, editing, changing, adding to, and subtracting from content are all important steps in writing a good resume. For this reason, I suggest that you write yours on a computer if you can, although that is certainly not essential.

EDIT, EDIT, EDIT

Every word has to count in your resume, so keep editing it until it is right. This may require you to make multiple passes and to change your resume many times. But, if you did as I said in the beginning of this book and created a simple but acceptable resume, your fretting over your "better" resume shouldn't delay your job search one bit.

GET SOMEONE ELSE TO REVIEW YOUR RESUME FOR ERRORS

After you have finished writing your resume, ask someone else who has good spelling and grammar skills to review your resume once again. It is simply amazing how errors creep into the most carefully edited resume...

TIPS TO DESIGN YOUR RESUME AND IMPROVE ITS APPEARANCE

Just as some people aren't good at resume writing, others are not good at design. Many resumes use very simple designs and this is acceptable for most situations. But there are things you can do to improve the appearance of your resume and I will cover some of the basics in this section.

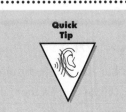

Quick
Tip

When looking at the sample resumes in Section 3, note how some have a better appearance than others. Some have borders and others do not. Some include more white space while others are quite crowded. Compromises are made in most resumes but some clearly look better than others. Note the resumes whose appearance you like and try to incorporate those design principles in your own resume.

WHAT TO DO IF YOU DON'T HAVE THE BEST EQUIPMENT

What do you do if you don't have a state-of-the-art computer and a laser printer? No problem. As I mentioned earlier, there are many people who can help you with the typing and design of your resume. If you do not regularly use a computer or don't have access to good equipment, it is often simpler and better to pay someone else who does have the proper equipment and knows how to use it. At the beginning of this chapter, there is some information on having others do your typing and design work.

INCREASE READABILITY WITH SOME SIMPLE DESIGN PRINCIPLES

People who design advertising know about what makes something easy or hard to read and they work very hard to make things easy. Following are some things that they have found to improve readability. You can apply these same principles in writing your resume.

✔ Short sentences and short words are better than long ones.

✔ Short paragraphs are easier to read than long ones.

✔ Narrow columns are easier to read than wide ones.

✔ Put important information on the top and to the left, since people scan materials from left to right and top to bottom.

✔ Using plenty of white space increases the readability of what remains. And it looks better.

✔ Don't use too many type styles on the same page.

✔ Use underlining, bold type, and bullets to emphasize and separate.

While you may not follow all these guidelines, you should try to use as many as you reasonably can in the design of your own resume.

Quick Alert

AVOID "PACKING" YOUR RESUME WITH SMALL PRINT

Sometimes it is hard to avoid including lots of detail but doing so can make your resume appear crowded and harder to read. In many cases, crowded resumes could be shortened with good editing which could allow for considerably more white space.

USE TWO PAGES AT THE MOST

One page is often enough if you are disciplined in your editing but two uncrowded pages are far better than one crowded one. Those with considerable experience or high levels of responsibility often require a two page resume but very, very few justify more than two.

EDIT AGAIN FOR APPEARANCE

Just as the writing of your resume requires editing, you should be prepared to review and make additional changes as needed to the design of your resume. After you have written the content just as you want it, you will probably need to make additional editing and design changes so that everything looks right.

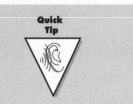

If someone else will help you with the typing and design of your resume, bring them copies of resumes you like as design examples. Be open to the suggestions that they have as well but be willing to assert your own taste regarding your resume's final appearance.

SELECT TOP QUALITY PAPER

Don't use cheap copy machine or other paper. After all your work, you should use only top quality paper. Most print shops are used to doing resumes and will have a selection of papers for you to choose from. The better quality papers often have a percentage of cotton or other fibers in them. I prefer an off-white or light cream color, as it gives a professional and clean appearance. Pastel colors such as gray and light blue are also acceptable but avoid bright colors such as pink, green, or red.

STATIONERY AND ENVELOPES

Envelopes made of the same paper as your resume present a professional appearance. Select an envelope of the same paper type and color at the time you select your resume paper. You should also get some blank sheets of this same paper for use in your cover letters and other job search correspondence. In some cases, you may also be able to obtain thank-you note envelopes and paper as well, though this is not essential.

PRODUCTION TIPS AND GETTING COPIES MADE

GOOD QUALITY PHOTOCOPIES AND LASER PRINTER COPIES ARE FINE

Many better-quality photocopy machines now create excellent images and these can be used to create your resume—as long as high grade paper is used. Check out the copy quality first. Most laser printers also create good-quality images and can be used to make multiple resume copies. Laser printers also have the highest quality output if you plan to include such things as borders and various type styles.

A good quality typewriter will also do a fine job on simple resume formats as will computer printers such as a daisy wheel, ink-jet, and some letter-quality (24 pin) dot-matrix computer printers. Use your judgment here and don't compromise. If it doesn't look better than good, then find a different way to get it done.

EVALUATING AND SELECTING A PRINT SHOP

If you plan on having a print shop print your resume, ask to see examples of their work first. Offset printing can vary in quality, so check out a few places before you decide. I prefer a printer who has more experience with small runs of resumes and who has a good selection of resume paper and envelopes on hand. There are many "quick print" shops in most locations (look in the *Yellow Pages* under "Printers"). These smaller shops are what you want rather than a commercial printer who tends to make longer print runs.

HOW MANY COPIES TO GET

Plan on having at least one hundred copies made; more is better. If you are having the resume printed, the big cost is getting the job on the press and additional copies are often quite inexpensive. The best use of a resume is to get them into circulation early and often, so have enough so that you don't feel you have to "save" them. Having 500 or so would certainly help you avoid that temptation.

If you have your resume photocopied, it is easy and cheap to get additional copies and you can keep a smaller number on hand. If you have access to a computer with a good printer, getting additional copies is also simple.

TIPS FOR USING A COMPUTER TO DO YOUR RESUME AND OTHER CORRESPONDENCE

I use a computer every working day, mostly for word-processing. If you have access to one, it can be a great help in handling correspondence and writing your resume, as you probably know. I also have a laser printer that allows me to print high quality letters and many other things. So I am reasonably computer literate and appreciate their value in doing tasks such as a resume. That is why I can say that, if you are not already familiar with how to use a computer for word-processing and you do not have easy access to one with a good printer, now is not the time to learn.

I say this because, unless you know how to use it, you can waste lots of time trying to get a computer to do simple things (like print out a letter). If computers are new to you, let someone else type and print out your resume. Once you have your resume, you might have someone show you how to use the computer for things like correspondence. But avoid the fancy stuff. Trust me on this.

**Quick
Tip**

Computers are everywhere. If you don't have good computer skills, you are at a great disadvantage in the job market since more and more employers require computer literacy at all levels. If you have not kept up with computer skills related to your career area, consider taking some classes on the applications used most in the jobs you want. This might be word processing, spreadsheets, database, graphics or some other type of program. Local adult education and community colleges often offer low cost courses. You should also read some of the computer magazines to familiarize yourself with the concepts, capabilities, and language. Do it regularly!

If you can use and have access to a computer, though, they do offer some distinct advantages. Most word processing programs can handle all your resume writing and correspondence needs. Some even have resume "templates" that provide one or more good designs that you can just fill out. You may also have access to a mailing list, card file, database, or other programs that can be used to organize your mailing lists and remind you to follow up on leads.

There are also a growing number of programs designed to assist you in your job search. These include programs to help you write a resume, to organize your job search, teach you career planning and job search skills, obtain information on major occupations, complete the complex federal application form (the dreaded FS 171), and other tasks. CD-ROM disks are also now available to help you look up information on thousands of careers and to obtain other information. And then there are the electronic resume databases where your resume can be searched by employers looking for specific skills. If all of this is new to you, go to a large computer software store and wander the business software shelves. There is a lot already there and more will come.

While all of this may appear exciting, I still believe that you should avoid spending too much time playing with programs and technology during your job search. Instead, go out and get interviews—that requires human communication, not electronic wizardry. Ultimately, effectively communicating your strengths is what will matter, though you can certainly use computers to assist you in the process.

Section Three

· ·

SAMPLE

RESUMES

· ·

Introduction

I've never felt that there was one and only one "right" way to do a resume. Each person has unique information to present and each resume can look and be different. Often there are good reasons for this. For example, some occupations (such as law) have more formal traditions and resumes in this area typically would be more formal. Someone looking for a job in graphic design or marketing might have a more colorful and non-traditional approach.

There are many reasons to use different writing and design styles and the resumes that I have included in this section show wide variety in all their elements. There are samples of chronological, skills, combination, and creative resumes. There are resumes for all sorts of people looking for all sorts of jobs. Some resumes include interesting graphic elements and others are quite "plain."

I think that this variety will help you with ideas for writing and creating your own resume. It will also give you "permission" to experiment and use whatever style best suits you.

Some Ways to Review the Sample Resumes

I have organized the resumes into clusters I thought would be helpful to you. These clusters include sample resumes in these groupings:

- Education & Human Services
- Office Jobs, Including Clerical
- Technical, Scientific, & Specialty
- Professional, Managerial, & Executive
- Recent Graduates and Still in School
- Marketing, Sales, Public Relations, & Retail
- Career Changers & Special Situations
- Creative, Writing, & Media
- Military to Civilian

One obvious way to use the samples is to turn to the section that seems most compatible with your career goals. Doing this will allow you to see how others in similar situations or seeking similar jobs have handled their resumes.

But I also encourage you to look at all the groupings since they provide interesting formats, presentation styles, and other ideas that you may be able to use in your own resume. For example, there are some resumes with superior graphic design elements that may inspire you, even though your job objective lies in a different area.

Where the Resumes Came From

The sample resumes came from several sources. I developed some of them and, in some cases, have used them in other books I have written.

Dave Swanson has kindly given me permission to use a number of resumes that originally appeared in his book, *The Resume Solution*. Dave's book is particularly strong on resume design and offers a step-by-step process that is very easy to follow. I recommend it! His resumes include those for Conner O'Brien, Amy Ann Townson and John Thomas.

One particularly interesting resume, that of Lili LiLu, is from Richard Lathrop's book *Who's Hiring Who?* He calls his approach to resumes a "Qualifications Brief," and it does a good job of presenting skills in an interesting way.

In addition, there are many sample resumes that have been provided by professional resume writers from across the country and Canada. Most are members of the Professional Association of Resume Writers and many are certified by that group as a "Professional Certified Resume Writer." I want to thank all those who submitted resumes for use in this book. They give the examples a diversity and range that would not have been possible otherwise.

When a resume is not mine, I credit its source on the bottom of the page. I've also included the full contact information for each source at the end of this section, organized by location. While I can't personally endorse the services of all the professional resume writers who have contributed the sample resumes, I encourage you to contact them for assistance, should you be in their respective areas.

In all cases, the names and other details on the resumes are "fictionalized" and do not present real people, although each and every one *is* based on an actual resume written for and by a real person. Because they are based on real resumes, written by a diverse group of people, they represent a wide range of styles, designs, and formats. I hope that this approach shows you that it is OK to "break the rules" and be a bit creative in writing your own resume.

I've Included Comments on the Resumes

I have included comments on many of the sample resumes to point out features I like or don't like, provide information on the person behind the resume, or to provide other information.

Since the resumes are reduced in size to fit on the book's pages, I wrote my comments on the resumes themselves to save space. I hope you like these comments and don't find them distracting.

Groupings of Sample Resumes	Page
Education & Human Services	169
Office Jobs, Including Clerical	174
Technical, Scientific, & Specialty	180
Professional, Managerial, & Executive	188
Recent Graduates & Still in School	196
Marketing, Sales, Public Relations, & Retail	206
Career Changers & Special Situations	214
Creative, Writing, & Media	221
Military to Civilian	227

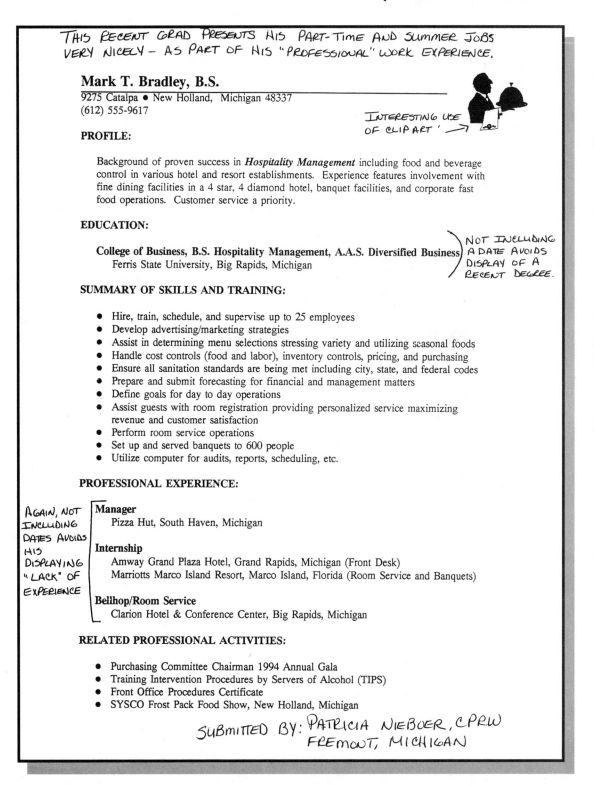

THIS RECENT GRAD PRESENTS HIS PART-TIME AND SUMMER JOBS VERY NICELY — AS PART OF HIS "PROFESSIONAL" WORK EXPERIENCE.

Mark T. Bradley, B.S.

9275 Catalpa • New Holland, Michigan 48337
(612) 555-9617

INTERESTING USE OF CLIP ART ⟶

PROFILE:

Background of proven success in *Hospitality Management* including food and beverage control in various hotel and resort establishments. Experience features involvement with fine dining facilities in a 4 star, 4 diamond hotel, banquet facilities, and corporate fast food operations. Customer service a priority.

EDUCATION:

College of Business, B.S. Hospitality Management, A.A.S. Diversified Business
Ferris State University, Big Rapids, Michigan

NOT INCLUDING A DATE AVOIDS DISPLAY OF A RECENT DEGREE.

SUMMARY OF SKILLS AND TRAINING:

- Hire, train, schedule, and supervise up to 25 employees
- Develop advertising/marketing strategies
- Assist in determining menu selections stressing variety and utilizing seasonal foods
- Handle cost controls (food and labor), inventory controls, pricing, and purchasing
- Ensure all sanitation standards are being met including city, state, and federal codes
- Prepare and submit forecasting for financial and management matters
- Define goals for day to day operations
- Assist guests with room registration providing personalized service maximizing revenue and customer satisfaction
- Perform room service operations
- Set up and served banquets to 600 people
- Utilize computer for audits, reports, scheduling, etc.

PROFESSIONAL EXPERIENCE:

AGAIN, NOT INCLUDING DATES AVOIDS HIS DISPLAYING "LACK" OF EXPERIENCE

Manager
Pizza Hut, South Haven, Michigan

Internship
Amway Grand Plaza Hotel, Grand Rapids, Michigan (Front Desk)
Marriotts Marco Island Resort, Marco Island, Florida (Room Service and Banquets)

Bellhop/Room Service
Clarion Hotel & Conference Center, Big Rapids, Michigan

RELATED PROFESSIONAL ACTIVITIES:

- Purchasing Committee Chairman 1994 Annual Gala
- Training Intervention Procedures by Servers of Alcohol (TIPS)
- Front Office Procedures Certificate
- SYSCO Frost Pack Food Show, New Holland, Michigan

*SUBMITTED BY: PATRICIA NIEBOER, CPRW
FREMONT, MICHIGAN*

PRESENTS VOLUNTEER AND LIFE EXPERIENCES HERE NICELY TO SUPPORT A TRANSITION TO AN ENTRY-LEVEL JOB WORKING WITH CHILDREN.

JENNIFER A. BLOOM

2236 East Oak Drive
Windfall, IN 46076
(317) 555-7649

PROFILE

Seeking a position working with children / providing office support in a day care or preschool setting. Responsible, dependable employee. Possess good interpersonal skills, and relate well to children.

A GOOD USE OF ADAPTIVE SKILLS HERE. IT WORKS WELL!!

RELEVANT VOLUNTEER EXPERIENCE

Preschool Teacher, Carroll Christian Church, Carroll, IN   9/90 - Present

Teach Sunday school to four-year-old children. Create a warm, relaxed learning environment for seven preschool students. Utilize the "time out" discipline approach. Plan lessons and craft projects appropriate for the season. Lead sing-a-long sessions; read Bible stories. Make progress reports to parents, and make recommendations to parents for home study. Plan and coordinate holiday parties.

Volunteer, at home   9/93 - Present

Assist my handicapped sister daily in special exercises and activities as directed by the occupational therapist from the Hope Treatment Center. Follow directions carefully and report results on a weekly basis.

WHY NOT? THIS IS GOOD INFORMATION TO INCLUDE HERE AS IT SUPPORTS HER JOB OBJECTIVE

CUSTOMER SERVICE EXPERIENCE

Provide polite, cheerful service to customers. Bag groceries, do price checks, and handle overstock. Help handicapped people do their shopping. Regularly complimented by customers for courteous service.

Received Kroger's commendation award for service above and beyond the ordinary.

OFFICE SUPPORT EXPERIENCE

Delivered medical records and charts, handled light typing, and filed records and charts.
Greeted customers, provided information, and opened safety-deposit accounts.

WORK HISTORY

Service Clerk	KROGER FOODS INC. Carroll, IN	10/91 - Present
Service Clerk	KROGER FOODS INC. Windfall, IN	4/86 - 10/91
Vault Clerk	WINDFALL STATE BANK Windfall, IN	5/84 - 4/86
Medical Records Clerk	TIPTON COUNTY MEDICAL CENTER Tipton, IN	6/80 - 5/84

EDUCATION

Tipton High School, Tipton, IN • GRADUATE

Hoosier Community College, Carroll, IN
Courses in continuing education • Earned certificate in BASIC COMPUTER OPERATIONS.

References will be provided upon request.

SUBMITTED BY: JENNIE R. DOWDEN FLOSSMORE, ILLINOIS

WHILE THIS RESUME IS TARGETED TO HEALTHCARE, IT COULD EASILY BE RE-FOCUSED TO MORE GENERAL FINANCIAL MANAGEMENT POSITIONS.

Robert H. Colombo

18 Milton Lane • Needham, MA 01532
(617) 444-6631

Objective

To obtain a position as a *Financial Manager* in the Health Care industry utilizing 16 years of demonstrated success and accomplishment.

Summary

- Outstanding knowledge and expertise in Health Care with particular emphasis in analyzing and resolving financial problems.
- Effectively reorganized a $20 million agency realizing a significant increase in Federal reimbursements.
- Excellent knowledge and experience in all phases of financial management including operations, financial reporting, internal controls, controllership and financial analysis.
- Achieved outstanding results through tenacious and persistent application of sound financial management techniques.
- Demonstrated ability to effectively lead and develop a skilled staff.
- Able to successfully manage multiple priorities and assignments.
- Approach problems in a highly creative and effective manner.

Experience
1992 to Present

INTERNATIONAL HEALTH SPECIALISTS, INC., Newton, MA
Controller

- Significantly reduced A/R (mostly with 120 day aging) through controls, staffing changes, MIS additions, and management direction.
- Designed and implemented more informative P&L reports for growing divisions of healthcare services.
- Responsible for Accounting, Billing, Collections, Payroll, MIS and Accounts Payable.

1987 to 1992

DIGITAL EQUIPMENT CORPORATION, Marlboro, MA
Finance Manager - U.S. Leasing and Remarketing (8/89 to Present)
Administrative Finance Manager - U.S. Sales (6/88 - 8/89)
Sales Finance Manager - Southern Area (4/87 - 6/88)

EFFECTIVE USE OF CAPITAL LETTERS, BOLD FACE, ITALIC AND BULLETS — A SIMPLE, BUT EYE CATCHING TOUCH.

- Developed and implemented a Performance Reporting System that is able to effectively evaluate the quality of sales and to keep the performance of the division on track to accomplish stated goals.
- Successfully implemented the Leasing Business Plan with total sales volume of $400 million accounting for 10% of all sales at DEC.
- Conducted financial analysis of all new U.S. Sales Administration programs.
- Conducted Profit & Loss performance analysis to determine sales trends.
- Accurately and effectively completed monthly sales forecasts, developed an ongoing quarterly book, and coordinated third balance sheet review for operations.
- Hire, train and develop a staff of 10 professionals.

SUBMITTED BY: STEVEN GREEN NORTHBORO, MASSACHUSETTS

Robert H. Colombo
Page Two

1986 to 1987	SAMSON & SAMSON, Needham, MA *Senior Consultant* • Accountable for consolidations and mergers in the health care field. Analyzed financial statements, conducted audits and prepared cost reports.
1983 to 1986	BOSTON AFFILIATES, Boston, MA *Chief Financial Officer/Controller* • Full financial responsibility for this $22 million agency including accounting, credits and collections and data control. Also managed the Administrative Services which included purchasing and MIS. Responsible for a staff of 50. Reported to the Executive Director. • Effectively reorganized the agency resulting in a substantial increase in Federal reimbursements. Realized a 20% savings through inventory controls and competitive purchasing techniques. • Successfully conducted Labor negotiations involving union employees in 5 locations. Conducted rental/lease contract negotiations.
1980 to 1983	VISITING NURSE ASSOCIATION OF WORCESTER, INC. Worcester, MA *Controller* • Responsible for the total Financial Management of the Association. Achieved a stabilized financial position and provided guidance to the Executive Director and Board of Directors.
1974 to 1980	MILFORD WHITINSVILLE REGIONAL HOSPITAL, Whitinsville, MA *General Accountant*
Education	Bryant College, Smithfield, RI M.B.A. 1982. B.S. in Accounting. 1975.

SUPERIOR CREDENTIALS THAT MIGHT JUSTIFY MORE DETAILS, THOUGH HIS SUBSTANTIAL EXPERIENCE MAKES IT LESS IMPORTANT.

Community Activites

• *Treasurer* and Board Member, Massachusetts Association of Community Health Agencies (MACHA);

• *Chairman* of the Regulatory Committee of MACHA.

--REFERENCES AVAILABLE UPON REQUEST--

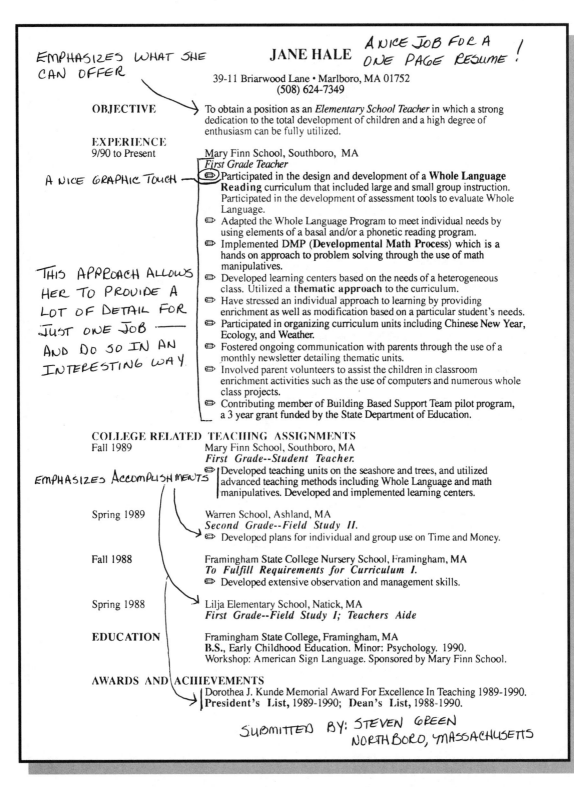

EMPHASIZES WHAT SHE CAN OFFER

JANE HALE

A NICE JOB FOR A ONE PAGE RESUME!

39-11 Briarwood Lane • Marlboro, MA 01752
(508) 624-7349

OBJECTIVE

To obtain a position as an *Elementary School Teacher* in which a strong dedication to the total development of children and a high degree of enthusiasm can be fully utilized.

EXPERIENCE
9/90 to Present

Mary Finn School, Southboro, MA
First Grade Teacher

A NICE GRAPHIC TOUCH

- Participated in the design and development of a **Whole Language Reading** curriculum that included large and small group instruction. Participated in the development of assessment tools to evaluate Whole Language.
- Adapted the Whole Language Program to meet individual needs by using elements of a basal and/or a phonetic reading program.
- Implemented DMP (**Developmental Math Process**) which is a hands on approach to problem solving through the use of math manipulatives.

THIS APPROACH ALLOWS HER TO PROVIDE A LOT OF DETAIL FOR JUST ONE JOB — AND DO SO IN AN INTERESTING WAY.

- Developed learning centers based on the needs of a heterogeneous class. Utilized a **thematic approach** to the curriculum.
- Have stressed an individual approach to learning by providing enrichment as well as modification based on a particular student's needs.
- Participated in organizing curriculum units including **Chinese New Year, Ecology, and Weather.**
- Fostered ongoing communication with parents through the use of a monthly newsletter detailing thematic units.
- Involved parent volunteers to assist the children in classroom enrichment activities such as the use of computers and numerous whole class projects.
- Contributing member of Building Based Support Team pilot program, a 3 year grant funded by the State Department of Education.

COLLEGE RELATED TEACHING ASSIGNMENTS
Fall 1989

Mary Finn School, Southboro, MA
First Grade--Student Teacher.

EMPHASIZES ACCOMPLISHMENTS

- Developed teaching units on the seashore and trees, and utilized advanced teaching methods including Whole Language and math manipulatives. Developed and implemented learning centers.

Spring 1989

Warren School, Ashland, MA
Second Grade--Field Study II.
- Developed plans for individual and group use on Time and Money.

Fall 1988

Framingham State College Nursery School, Framingham, MA
To Fulfill Requirements for Curriculum I.
- Developed extensive observation and management skills.

Spring 1988

Lilja Elementary School, Natick, MA
First Grade--Field Study I; Teachers Aide

EDUCATION

Framingham State College, Framingham, MA
B.S., Early Childhood Education. Minor: Psychology. 1990.
Workshop: American Sign Language. Sponsored by Mary Finn School.

AWARDS AND ACHIEVEMENTS

Dorothea J. Kunde Memorial Award For Excellence In Teaching 1989-1990.
President's List, 1989-1990; **Dean's List,** 1988-1990.

*SUBMITTED BY: STEVEN GREEN
NORTHBORO, MASSACHUSETTS*

SUSAN WHITAKER
1227 Juniper Drive
Bloomington, Indiana 47401
(812) 555-9445

HIGHLIGHTS OF QUALIFICATIONS

- Four years experience in administrative/clerical support positions.
- Easily establish rapport with managers, staff, and customers.
- Proficient at analyzing statistics and market trends to develop accurate forecasts and effective sales presentations.
- Excellent problem solving, project management and decision making skills.
- Proven ability to prioritize and complete multiple tasks.

COMPUTER SKILLS

Software:	WordPerfect, Microsoft Word for Windows
Graphics:	Harvard Graphics, Powerpoint for Windows
Database:	Telemagic
Hardware:	Apple IIE, HP and most IBM compatibles
Spreadsheets:	Lotus 1-2-3, Microsoft Excel, Quattro Pro

IMPORTANT DETAILS TO EMPHASIZE

OFFICE SKILLS

65+ wpm typing, 75 wpm word processing, 70+ wpm shorthand, CRT, dictation, 10-key adding machine, statistical analysis

PROFESSIONAL EXPERIENCE

PEPSI-COLA COMPANY, Indianapolis, Indiana   1988 - Present
Administrative Assistant

- Analyze sales volume and profit.
- Finalize and package forecasting reports for more than $100 million in annual sales.
- Monitor monthly spending and reconciliation for $8 million budget.
- Manage $300,000 in advertising and promotional materials.
- Interact with sales staff impacting service to 1200 customers.

EVERY LINE INCLUDES SOME NUMBERS

EDUCATION

Executive Secretarial Certificate, 1988
ITT TECHNICAL INSTITUTE, Indianapolis, Indiana
- Dean's List, 3.7/4.0 GPA
- Maintained perfect attendance record

EXCELLENT DETAILS TO ADD !!

REFERENCES AVAILABLE UPON REQUEST

SUBMITTED BY: JOHN A. SUAREZ ST LOUIS, MISSOURI

THIS RESUME PRESENTS SUBSTANTIAL EXPERIENCE BY USING BRIEF, WELL-SELECTED STATEMENTS.

JESSIE W. FOLGER

783 Calhoon Drive
Greencastle, Indiana 46305
(317) 635-8824

EXPERTISE: PURCHASING / MATERIALS MANAGER

EXPERIENCE:

Simple, short statements, but they present him well →

Cast Metal Products, Inc., Greencastle, Indiana   3/88-Present

PURCHASING AGENT: Organize, manage, and supervise purchasing department for $30,000,000 manufacturer of die cast aluminum transmission housings.

ACCOMPLISHMENTS/PRIMARY FUNCTIONS:
- Consistently obtain 3%-5% annual cost reduction from vendors.
- Certified Instructor, "Working" Class; increase productivity/worker efficiency daily.
- Member, National Association of Purchasing Managers.
- Negotiate contracts for major commodities; emphasis in $23,000,000 of aluminum annually.
- Cost analysis for numerous items.
- Quality Circle Team Leader, commitment of team leadership/management philosophy.
- Extensive customer relations experience.
- In-depth knowledge of daily workings in manufacturing operation.

Myers Electric Equipment Company, Martinsville, Indiana   6/87-3/88

OUTSIDE ELECTRICAL SALES ENGINEER: Extensive customer interaction for major electrical distributor with four divisions.

ARCO Electric Products Corporation, Martinsville, Indiana   1/76-5/87

VICE PRESIDENT, CUSTOMER RELATIONS: Designed product compatibility systems for consumer needs. In-house and on-site troubleshooting application and engineering assistance.
VICE PRESIDENT, MARKETING: Administered guidance to 23 field agents. Developed new product literature.
NATIONAL SALES MANAGER: Ensured continuity of policies and practices for nationwide distribution market. Developed and implemented training program for representatives.
PURCHASING AGENT/BUYER: Improved inventory control system. Analyzed bids from different suppliers. Assessed and selected raw materials for use in all aspects of production.

EDUCATION:

Bachelor of Science, Education, Indiana University, Bloomington, Indiana

Continuing Education:
- Advanced Purchasing Strategies, Cast Metal Products, Inc.
- Successfully completed three in-house training programs, Cast Metal Products, Inc.
- Dale Carnegie, Simon D. Yancy Associates, Indianapolis, Indiana
- Accounting I, Indiana Vocational Technical College, Indianapolis, Indiana

CIVIC ACTIVITIES:

- Immediate Past President, Kiwanis Marks Club of Greencastle
- Member, Board of Directors, Brothers, Inc. of Morgan County
- Sub-committee Chairman, Partners-in-Education, Monroe County Chamber of Commerce
- Member, Monroe County Chamber of Commerce

SUBMITTED BY: CAROLE PERLEY INDIANAPOLIS, INDIANA

SKILLS AND STRENGTHS ON PAGE ONE, CREDENTIALS ON PAGE TWO. THIS MAKES A GOOD ONE-TWO "PUNCH," EACH PAGE USING DIFFERENT FORMATS.

DIANA MOSS

184 Crestview Court • Freehold, New Jersey 07728 • (908) 431-8965

OBJECTIVE

An administrative position in the area of rehabilitation/geriatric health care utilizing my knowledge of clinical, community, and patient services.

SUMMARY OF QUALIFICATIONS

Increasing responsibilities in areas including:

- Medical Rehabilitative Services
- Speech and Language Pathology
- Contract Sales
- Rehabilitative Marketing Services
- Treatment Coordinator and Liaison
- Public Relations

PROFESSIONAL ACCOMPLISHMENTS

Administration

- Supervised treatment programs at numerous skilled nursing facilities throughout the states of New Jersey and Pennsylvania.

- As Clinical Coordinator for PermaCare, responsible for direct patient care, planning, patient and family counseling.

- In charge of Medicare documentation lending to reimbursement for each facility. Assist in budgeting for rehabilitative services.

- Plan restorative nursing programs and provide consultation to appropriate agencies.

- Write program goals.

- CFY supervision.

Speech and Language Pathology

- Responsible for patient identification, evaluation, case consultations, goal setting, and direct care.

- Receive referrals from within the facility and from outside referring agencies.

- Conduct public and private speech-language, and hearing screenings. Involved in public education of communication disorders; knowledge of OBRA regulations.

Sales/Marketing/Public Relations

- Work with patients, families, and community agencies. Communicate facility's services; advertise availability and quality of services.

- Perform public relations functions in both corporate and hospital environments.

SUBMITTED BY: BEVERLY BASKIN, CPRW
MARLBORO, NEW JERSEY

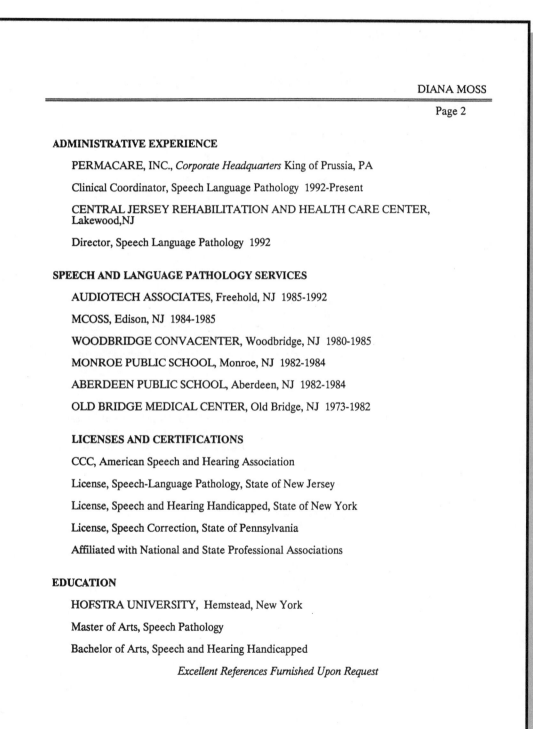

DIANA MOSS

Page 2

ADMINISTRATIVE EXPERIENCE

PERMACARE, INC., *Corporate Headquarters* King of Prussia, PA

Clinical Coordinator, Speech Language Pathology 1992-Present

CENTRAL JERSEY REHABILITATION AND HEALTH CARE CENTER, Lakewood,NJ

Director, Speech Language Pathology 1992

SPEECH AND LANGUAGE PATHOLOGY SERVICES

AUDIOTECH ASSOCIATES, Freehold, NJ 1985-1992

MCOSS, Edison, NJ 1984-1985

WOODBRIDGE CONVACENTER, Woodbridge, NJ 1980-1985

MONROE PUBLIC SCHOOL, Monroe, NJ 1982-1984

ABERDEEN PUBLIC SCHOOL, Aberdeen, NJ 1982-1984

OLD BRIDGE MEDICAL CENTER, Old Bridge, NJ 1973-1982

LICENSES AND CERTIFICATIONS

CCC, American Speech and Hearing Association

License, Speech-Language Pathology, State of New Jersey

License, Speech and Hearing Handicapped, State of New York

License, Speech Correction, State of Pennsylvania

Affiliated with National and State Professional Associations

EDUCATION

HOFSTRA UNIVERSITY, Hemstead, New York

Master of Arts, Speech Pathology

Bachelor of Arts, Speech and Hearing Handicapped

Excellent References Furnished Upon Request

A GOOD APPEARANCE AND LAYOUT TO THIS MODIFIED CHRONOLOGICAL RESUME.

Jane E. Doe

P.O. Box 666 - Towny, Illinois 62222 - (217) 555-0000

SUMMARY OF QUALIFICATIONS:

- Strong accounting and recordkeeping aptitude experience.

- Effective planning and organization skills.

- Ability to work well both independently and in a team environment.

A NICE TOUCH →

- Takes great pride in completing a job with accuracy, proficiency and effectiveness.

EXPERIENCE: *FROM HERE ON, THIS IS A TRADITIONAL CHRONOLOGICAL RESUME*

March 1988 to December 1993

JOE'S BUILDING, INC., Towny, Illinois
Office Manager
Responsible for managing all accounts receivable, accounts payable, order entry, inventory, purchase order receivings and general ledger transactions utilizing the Great Plains Accounting System on an IBM compatible computer. Balanced manual checkbook to reconcile bank statements. Handled multi-line phone for customer inquiries, organized filing system and balanced cash drawer completing deposits.

April 1985 to February 1988

TOWNY ENERGY, Towny, Illinois
Secretary
Maintained employee payroll and tax records. Responsible for entire paper trail of business including accounts payable and receivable. Provided customer service by scheduling appointments and answering telephone questions. Utilized Apple computer.

October 1984 to April 1985

JILL'S FAST FOOD, Towny, Illinois
Assistant Head Cashier
Maintained daily deposits and balances of all cash registers. Opened and closed the store. Accountable for office paper trail of daily balances.

August 1976 to April 1984

GROCER'S, Towny, Illinois
Cashier/Office Assistant
Customer service representative through phone inquiries and office work. Relied on to close and balance cash registers and to make daily deposits.

EDUCATION: HER ACADEMY, Towny, Illinois
Diploma

GREAT PLAINS ACCOUNTING SYSTEM, Poorboy, Texas
Certificate

REFERENCES: Available upon request.

SUBMITTED BY: LAURA G. LICHTINSTEIN SPRINGFIELD, ILLINOIS

A VERY EASY TO READ RESUME WITH A CLEAN FORMAT

S. OLIVIA HANSON
4444 Kitz Road
Evansville, Indiana 47711
(812) 555-5555

PROFILE

STRONG STATEMENTS OF ABILITIES — A GOOD OPENING

Highly skilled Executive Secretary with outstanding, professional experience including:

▸ Ability to communicate with all levels of management and employees.
▸ International communication liaison with subsidiary companies.
▸ Contract Negotiation Bargaining Team member.
▸ Use of word processing, windows and training on Lotus 1-2-3.

EXPERIENCE

PIONEER CORPORATION Evansville, Indiana
Executive Secretary 5/88 - 8/93
• Served as secretary to the Director of Plant Operations and to the Director of Engineering.
• Assisted in start-up of two branches of the company (Brazil, S.A., Ft. Smith, AR).
• Arranged all aspects of international and domestic travel for Engineering Department.
• Member of bargaining unit representing the Company during contract negotiations.
• Maintained executive calendars, scheduled appointments, and fielded phone calls.
• Prepared draft of monthly reports regarding current capital engineering projects.
• Routed all incoming company mail to appropriate department.
• Assisted in the preparation and editing of the company newsletter.
• Provided visitor assistance and arranged departmental luncheons.

SEIGNMAN ENGINEERING Evansville, Indiana
Part-Time Secretary/Receptionist 1983 - 1985
• Assisted with compiling legal data and putting it in chronological order.
• Prepared court exhibits.
• Typed correspondence and legal documents.
• Answered phones and greeted clients.

CENTRAL SERVICE Evansville, Indiana
Customer Service Representative 1978 - 1980
• Located overages/shortages at main store.
• Answered service calls, scheduled appointments, and resolved customer complaints.
• Performed clerical and cashier duties.

PET MEDICAL CENTER Evansville, Indiana
Veterinarian Assistant 1972 - 1978
• Assisted in surgery with anesthesia and instruments.
• Provided pre- and post-operative animal care.
• Performed administrative clerical and reception duties.

EDUCATION

INDIANA VOCATIONAL TECHNICAL COLLEGE Evansville, Indiana
Professional Secretary Certification November 1993

References Available Upon Request

SUBMITTED BY: TERESA COLLINS, CPRW +ERICA HANSON
EVANSVILLE, INDIANA

THIS RESUME PRESENTS MR. RILEY AS IF SOMEONE ELSE WAS PRESENTING HIS BACKGROUND — AN INTERESTING APPROACH.

PROFESSIONAL PROFILE

CHARLES B. RILEY, CEI/CES

BACKGROUND

Charles B. Riley has had over 25 years of diversified experience in the technical and engineering field. His qualifications include having worked in Manufacturing/Industrial Management, Engineering Sales and Management; in addition to his positions as a Management Consultant Engineer, Safety Director, and more recently, Environmental Consultant.

PROFESSIONAL EXPERIENCE

A Professional Environmental Consultant since 1988, Mr. Riley specializes in the marketing of services related to:

- Contamination Assessments and Remediation at Hazardous and Non-hazardous sites.
- Underground Storage Tank (UST) Evaluations.
- Phase I, II and III Assessments.
- Asbestos Abatement/Radon Testing.
- OSHA 40-Hour Haz-Met School.
- Personnel Placement of Engineers and Technicians.

NOTICE THAT NO DATES ARE INCLUDED. THIS ALLOWS HIM TO PRESENT HIS EXPERIENCE WITHOUT DISPLAYING HIS AGE

Mr. Riley's professional background includes prior employment with the following companies:

Donahue Groover & Associates, Staff Engineer/Consultant. Coordinated financial budget (P&E); marketing and logistics; Industrial Relations; general overall monitoring of organizational activities.

INA Insurance Company of North America (now Cigna), Senior Marketing Technical Representative. Responsible for monitoring total loss control, in conjunction with 30 insurance agencies. Instructed insurance officials, their insureds, and prospective clients on the OSHA Regulations and the implementation of safety programs to insure governmental compliance.

Hayes Aircraft, Senior Project Engineer. Supervised eight engineers. Coordinated research and design problems on Saturn V Swing Arms. Worked closely with NASA Engineers in reviewing and resolving problem areas.

Bendix Corporation, Supervisor of 50 personnel at John F. Kennedy Space Center, Florida. Coordinated refurbishment of Saturn V Swing Arm. Supported NASA Contractors and directed all operations. Training instructor for mechanical and pneumatic personnel involved in Swing Arm project. Instructor at Ground School for Heavy Equipment and Launch Control Systems.

Honeywell, Inc., Industrial Engineer/Cost Estimator. Worked on various "classified assemblies" and military electronic devices. Prepared cost estimates for bidding.

EDUCATION

Mr. Riley studied Industrial Engineering at Ohio University and is also a graduate of the International Safety Academy. In July, 1992, he received a 40-Hour OSHA Certification from the Technical Environmental Training Institute. During his career, he has participated in a variety of certified, specialized training and management programs; together with being an instructor for a Welding School and the Saturn V Ground Support School. He has conducted seminars and given speeches on OSHA Regulations and Procedures; Safety Programs to Insure Compliance with OSHA; Environmental Work - Air Quality, Smoke Stack Emissions, and Water Contamination.

PROFESSIONAL MEMBERSHIPS/AFFILIATIONS

- Environmental Asssessment Association (EAA)
- Environmental Conservation Organization (ECO)
- Lifetime Member - Methods Time Management Association (MTM)

SUBMITTED BY: DIANE McGOLDRICK TAMPA, FLORIDA

WHILE I'VE NOT INCLUDED MANY RESUME "COVER SHEET" SAMPLES, THIS ONE SHOWS YOU A SIMPLE, BUT WELL DONE ONE. THE GRAPHIC IS A NICE FEATURE, AS IS THE FACT THAT IT WAS INDIVIDUALLY PERSONALIZED FOR THE EMPLOYER WHO RECEIVED IT. THIS SORT OF "ATTENTION TO DETAIL" CAN PAY OFF IN CREATING A GOOD FIRST IMPRESSION.

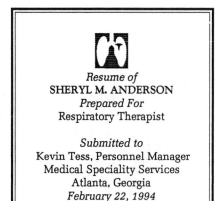

Resume of
SHERYL M. ANDERSON
Prepared For
Respiratory Therapist

Submitted to
Kevin Tess, Personnel Manager
Medical Speciality Services
Atlanta, Georgia
February 22, 1994

SUBMITTED BY: MICHAEL ROBERTSON
ALEXANDRIA, LOUISIANA

GOOD DESIGN, GOOD LAYOUT
GOOD PRESENTATION OF
SPECIFIC DETAILS.

SHERYL M. ANDERSON
1010 5th Street
Alexandria, Louisiana 71306
Phone: (315) 441-1234

CAREER OBJECTIVE: Certified Respiratory Therapist seeks position with progressive hospital/medical center or respiratory agency in need of a challenge-oriented individual with entry-level skills in all areas of respiratory care.

Interested in position which offers broad participation, immediate challenges and career opportunity to apply academic experience and employment background in job setting that provides future potential based upon an individual's initiative and abilities.

Personal attributes include an ability to adapt easily to new organizational environments and function independently with own decision making responsibilities under hospital medical direction.

SYNOPSIS OF WORK EXPERIENCE: Graduate of AMA approved school for respiratory care therapy, including extensive and diversified work experience in:
- Neonatal Intensive Care-Level III Nursery
- Adult Critical Care Units
- Emergency Transport Units
- Arterial Blood Gas Analysis
- Assisting in Intubation procedures
- Worked with expert Open Heart team

EMPLOYMENT HISTORY

9/90-Present
DEEP SOUTH MEDICAL STAFF, Metairie, Louisiana
Respiratory Care Technician, Contract Service Division
Position required adaptability to different hospitals' staffs and routines in a wide variety of assignments calling for complete knowledge of all phases of respiratory care.

4/89-9/90
ST. FRANCIS CABRINI HOSPITAL, Alexandria, Louisiana
Respiratory Care Technician, Cardiopulmonary Department
Responsibilities included adult & neonatal-level III nursery ventilator management, arterial blood gas sampling, bronchoscopy assistance, pulmonary functions, pulmonary stress testing, EKG & Holter monitoring set-ups, routine floor care, charge technician for shifts, Open Heart Teams assistance and Transport Units for adults and neonates.

1/90-5/90
HUMANA HOSPITAL, Natchez, Mississippi
Respiratory Care Technician
Worked part-time as a PRN Pool person to 100 bed hospital-all phases of respiratory care, only one therapist per 12 hour shift.

9/88-3/89
OFFICERS CLUB, ENGLAND A.F.B., Alexandria, Louisiana
Club Operations Assistant

4/88-6/88
JOSTENS, Memphis, Tennessee
Inventory Control Clerk (Temporary position)

4/84-2/88
SHERATON INN, Alexandria, Louisiana
Front Office Manager/Reservations

11/81-4/84
OFFICERS CLUB, ENGLAND A.F.B., Alexandria, Louisiana
Banquet Supervisor

CERTIFICATIONS:
Respiratory Therapy Technician (1990)
Louisiana State Board of Medical Examiners

Respiratory Therapy Technician (1990)
The National Board of Respiratory Care

SHERYL M. ANDERSON
Page 2

EDUCATION & TRAINING:	Currently working toward **Registry Program** completion *Status: 75% complete*

Respiratory Care Practioner Tutorial Program   *Graduated 3/31/90*
California College for Health Sciences, through St. Francis Cabrini Hospital,
Alexandria, LA

Nursing - Louisiana State University, Alexandria, LA *(GPA: 3.0)* *1983-85*

Accounting: Delta Business College, Alexandria, LA   *1981-1982*

PROFESSIONAL AFFILIATIONS:
- **American Association for Respiratory Care**
- **LAMBDA BETA Society** - National Honor Society for the Profession of Respiratory Care

ADDITIONAL QUALIFICATIONS:

1. Able to perform CPR and maintain current documentation of skill
2. Posses didactic and clinical knowledge of current respiratory care medicines including, but not limited to, isoetharine, metaproterenol, beclamethazone, cromolyn sodium, albuterol, racemic epinephrine, ribavirin, and pentamadine.
3. Able to instruct patients in proper use of metered dose inhalers and spacers.
4. Safely administer postural drainage and percussion in proper therapeutic positions.
5. Safely administer IPPB and hand-held (ACORN) nebulizer delivery systems.
6. Safely induce sputum specimens using proper agents and equipment.
7. Posseses clinical knowledge of incentive spirometry devices.
8. Able to safely setup humidifiers and nebulizers.
9. Posseses clinical knowledge in the administration of oxygen via high-flow devices like mask/nasal CPAP and manual resuscitators.
10. Able to properly assess endotracheal tube placement.
11. Able to setup, maintain, and monitor patients on mechanical ventilation.
12. Able to draw and analyze arterial blood gases.
13. Able to suction and care for endotracheal and tracheostomy patients on ventilators.
14. Able to perform weaning procedures, such as maximal inspiratory force, vital capacity, and minute volume.
15. Able to adjust ventilator parameters according to physician orders.

[handwritten note: PROVIDES SPECIFIC "CAN DO" SKILLS RELATED TO THE JOB OBJECTIVE.]

AVAILABILITY: Two weeks following acceptance of position offer. *[handwritten: — A GOOD DETAIL TO ADD]*

REFERENCES:

Flora Neal, Director of Respiratory Care School, St. Frances Cabrini Hospital
7770 Masonic Drive, Alexandria, LA 71302   (318) 444-1238

Mark Hallard, Director of Respiratory Care, Humana Hospital
P.O. Box 9703, Jefferson Davis Blvd., Natchez, MS 31120 (801) 447-6746

Steven McDonald, Manager of Respiratory Care Services
1569 Lake Avenue Suite 203, Metairie, LA 70005   (104) 936-6900

A HIGHLY SPECIFIC JOB OBJECTIVE FROM A PREVIOUS BUSINESS OWNER.

KEN ARTHUR

RR1, Box 3935
Freedom, Maine 04000

AN INTERESTING AND SENSIBLE ADDITION

(207) 782-5513 (Telephone)

(207) 782-2131 (Facsimile)

A VERY CLEAN AND BOLD JOB OBJECTIVE

INDUSTRIAL FABRIC STRUCTURES ENGINEER

QUALIFICATIONS: *A GOOD WAY TO PRESENT HIS YEARS OF EXPERIENCE WITHOUT REVEALING ANY LIABILITIES.*

Extensive and proven hands-on experience in fabrication, maintenance, and rental of advanced architectural fabric structures since 1979; projects have been of varying sizes and complexities. Responsibilities have included total business and project management and administration.

- Experience has included hands-on fabrication through completion of structures, material selection and purchasing, contract negotiations, job costing, personnel selection and supervision, quality control, and customer relations (with an excellent track record for customer satisfaction).

- Have received recognition for excellence in fabrication work performed throughout the country; many projects have come as a result of referrals from satisfied clients from varying industries and geographic locations.

- Ability to interpret and convert engineer's patterns and designs into working patterns and seamed fabric shapes upon completion; in some cases, have made some (correction) recommendations for appropriate changes to engineering designs.

- Skilled in the areas of peripherals (all tools, materials, machinery, equipment, and transportation means) relating to fabric fabrication requiring earth work, plumbing, air conditioning, and structural steel erection.

- Introduction to industrial fabrics in 1979 started with the fabrication of awnings (commercial and residential), tents (including rentals of varied sizes), carnival ride tops including a specialty top fabricated for a merry-go-round built in 1888.

- Have been contracted (in the past) to fabricate new fabric structures to replace those inadequately manufactured by other companies; projects were always successfully completed and (in some cases) this was done under very poor working and weather conditions.

- Contracted with various companies as an independent consultant in training employees in varied specialty fabrication processes including the patterning and welding of nylon and polyester fabrics for their particular needs.

In addition to engineering and designing skills, have extensive business and financial management and sales and marketing experience as a business owner for many years.

SUBMITTED BY: ROLANDE L. LAPOINTE, CPRW
AUBURN, MAINE

KEN ARTHUR   PROFESSIONAL RÉSUMÉ (Page Two)

WORK EXPERIENCE:

- **GENERAL MANAGER &**   1992 to Present
  FABRIC STRUCTURES ENGINEER
  Fabric Design Shop, Inc. (Freedom, Maine)
  Total Business and Project Management
  Including Sales, Marketing, and Public Relations

- **FABRIC STRUCTURES ENGINEER**   1979 to 1992
  BUSINESS CO-OWNER (1987 to 1992)
  Worked at Varied Locations (to be discussed at an interview)
  Started Air Structure Design Engineering Work in 1983

- **OWNER/MANAGER - TRAILER TRUCK COMPANY**   1971 to 1977
  Total Business and Financial Management
  3-Truck Operation

BESIDES EMPLOYERS, HE IS USING PREVIOUS CUSTOMERS AS REFERENCES — AN EXCELLENT IDEA FOR THIS KIND OF JOB OBJECTIVE.

PROFESSIONAL ACCOMPLISHMENTS:

Partial listing of major projects completed through the years. Additional information is available upon request.

- **DOME SYSTEM FOR ENGINEERED SPECIALTY FABRICS. INC.**   **$56,000**
  Also, Project Manager for Fabrication of Fabric Utilized **$10,000**
  Air Form 263' Diameter Dome Fabrication
  125' Diameter Silo Air Form
  Straight Wall 76' Dome on Top
  Contact: John McCormack   (212) 987-4145

- **GREENWICH, NEW YORK MUSIC PAVILION**   **$40,000**
  Architecturally Designed Tension Structure
  Acoustical Fabric Shell
  Fabric Design Structures, Inc.
  Contact: Bob Mulligan   (202) 778-2859

- **BOUNDARY RECREATION DEPARTMENT - BOUNDARY, UTAH**   **$145,000**
  135' X 240' Air Supported Structure
  Over Olympic Size Swimming Pool
  Contact: Don Grant   (207) 398-7220
  Contact: Robert Jones   (207) 398-7220

- **COMBUSTION ENGINEERING**   **$48,000**
  Metro Business District, Groton, Connecticut
  Explosion Roofs
  Contact: Tim Daley, TFL   (213) 832-4791
  Contact: Bill Murrell, Fabric Structures Inc.   (213) 764-2869

THIS GRAPHIC IS NOT THE ONLY INTERESTING FEATURE ON THIS RESUME. THE SIMPLE "HERE ARE THE FACTS" PRESENTATION WORKS VERY WELL HERE FOR THIS JOB OBJECTIVE

GARY D. RIETER
1210 Shore Lane, Elkhart, ID 46524
Phone (209) 634-4261

JOB OBJECTIVE: *Pilot position*

RATINGS/CERTIFICATES

Airline Transport Pilot - Multiengine
Commercial - Single Engine Land
Commercial - Single Engine Sea
Certified Flight Instructor
Certified Flight Instructor (Instrument)
Medical Certificate: FAA Class I - No Restrictions

FLIGHT TIME:

Total Flight Time	2683	Total Alaska Time	1000
Pilot in Command	1800	Instrument	250
Multiengine Land	412	Instrument Simulator	50
Single Engine Land	600	Military Flight Engineer	829
Single Engine Sea	810		

QUALIFICATIONS

<u>Owner-Operator Line Pilot</u>, <u>Chief Flight Instructor</u> and <u>Company Safety Supervisor</u>, Seahawk Air, Kodiak, Alaska, 1992-1993
<u>Flight Engineer</u> HC130H, U.S. Coast Guard, Florida & Alaska, 1989-1992. Safely logged 829 hours flight time. Member of Total Quality Management Team and Civil Rights Committee
<u>Chief Flight Instructor</u>, U.S. Coast Guard Flying Club, Kodiak, Alaska, 1990-1992. Implemented and monitored training and safety procedures
<u>Flight Instructor</u>, Keys Air Flight Training, Florida, 1989

SPECIALIZED TRAINING AND EDUCATION

Cockpit Resource Management, U.S. Air Force, completed annually 1987-1992
HC130H Advanced Electrical System, Dyess AFB, Texas, 1990
Basic & Advanced Flight Engineer, Little Rock AFB, Arkansas, 1989. Graduated top 10% of class. Course topics: turbine engine theory; systems - pressurization, bleed air, electrical, hydraulic, fuel, anti-ice, de-ice; and emergency procedures
University of Montana, Missoula, MT, 1982-1984

COMMUNITY AFFILIATIONS

Kodiak Civil Air Patrol, 1990-1992
Kodiak People for Pets (Humane Society)

SUBMITTED BY: JACQUELINE K. HERTER, CPS KODIAK, ALASKA

References available upon request

A TRADITIONAL FORMAT THAT WAS TYPED ON A TYPEWRITER.

KIM CHAN
88-35 Goodwill Boulevard, Apt. 3F
Bayside, New York 11355
(718) 444-7777

OBJECTIVE
Seeking a position as a Registered Nurse where I can be most
effective in helping other medical personnel assist patients and
provide quality health care.

EDUCATION
MANHATTAN COMMUNITY COLLEGE, New York, NY
Associates in Applied Sciences - Nursing, February, 1994
Curriculum included: Nursing Care Planning and Assessment,
Fundamentals of Nursing, Medical, Surgical, Pediatrics and Obstetrics
(68 credits) G.P.A.: 3.7

LICENSES
Registered Nurse - to sit for board March 1994
Licensed Practical Nurse - results pending from exam November 1993

PROFESSIONAL DEVELOPMENT
QUEENS HOSPITAL MEDICAL CENTER, Rosedale, NY   3/91 - Present
Transporter (3/93-present)
Transporting in-house patients to Radiology Department for CT,
Ultrasound and Nuclear Medicine. Work with OB/GYN patients, Cardiac
patients and bone fractures. This includes scanning for etopic
pregnancy, tumor diagnosis, etc. (To take time for school studies,
requested this part-time position).

Nursing Assistant (5/91-2/93)
Assisted Doctors and Nurses in the emergency room while attending to
various situations, i.e, accident victims, cardiac arrest, fractures,
etc. Responsible for taking blood pressure and temperature. Aided
Doctors while diagnosis was being made. (Full-time)

UNITED LANGUAGE SCHOOL, Bronx, NY   3/90 - 4/91
As a Chinese Instructor assisted English speaking lawyers who wanted
to learn Mandarin in order to be able to conduct business in the
Oriental community. Worked on a one-on-one basis. (Part-time)

QUEENS COUNTY HOSPITAL, Rego Park, NY   3/89 - 2/90
As an Interpreter worked with other medical practitioners to
determine the problems confronting patients admitted on various wards
throughout the facility. These patients were unable to speak good
English and many of the psychiatric patients were in a very confused
state of mind.

ADDITIONAL EDUCATION
SINGAPORE MEDICAL UNIVERSITY, Singapore, China   1984 - 1986
Completed four years of medical school curriculum which covered the
areas of internal medicine, general surgery, obstetrics, gynecology
and pediatrics. Received full scholarship and graduated with honors.
Credits received for basic medical courses were transferred to
Brooklyn Community College. Completed Medical Internship during the
fourth year at the Singapore Pie Jin and Singapore Da Pin Hospitals.

CERTIFICATE
CPR - American Heart Association, expiration date February 1993.

SUBMITTED BY: JAMES VOKETAITIS
FLUSHING, NEW YORK

USES SMALL TYPE TO FIT ALL DETAILS ON TO ONE PAGE- BUT USE OF WHITE SPACE, BULLETS AND OTHER DESIGN FEATURES KEEP IT FROM LOOKING TOO "CROWDED".

Johanna Breitmorgan

2110 Sneckner Court
Morro Bay, California 90044
Telephone (213) 327-6111

Experience and education have provided detailed working knowledge of these key areas:

Financial Services	**Business Strategies**
Organization Development	**Customer Service**
Program Development	**Staffing & Training**
New Product Introductions	**Employee-Community Relations**

AN EFFECTIVE WAY TO PRESENT HER STRENGTHS

Highly motivated, results-oriented business professional with sixteen years of progressive accomplishments. Highly effective leadership skills, with an established track record of achievements. Fluent in French, German and English.

HANDLES SEVERAL POSITIONS WITH SAME EMPLOYER AS DIFFERENT JOBS

CRÉDITE INTERNATIONALE Morro Bay, California 1977 - Present
Have played key roles in managing change, building organizations, and working with senior management throughout this financial services organization that has 300 million cardholders in 240 countries and sales of $500 billion.

Director - Management Communications 1989 - Present
Partnering with the president and senior management of this 2,500-employee organization, created and launched programs for an executive speaker's bureau, employee communications, and community relations.

* Aggressively capitalized on opportunities and doubled the first year's number of speeches given by executive management; grew the total four-fold within three years.
* Developed and introduced a successful speech-merchandising program that, through press releases, op-ed articles, and reprints, delivered a strengthened image of Crédite as an industry leader.
* Developed a community relations program that made grant money available to non-profit organizations in which Crédite employees were working as volunteers.
* Recruited and worked closely with some 10 external speech writers.
* Planned and directed a complete re-design of the employee newsletter from improved graphics to an editorial planning calendar to meet the needs of multiple levels of management and staff.

Executive Assistant to the COO 1988 - 89
Pro-actively identified several significant corporate issues and, working with senior managers, developed plans to effect improvement.

* Resolved a growing problem of compliance between merchants and banks issuing the Crédite card.
* Revamped an out-moded mailing system to assure prompt delivery of important communications to banks.
* Prepared new policy and guidelines for employees to communicate with customers.

Director - Member Services 1985 - 88
Called in to manage a troubled, 35-employee unit that had an operating budget of $2 million and supported 80 major data centers, representing 1,500 banks, in the Western U.S. and Asia-Pacific.

* Restored high level of morale to the unit and reduced turnover to near zero.
* Managed and oversaw two complete changeovers in system software that enhanced productivity.

Earlier in member services (1981-85), presented trainings and seminars in the U.S. and Asia to enhance effectiveness and profitability of Crédite's computer systems.

Operations Coordinator 1979 - 81
Championed the development of an Fast-Pay Refund System when Crédite introduced travelers checks in 1982 and played a vital part in the worldwide implementation as liaison between the business unit and operations center.

Joined the company in Strasbourg, France, in 1977.

BA Degree - Psychology
STANFORD UNIVERSITY California

SUBMITTED BY: TED BACHE PORTOLA VALLEY, CALIFORNIA

THIS DEMONSTRATES THAT A ONE-PAGE RESUME CAN BE USED FOR AN EXECUTIVE POSITION.

ROBERT L. CARROLL
1670 Orange Grove Avenue
Winter Haven, Florida 32789
(407) 749-8381

OBJECTIVE

Seeking expanded opportunities within selected organizations where I can utilize my expertise to implement profit-oriented results.

PROFESSIONAL PROFILE

Extensive experience at the Senior Executive level in marketing multi-faceted services for a NASDAQ publicly-held company consisting of 53 drug store units, 6 home/health care convalescent centers, a drug store distribution center, 125 one-hour dry cleaning stores, a dry cleaning distribution center, and a manufacturing subsidiary of windows for drive-in service. Qualifications include a background in progressively responsible positions initiating from entry level management to CEO and President/Chairman of the Board. Established a successful history in the development and expansion of a diverse market reach resulting in a significant increase of annual gross revenues from $36 million to $80 million. Company was acquired by a national corporation in 1988.

EMPLOYMENT HISTORY

PHARMACEUTICAL/MANUFACTURING CO., Tampa, FL   1993
Director of Trade Relations / Assistant to the C.E.O.

> Public Relations and Corporate Marketing involving assimilation of conceptual and long-range planning strategies for a small, Bay-area, pharmaceutical/manufacturing company.

MANAGEMENT CONSULTANT, Knoxville, TN   1988 - 1993
Multiple Industries

> Provided consulting services to Retailers, Manufacturers and Distributors in the Southeast and Mid-West Territory of the U.S.

CARROLL ENTERPRISES, Lexington, KY   1962 - 1988

Chairman of the Board/President/CEO	1979-1988
President	1974-1979
Vice President - Advertising/Merchandising/Merchandise Distribution	1972-1974
Vice President - Drug Operations	1968-1972
Director of Merchandise / District Store Supervisor	1967-1968
Elected to Board of Directors	1967
Warehouse Manager / Seasonal & Promotional Buyer	1963-1967
Merchandise Manager	1962-1963

EDUCATION

UNIVERSITY OF CINCINNATI SCHOOL OF PHARMACY

UNIVERSITY OF KENTUCKY

PAST PROFESSIONAL AFFILIATIONS

Vice Chairman of the Board, Executive Committee Member, Board Member, Treasurer, Chairman of Finance Committee, and of Chairman of Government Affairs Committee for the **National Association of Chain Drug Stores (NACDS)**, Washington, D.C.

Chairman of **Kentucky Retail Federation**.

References and Detailed Resume Available Upon Request.

SUBMITTED BY: DIANE McGOLDRICK TAMPA, FLORIDA

A GOOD RESUME FROM SOMEONE WITH A LOT OF EXPERIENCE AT SAME COMPANY.

JAMES L. GREGG
89 Glenwood Road
Marlboro, New Jersey 07746
(908) 536-7521

SUMMARY OF QUALIFICATIONS

Twenty years of financial management experience encompassing a steady progression of increasing accomplishments and responsibilities and active involvement in many major strategic decisions. Background also includes International Finance and management of a data processing organization. Primary strengths are excellent leadership, analytical, communication, and interpersonal skills.

EXPERIENCE

1975-Present   **H&H CHEMICALS, INC.** - A diversified International chemical company with sales of $500 million.

1986-Present   **VICE PRESIDENT, FINANCE & CONTROLLER**
Responsible for all finance and control functions, including data processing. **CHIEF FINANCIAL OFFICER** and member of the Executive Committee, which sets policies and strategic direction for the Corporation. Supervises several departments including 65 employees.

SHOWS PROMOTIONS UP

1979-1985   **CORPORATE CONTROLLER**

1977-1978   **DIRECTOR OF COST ACCOUNTING AND DATA PROCESSING**

1975-1976   **MANAGER OF COST ACCOUNTING**

ACCOMPLISHMENTS - *SHORT, SPECIFIC, IMPRESSIVE STATEMENTS*

- Significantly upgraded the Company's information systems (EDP) capabilities while at the same time reducing data processing costs by more than 20%.

- Initiated and led a program that reduced working capital by 5% of sales, thereby lowering interest and operating expenses by $3 million.

- Analyzed and participated in negotiation of many major acquisitions and divestitures which enhanced the strategic thrust of the Company.

- Significantly reduced accounting errors, accelerated the monthly closing cycle, and eliminated "surprises". Consistently had clean audit reports.

- Implemented financial statement reporting by major product line. This enhanced decision-making and focused business managers' attention on the "bottom line" for their products.

- Streamlined and enhanced the Corporate budgeting process and made it the cornerstone upon which the Company's operations are measured.

SUBMITTED BY: BEVERLY BASKIN MARLBORO, NEW JERSEY

JAMES L. GREGG   Page 2

ACCOMPLISHMENTS (Continued)

- Restructured foreign subsidiaries' balance sheets and updated transfer prices and management fees so that the Corporation's tax payments were reduced by over $1 million.

- Significantly improved the financial reporting systems to make them more responsive to the needs of the Business.

- Standardized cost accounting practices at all locations. This greatly enhanced controls and aided in decision-making.

- Developed and conducted financial seminars for Business Management to aid them in the use of financial concepts for decision-making.

1973 - 1975   LONDON CORPORATION - ESSEX DIVISION

MANAGER OF FINANCIAL PLANNING & ANALYSIS - Supervised a department of eight. Responsible for preparation and review of the annual budget and long-range plans; operational analysis of monthly results and trends; preparation and analysis of capital expenditure requests; monthly closings.

1966 - 1973   STAMCO, INC.

SENIOR FINANCIAL ANALYST (1970-1973) - Analyzed and prepared all major capital expenditure requests for submission to the Board of Directors; learned both Fortran and Basic programming languages and developed timesharing computer models such as plant production simulation studies and Monte Carlo investment risk analysis.

CHEMICAL ENGINEER (1966-1969)

EDUCATION

MASTER OF BUSINESS ADMINISTRATION, 1975 - Rutgers University

BACHELOR OF CHEMICAL ENGINEERING, 1966 - City College of New York (CCNY)

- Captain of City College Tennis Team
- President of Omega Tau Alpha Fraternity

PERSONAL

Married, two children, excellent health, likes to participate in athletic activities.

WITH SEVERAL JOBS IN THE SAME OCCUPATION, A CHRONOLOGICAL
APPROACH MAKES GOOD SENSE.

IRMA M. WELSH
5206 Hampton Court
Sarasota, Florida 34692
813-242-3398

OBJECTIVE

To obtain an enhanced **Real Estate Property Management** position providing a challenging opportunity for the utilization of my expertise within this industry.

THE SUMMARY PULLS TOGETHER
HER EXPERIENCE IN AN
EFFECTIVE WAY.

SUMMARY OF QUALIFICATIONS

Extensive experience at the Property Management level maintaining commercial real estate portfolios totaling from 500,000 S.F. to 1 million S.F. of space. Qualifications include a background of progressively responsible positions with a demonstrated performance record, and cost-effective monitoring of budgets over $1 million. Excellent communication, leadership, and motivation skills that effectively interact with staff, clients and executive management. Bilingual - fluent English and Spanish.

PROFESSIONAL EXPERIENCE

HENDERSON PARTNERS, Sarasota, FL   **2/92 - Present**
Property Manager
- Maintain portfolio consisting of 500,000 S.F. in office buildings and industrial service centers; **Increased commercial lease occupancy to 100%.**
- Directly responsible for overseeing annual budget, property accounting, preparation of 5-year forecasts and monthly operating reports; tenant relation programs; and contracted services.
- Coordinate tenant improvements and lease negotiations.
- Instrumental in complying with ADA (American Disabilities Act) renovation requirements.
- Supervise on-site personnel.

CDM COMMERCIAL REAL ESTATE, INC., Sarasota, FL   **1/91 - 2/92**
Real Estate Manager / Special Services
- Performed all management services for 3 shopping centers and 2 industrial parks totaling 500,000 S.F.
- Created annual budgets and quarterly reforecasts.
- Provided consulting services; assisted in special projects.
- Automated property management accounting for 13 properties.

USA GROUP LIMITED, Tampa, FL   **4/86 - 1/91**
Property Manager
- Commercial portfolio included management of an office park, service center and high-rise office building; liaison between brokers and prospective tenants; structured renegotiation of leases.
- Hired and supervised support staff; coordinated operations and maintenance plans for a building containing asbestos.

ACORN DEVELOPMENT CORPORATION, Tampa, FL   **8/81 - 4/86**
Property Management Administrator / Data Control
- Instrumental in the establishment of a Property Management Division responsible for overseeing a real estate portfolio consisting of 8 commercial properties totaling 1 million S.F.
- Selected and implemented a Data Base Management System (hardware and software) facilitating accounting cost controls for Corporate and 13 Regional Offices. Conducted in-house training program.

EDUCATION / SPECIALIZED TRAINING

BUILDING OWNERS & MANAGERS ASSOCIATION (BOMA)   **1988**
Real Property Administrator (RPA)

FLORIDA REAL ESTATE SALESPERSON'S LICENSE   **1988**

NEW YORK UNIVERSITY, New York, NY   **1980**
Bookkeeping Certificate

BRONX COMMUNITY COLLEGE, New York, NY   **1972 - 1974**
Associate Degree - Liberal Arts

SUBMITTED BY: DIANE McGOLDRICK
TAMPA, FLORIDA

John Doe

555 Merry Lane ◻ Player, Ohio 00000 ◻ Telephone: (000) 555-0000

OBJECTIVE: To secure the challenging position of the **Sales and Use Tax Consultant** within your organization that will utilize my education, experience, and unique abilities to further my career opportunities.

SUMMARY OF QUALIFICATIONS:

KEY SKILLS ARE IN BOLD, GIVING THEM ADDITIONAL EMPHASIS.

- ◆ Possesses over **16 years** experience in accounting, auditing, and financial management. **Eleven** years as an Auditor for the Cool Money Department.
- ◆ Outstanding **management and supervisory** skills - the ability to coordinate multi-faceted activities; determine, analyze problems; and develop and implement productive corrective actions.
- ◆ Outstanding **Communication** skills - proficiently utilizes inter-personal skills in relating with others.
- ◆ Effective **Planning and Organizational** skills - Expertise in business administration, recordkeeping, planning, policies and procedures, researching, scheduling, and related acts to ensure productive operations.
- ◆ In-depth knowledge of automated accounting system design and set-up.

EDUCATION:

PLAYERSTATE UNIVERSITY, Player, Ohio
Bachelor of Applied Science in Management - 1978

PLAYERCOMMUNITY COLLEGE, Player, Ohio
Associate in Applied Science in Business Management - 1976

Additional Training:

JOE DEERECAREER CAMPUS:
Operation Lotus 1-2-3   Certificate, March 1987
Business Writing Skills   Certificate, March 1987

CADRE PROGRAM (8/85-11/87)
This program was devoted to training in managerial skills, human resources development and behavioral sciences.

EXPERIENCE:

November 1987 to November 1993

DECORATOR INC., Cowtown, Illinois
President/CEO
Successfully managed the overall activities of an automobile leasing operation. Responsible for the day to day operations, personnel administration, sales, accounting, ordering, purchasing, budgeting, advertising, marketing, and customer service.
- ◆ Recognized in Who's Who.
- ◆ Recipient of the Business of the Month Award.

August 1978 to November 1987

COOL MONEY DEPARTMENT, Cool, Pennsylvania
Revenue Senior Auditor
Expertly conducted and/or reviewed selected, highly complex Pennsylvania and out-of-state audits of multi-national corporations, businesses, partnerships, and individuals to ensure compliance to tax regulations. In charge supervising and training an audit staff of 3-4 auditors. Coordinated, assigned, directed, and reviewed the activities of the audit team. Effectively conferred and corresponded with taxpayers and/or representatives regarding various issues and findings. Thoroughly interpreted and resolved technical problems and prepared/reviewed/approved audit reports. Testified as an expert witness at informal hearings or in court. Meticulously researched tax laws, rules, regulations and other resources in relation to applicable cases.
- ◆ Progressed through the ranks from Auditor A, to Auditor B, to Auditor C, to finally Revenue Senior Auditor.

PERSONAL:

Hobbies/Interests: Tennis, Basketball, Travel, Reading, and Community Involvement.
Willing to travel.

REFERENCES: Available upon request.

SUBMITTED BY: LAURA G. LIEHTENSTEIN SPRINGFIELD, ILLINOIS

A COMBINATION RESUME THAT PROVIDES A LOT OF DETAILS THAT A MORE LIMITED FORMAT WOULD NOT PRESENT AS WELL.

Susan Steinfeld

GOOD USE OF WHITE SPACE)

12 Browertown Road
Little Falls, NJ 07424
(201) 785-3011

Objective

Senior administrative management position with an innovative company, where the professional execution of their special events and various marketing programs will be valued.

Personal Profile

Entrepreneurial, creative manager with strong leadership and motivational skills; extremely service oriented; unique combination of intuitive and analytical abilities; astute at recognizing areas in need of improvement, with the vision to develop action steps and see them through to a prompt and successful completion, well within budgetary framework; knowledge of conversational French.

Areas of Expertise

Special Event/Meeting Planning

- Eleven years of experience in the start to finish management of high budgeted, multi-faceted projects for the hospitality, franchise and other industries.

- Demonstrated exceptional ability to plan and organize a broad range of considerations from site negotiations to finishing details and amenities, with the style and panache befitting events such as grand openings, major conferences, fundraisers and employee/corporate functions.

- Screen and select agency personnel, freelancers and in-house staff, promoting harmonious working relationships throughout entire event staging process. Scope of involvement includes: coordination of attendees and presentors, travel/accommodations planning, theme-oriented decor, room set-up, food and beverage services, entertainment, audio-visual productions, and more.

Marketing Communications

- Heavy exposure to the entire creative execution of corporate marketing plans, guided only by minimal directives from management.

- Contract for and direct the activities of implementation teams which include: communications consultants, print and audio-visual production houses, photographers, artists, designers and public relations agencies, in addition to internal support staff, to produce creative promotional materials reflective of the corporate image.

- Awarded recognition for multiple print and other corporate communications pieces such as annual reports, franchise brochures, videos, consumer information bulletins, and company newsletters.

... Continued

*SUBMITTED BY: MELANIE NOONAN. CPS
WEST PATERSON, NEW JERSEY*

Susan Steinfeld

Page 2

Professional Experience

HOST SERVICES INTERNATIONAL, New York, NY   1991-Present

Director of Event Marketing for hotel property franchisor controlling 2500+ Howard Johnson's, Days Inn and Ramada facilities. Report to Executive Vice President of Marketing. Responsible for planning and executing major special events including annual conferences, cause related marketing, corporate meetings, and creative contributions to marketing plans.

- Within six months, orchestrated two successful major meetings normally requiring two years from inception of plans.
- Utilized economics of scale to produce two corporate functions with similar themes, back to back at the same location, saving the company at least $500,000 had they taken place at different times of the year.

BILLY BOB'S CHUCKWAGON, INC., Houston, TX   1981-1991

Director of Marketing Communications Services (1988-91) at Corporate Headquarters of $1.4 billion, 2400+ unit international restaurant chain.

- Reported to the Vice President of Corporate Communications and managed a staff of four in the areas of corporate communications/public relations, special events, publications, audio-visuals, and large scale meetings. Controlled a $1.2MM meeting budget.
- Promoted through the ranks of the marketing organization to director post by proving ability to take charge of problem areas and effect beneficial solutions.
  - ... Initiated marketing information center to answer various inquiries from individual franchise operators; published a quarterly directory listing contacts for available services.
  - ... Facilitated distribution of newly introduced but difficult to obtain marketing items. Traced cause of problem to short term lack of inventory and developed monitoring system to prevent recurrences.
  - ... Took over meeting planner responsibility upon former incumbent's resignation three months before annual convention. With brand new management, developed and executed plans quickly, smoothly and to their satisfaction.
- Assumed permanent charge of event planning for the next seven years, each year progressively improving it with regard to increased attendance, quality of service and graphic design.
- Received Billy Bob's Outstanding Performance Award (four years) for quality and prompt execution of projects and recognition for award-winning annual reports.

Education

McGill University, Montreal, Canada (1975-77). Major in Marketing and Advertising. Management and Creative Writing seminars while at Billy Bob's.

Memberships

Meeting Planners, Inc.
Women in Communications

References and portfolio available upon request.

[handwritten note:] CHRONOLOGICAL LISTING OF JOBS INCLUDES GOOD EMPHASIS ON RESULTS

George A. Munroe

Campus : 293 Harper Hall West Lafayette, IN 47000 (317) 555-1212	← A GOOD WAY TO HANDLE → A TEMPORARY ADDRESS *Permanent :*	433 Lafayette Road Rossville, IN 47000 (317) 555-1212

Career Focus

Manufacturing/production. Current areas of interest for entry-level opportunities include quality control for polymer processing.

Education

GOOD GRADES!!

Bachelor of Applied Science in Industrial Technology, May 1994
Purdue University School of Technology
HIS COURSES ARE SPECIFIC AND DIRECTLY SUPPORT HIS JOB OBJECTIVE.
COMPUTER SKILLS ARE A PLUS.
- Focus on Quality Assurance and Polymer Materials Processing
- Major GPA: 5.5/6.0

Areas of Emphasis

- Industrial and Manufacturing Quality Control, Statistics, SPC
- Plastics -- Injection Molding, Blow Molding, Extrusion, Thermoforming, etc.
- Manufacturing Processes
- Materials Handling and Distribution -- JIT
- Facilities Planning -- Designed a manufacturing process for a new product.
- Production Management, Safety and Health, Technical Communications

Computer Skills: VanDorn Molder, Excel, Lotus 1-2-3, VersaCAD, AutoCAD, MacBRAVO, Basic, Pascal

Manufacturing Experience

SUMMER JOBS SUPPORT HIS JOB OBJECTIVE IN A DIRECT → WAY.

Royal Die Casting, South Bend, IN
A leading manufacturer of transmission and a/c casings for the automotive industry.
Machinist, Summers 1993 and 1992
- Assisted in quality assurance and analysis. Helped train new employees and demonstrate proper techniques. Proficient on a variety of industrial machines.
- Personally initiated a study of misfiled parts. Submitted a 25-page analysis to management, recommending systems and training solutions.

Cool-Comp Incorporated, Rossville, IN
A manufacturer of coolant compressors for refrigeration and air conditioning.
Machinist and Laborer, Summers 1991 and 1990
- Acquired assembly line, packaging, and machining techniques.
- Coordinated parts schedules for distribution and storage.
- Helped implement a computerized inventory control system.

Leadership Experience

MORE DETAILS ON HIS EDUCATION RELATED EXPERIENCE.

Purdue University Residence Halls
Student Office Manager, August 1992 - present
- Self-supervised position providing services for 850 residents. Requires decision-making, flexibility, and communication through personal service skills.
- One of 16 selected (from 100 candidates) to staff a new residence hall.

Professional Affiliations

American Society for Quality Control   Society of Industrial Technology
National Society of Professional Engineers

SUBMITTED BY: ALAN D. FERRELL
LAFAYETTE, INDIANA

THIS RECENT GRADUATE DEMONSTRATES HER CREATIVE
LAYOUT AND GRAPHICS BACKGROUND WITH HER RESUME.

MICKEY LYNNE
25 South Charles Street, #32
Belleville, IL 62220
(418) 555-6297

HIGHLIGHTS OF QUALIFICATIONS	

- Creative design and layout skills
- Experienced copy writer and editor
- Strong knowledge of production processes and editorial considerations
- Familiar with IBM (Pagemaker) and Macintosh (Word) software applications

EDUCATION

degree: **B.S., Speech Communication, Journalism,** 1990
Southern Illinois University at Carbondale

emphasis: Public Relations, Advertising

honors: GPA 3.8/4.0, Dean's List all semesters, SIUC Foundation Merit Scholarship, Carrie M. Bunn Scholarship

activities: Student Alumni Council, Gamma Beta Phi Honor Society

internship: **Editorial Assistant,** University Print Communications. Proofread, researched and wrote articles for alumni magazine. Prepared production schedules.

PROFESSIONAL EXPERIENCE

Graphics Assistant
University Bookstore, Carbondale, IL
· Scheduled, designed and wrote copy for newspaper advertisements.

Assistant Copy Editor
Public Relations Student Society, Carbondale, IL
· Edited national newsletter for grammar, clarity and style.

REFERENCES AND PORTFOLIO AVAILABLE UPON REQUEST

SUBMITTED BY: JOHN A SUAREZ
ST. LOUIS, MISSOURI

THIS NEW GRADUATE INCLUDES AN INTERESTING GRAPHIC THAT LIKELY SUPPORTS HER OBJECTIVE. CLEVER!!

A. MAERIE JOSEPH
605 Pine Street
Alexandria, Louisiana 71306
(318) 443-9876

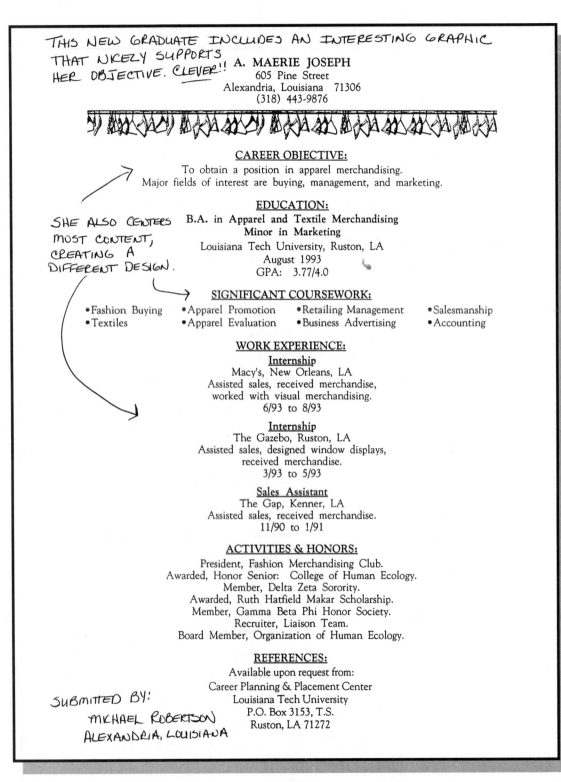

CAREER OBJECTIVE:
To obtain a position in apparel merchandising.
Major fields of interest are buying, management, and marketing.

SHE ALSO CENTERS MOST CONTENT, CREATING A DIFFERENT DESIGN.

EDUCATION:
B.A. in Apparel and Textile Merchandising
Minor in Marketing
Louisiana Tech University, Ruston, LA
August 1993
GPA: 3.77/4.0

SIGNIFICANT COURSEWORK:

- Fashion Buying
- Textiles
- Apparel Promotion
- Apparel Evaluation
- Retailing Management
- Business Advertising
- Salesmanship
- Accounting

WORK EXPERIENCE:

Internship
Macy's, New Orleans, LA
Assisted sales, received merchandise,
worked with visual merchandising.
6/93 to 8/93

Internship
The Gazebo, Ruston, LA
Assisted sales, designed window displays,
received merchandise.
3/93 to 5/93

Sales Assistant
The Gap, Kenner, LA
Assisted sales, received merchandise.
11/90 to 1/91

ACTIVITIES & HONORS:
President, Fashion Merchandising Club.
Awarded, Honor Senior: College of Human Ecology.
Member, Delta Zeta Sorority.
Awarded, Ruth Hatfield Makar Scholarship.
Member, Gamma Beta Phi Honor Society.
Recruiter, Liaison Team.
Board Member, Organization of Human Ecology.

REFERENCES:
Available upon request from:
Career Planning & Placement Center
Louisiana Tech University
P.O. Box 3153, T.S.
Ruston, LA 71272

SUBMITTED BY:
MICHAEL ROBERTSON
ALEXANDRIA, LOUISIANA

WHILE I'D PREFER TO SEE A JOB OBJECTIVE, HIS DEGREE
REQUIRES BEING FLEXIBLE IN WHAT JOBS TO CONSIDER AND
HIS RESUME KEEPS HIS OPTIONS OPEN.

VINCENT TUCCOLA

26A Denshire Place
St. Louis, MO 63109
(314) 555-3447

SUMMARY OF QUALIFICATIONS

WHILE HE DOES NOT HAVE "PROFESSIONAL"
WORK EXPERIENCE, HE PRESENTS A GOOD
CASE FOR BEING "EXPERIENCED".

- Seven years of responsible working experience
- Excellent communication and customer service skills
- Track record of success and leadership in academic and professional endeavors

EDUCATIONAL BACKGROUND

degree:
B.A., Psychology   May 1993
University of Missouri - St. Louis
Financed 100% of education — INDICATES A HARD WORKER

leadership:
- University Senate
- Student Government Association
- Missouri Governor's Leadership Forum
- Vice Chair, Lecture Committee Chair, University Program Board

GIVES A LOT OF SPACE
TO SCHOOL ACCOMPLISH-
MENTS.

honors:
- Student Affairs Leadership Award, 1990 & 1991.
- Man of the Year Award, Delta Zeta Sorority.

activities:
UM - St. Louis "First Choice" Promotion.   Assisted with recruiting efforts.

PROFESSIONAL EXPERIENCE

SHONEY'S RESTAURANT, Sunset Hills, MO   9/90-8/93
- Earned awards for quality customer service.

THE PASTA HOUSE COMPANY, Crestwood, MO   2/90-5/92
- Won Employee of the Month honors.

SCHNUCKS MARKETS, INC., St. Louis, MO   5/86-9/90
- Won service award for consistent sales volume, checkout speed and accuracy.

REFERENCES AVAILABLE UPON REQUEST

PROVIDES SOME GOOD SAMPLE ACCOMPLISHMENTS BUT, IF HE
HAD INCLUDED A JOB OBJECTIVE, HE COULD HAVE INCLUDED
ADDITIONAL DETAILS TO SUPPORT IT.

SUBMITTED BY: JOHN A SUAREZ
ST. LOUIS, MISSOURI

J'ANNE KONELLY

WHILE VIRTUALLY ALL OTHER JOB-RELATED EXPERIENCE IS CONNECTED WITH HER EDUCATION, THIS RESUME PRESENTS THIS BACKGROUND TO THE BEST EFFECT.

14 Briar Ridge, Suite X
Houston, Texas 77057
(713) 555-3281

OBJECTIVE: Obtain a challenging entry-level position in Broadcast Journalism, with a special interest in reporting, anchoring and producing with a commercial television station.

EDUCATION: **Bachelor of Liberal Arts**, May 1993
University of Mississippi, Oxford, Mississippi
Major: Broadcast Journalism   Minors: History and Spanish
● Dean's Honor Roll

RELATED BROADCAST EXPERIENCE:

Intern
● WCBI, Channel 4, Tupelo, Mississippi
July 1993 - October 1993

Reporting
● UMTV Channel 12 News, University of Mississippi
- Developed contacts and stories; responsible for covering stories on a regional and local level
- Developed and researched feature stories reflecting community interest
- Interviewed educational and business leaders concerning newsworthy events
- Developed ability to work under pressure and meet deadlines

● News Anchor, UMTV Channel 12 News, University of Mississippi
- Monitored Associated Press releases and wrote news scripts for station
- Produced and managed technical staff for newscast
- Covered fast-breaking news stories

● Weather Director, UMTV Channel 12 News, University of Mississippi
- Create local and regional map generation for nightly newscast
- Interpreted weather information from field communications
- Working knowledge of AT&T FC5 weather computer

Producing
● "Southern Review", University of Mississippi
- Produced and directed a monthly news magazine featuring both hard and soft news
- Supervised all aspects of project including story developments, creative style of magazine and development of script introduction to all magazine stories

Technical Experience
- Developed a working knowledge of videotape editing equipment, videotape camera equipment, videotape recording equipment, studio camera, character generation machine, and audio mixing board

HONORS & ACTIVITIES:
● Radio and Television News Directors Association
● Society of Professional Journalists
● Campus Political Organization
● Habitat for Humanity
● Editor of Angelia, Ole Miss Greek Publication
● Kappa Alpha Theta Sorority Member
  - Publications Chairman and Editor, 1992-1993
  - Panhellenic Representative, 1989-1990

REFERENCES: Terry Aberly, WXBI Tupelo Bureau Chief, (601) 555-0044
Ralph Braswell, Professor of Journalism, Oxford, Mississippi, (601) 555-4496
Palmer Alving, Owner, City Grocery, Oxford, Mississippi, (601) 555-8888

SUBMITTED BY: LEO J. LAZARUS OXFORD, MISSISSIPPI

THIS RESUME PRESENTS PART-TIME WORK EXPERIENCE EFFECTIVELY

MARK M. SCOVILLE
1452 4th Avenue North ← *TEMPORARY AND*
St. Cloud, Minnesota 56301 *PERMANENT* →
(612) 555-8201
ADDRESSES ARE A
NECESSARY FEATURE
IN THIS SITUATION

Permanent Address:
31 Overlook Road
Blue Sky, Minnesota 55352
(612) 555-3574

Job Objective: Entry Level Financial Analyst
with Portfolio Management or Financial Organization

EDUCATION

Bachelor of Science Degree in Business Administration
St. Cloud State University, St. Cloud, Minnesota
Major: Finance, Minor: Economics
Date of Graduation: November, 1995

WORK EXPERIENCE — *SHORT STATEMENTS, BUT THEY SUPPORT HIS JOB OBJECTIVE AND PRESENT HIS SKILLS*

October, 1993
to
Present

Park National Bank
St. Cloud, Minnesota

Computer Operator. Work nights; update daily files, process reports, back-up complete computer system, print notices, sort checks on reader sorter.

March, 1992
to
September, 1992

Able Charlie Manufacturing Corporation
Bloomington, Minnesota

Project Worker. Processed insurance claims in excess of $1,000,000. Used Lotus 1-2-3 and dBase III extensively.

March, 1991
to
December, 1991

Topper Automotive of Minnesota, Inc.
Goldenrod, Minnesota

Data Processing. Responsible for updating files, inventory control, processing of reports, some data entry. Received training at corporate office in Kansas City, Kansas.

ACTIVITIES & INTERESTS

DIVERSE ACTIVITIES DEMONSTRATE ENERGY

Selected for President's Round Table (all-university plan board)
Vice-President, Delta Sigma Pi (business fraternity)
President, Financial Management Association, SCSU
Advisor, Junior Achievement; voted "Company of the Year"
Selected and secured national speaker for Career Days
Hobbies: sports, camping, fishing, music

FROM THE RESUME SOLUTION, BY DAVID SWANSON

SHORT CAREFULLY SELECTED STATEMENTS ALL SUPPORT THE JOB OBJECTIVE OF THIS SOON-TO-GRADUATE STUDENT

Ronald P. Andrews
1437 Richer Avenue
East Town, Maryland 21602
(805) 555-8943
Leave messages: (805) 555-6562

Job Objective: Computer Repair Technician

EDUCATION

International Computer Institute
Washington, D.C.
Diploma in Computer Repair, June, 1995
Completed 18-month training program; "B" average

Walter Raleigh High School
East Town, Maryland
Graduated in June, 1993

LOTS OF WHITE SPACE

WORK HISTORY

September, 1993
to
Present

ArData Computer Systems: "The Computer Store"
Washington, D.C.

Troubleshoot and repair IBM-compatible MS-DOS computer
systems, including hard disk drives; dot matrix, inkjet and laser
printers; laptop portables and desktop models.

Familiar with various brands of equipment; able to diagnose
simple or complex malfunctions. Read schematic diagrams. Enjoy
mechanical as well as electronic work. Worked part-time to earn
tuition and expense money for computer school.

June, 1991
to
September, 1993

CopyQuick Instant Printers
East Town, Maryland

Counter clerk and printer at instant print shop. Waited on
customers. Advised on paper, ink, quantities, paper selection, and
binding. Ran printing equipment for hundreds of different types of
print jobs, including multi-color work. Worked after school and
weekends as needed.

MEMBERSHIPS, CLUBS, AND ACTIVITIES

- Varsity baseball team, Letterman's Club officer
- Member, Electronics Club, Ham Radio Club
- Volunteer Camp Counselor, summer church camp

FROM THE RESUME SOLUTION BY DAVID SWANSON

A VERY CLEAN OPEN FORMAT THAT USES A LOT OF WHITE SPACE
AND FEW, BUT WELL CHOSEN WORDS.

Thomas J. Thurgood

444 E. Cincinnati
Fresno, CA 93722
(209) 222-2222

■■ Career Focus: International Business ■■

IN THIS CONTEXT SUCH A GENERAL JOB OBJECTIVE KEEPS HIS OPTIONS OPEN

EDUCATION

CALIFORNIA STATE UNIVERSITY, FRESNO

B.S., Business Administration (12/92)
Emphasis: **International Business**

MORE DETAILS ABOUT ANY RELATED EXTRA-CURRICULAR ACTIVITIES OR ACCOMPLISHMENTS WOULD BE NICE HERE.

REPRESENTATIVE COURSEWORK

Intro to International Business
Management of Multinational Enterprises
World Commerce and Development

International Finance
International Marketing
International Management

RELATED EXPERIENCES

PRESENTS HIS LIMITED EXPERIENCE EFFECTIVELY AND EMPHASIZES INTERNATIONAL ASPECTS WELL

- **Pacific Rim Trip:** Visited Hong Kong, Bangkok, Thailand, Singapore, and Seoul, Korea in connection with CSUF coursework. Opportunity provided exposure to conducting business in the Pacific Rim.

- **International Business Internship:** Under direction of CSUF Department Chair, worked with entrepreneurs from Ireland in researching, identifying, and contacting companies offering potential for import/export business.

- **Import Experience:** Presently employed with Skorich International which specializes in importing watches from Hong Kong, Malaysia, and India; make buying recommendations and organize shows for sales in five western states.

COMPUTER — *COMPUTER LITERACY IS INCREASINGLY IMPORTANT, SO INCLUDING DETAILS AS A SEPARATE SECTION MAKES SENSE.*

Extensive computer coursework (60+ hours) with knowledge of various desktop hardware and software applications, including Lotus 1-2-3, WordPerfect, and D-base III+ and IV.

EMPLOYMENT SUMMARY *A GOOD STATEMENT SINCE IT SHOWS A GOOD WORK ETHIC AND JUSTIFIES MISCELLANEOUS JOBS.*

Personally financed 100% of education through the following employment:

Import/Sales: Trade International	1992-Present
Assistant Manager/Driver: Best Courier Services	1989-1990
Shift Supervisor/Waiter: Holiday Inn	1988-1989
Banquet Supervisor: The Marriott	1986-1988

AFFILIATIONS

International Business Association
Central California International Trade Association
Toastmasters International

Available for Relocation • **References Upon Request**

SUBMITTED BY: SUSAN BRITTON WHITCOMB, CPRW
FRESNO, CALIFORNIA

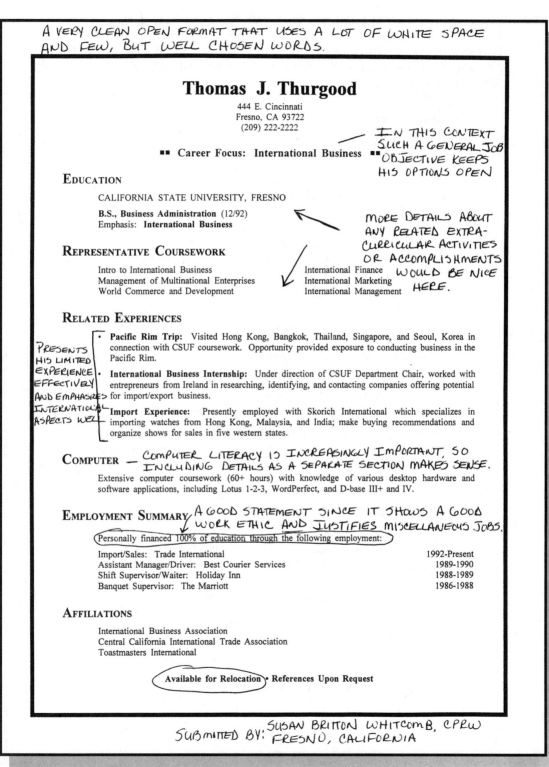

NO JOB OBJECTIVE WAS NEEDED HERE SINCE HER RECENT LAW DEGREE DEFINES HER PREFERENCES. THIS IS A SHORT RESUME. IT PRESENTS A PERSON WHO SHOWS ENERGY, DRIVE, AND TALENTS IN DIFFERENT AREAS.

Karen E. Mulligan
669 Dart Drive
Marietta, Georgia 30033
(404) 555-1571
(404) 555-4534 (alternate phone)

EDUCATION

Emory University School of Law
Atlanta, Georgia
Class of 1994

University of Alabama, Huntsville
Graduated February, 1991, with high honors: "Magna Cum Laude"
Bachelor of Arts degree; Major, psychology; minor, political science

Decatur High School, Decatur, Alabama
Class of 1986

HONORS, AWARDS AND ACHIEVEMENTS

"Outstanding Graduate," Department of Psychology, University of Alabama

Elected to Pi Sigma Alpha, political science honor society

Elected to Alpha Lambda Delta, freshman honor society

Elected to Senior and Junior Honor Societies, high school

Won varsity tennis letter, 2 years; basketball letter, 2 years

Selected for all-university Concert Committee; worked for four years to help select concerts for campus and community

WORK EXPERIENCE

Cabaret Director, University of Alabama   September, 1989 to February, 1991

Scheduled bands, comedians and other talent acts for university performances. negotiated contracts, prices, arrangements; handled details for university; supervised productions; hosted artists and performers. Attended regional and national Student Activities Conventions.

Self-employed Leather-crafter   1983 - 1991

Filled custom orders for leather goods (wholesale and retail). Sold several large orders to local specialty shops.

Bartender, T.G.I. Friday's   1990 - 1992

Earned college tuition and expense money with part-time work: later promoted to full-time status.

FROM "THE RESUME SOLUTION" BY DAVID SWANSON

THIS IS AN EXTRA ORDINARY RESUME IN ITS USE OF VERY BRIEF STATEMENTS AND OPEN DESIGN. EVEN SO, THERE IS ENOUGH HERE TO CREATE INTEREST - WHICH IS WHAT REALLY MATTERS.

Kevin Wong
4350 Highland Avenue
Tucson, Arizona 85772
(602) 555-7876
(602) 555-2232 (message service)

<u>Job Objective: Electronics Technician</u>

EDUCATION

Arizona Electronics & Technical Institute
Phoenix, Arizona
Associate Degree in Electronics Technology
Grade point average: 3.56 on 4.0 scale
Graduated June, 1995; courses included:

- Digital Electronics
- Microprocessors
- Circuit Design
- Hands-on Repair
- AF & RF analog Electronics
- Fabrication
- Design Applications
- Communications

Tucson North High School
Honors Grades in Math, Science, and Drawing
Received diploma in May, 1993

WORK EXPERIENCE

- <u>Unified Telephone Company</u>   September, 1993 to Present

Responsible for troubleshooting and repairing various types of telephones including cordless, dial, touchtone, and full-feature desk phones.

- <u>Bob's Big Boy Restaurant</u>   Two years - part-time after school

Busboy/Waiter. Commended as "one of my best workers" by management.

SCHOOL AND COMMUNITY ACTIVITIES

- Member, Math Club, Kit Car Club, Letterman's Club
- Assistant coach for Cub Scout Baseball Team

FROM "THE RESUME SOLUTION" BY DAVID SWANSON

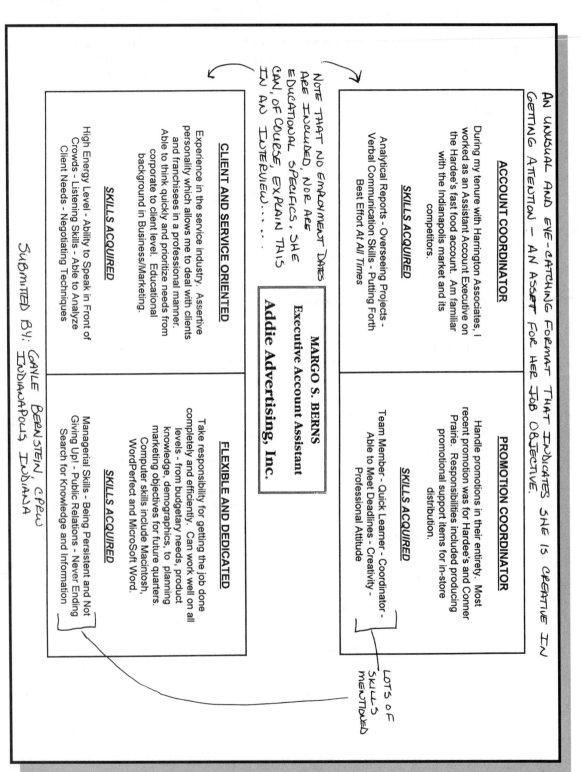

An unusual and eye-catching format that indicates she is creative in getting attention — an asset for her job objective.

ACCOUNT COORDINATOR

During my tenure with Harrington Associates, I worked as an Assistant Account Executive on the Hardee's fast food account. Am familiar with the Indianapolis market and its competitors.

SKILLS ACQUIRED

Analytical Reports - Overseeing Projects - Verbal Communication Skills - Putting Forth Best Effort At All Times

---

MARGO S. BERNS
Executive Account Assistant
Addie Advertising, Inc.

PROMOTION COORDINATOR

Handle promotions in their entirety. Most recent promotion was for Hardee's and Conner Prairie. Responsibilities included producing promotional support items for in-store distribution.

SKILLS ACQUIRED

Team Member - Quick Learner - Coordinator - Able to Meet Deadlines - Creativity - Professional Attitude

CLIENT AND SERVICE ORIENTED

Experience in the service industry. Assertive personality which allows me to deal with clients and franchisees in a professional manner. Able to think quickly and prioritize needs from corporate to client level. Educational background in Business/Marketing.

SKILLS ACQUIRED

High Energy Level - Ability to Speak in Front of Crowds - Listening Skills - Able to Analyze Client Needs - Negotiating Techniques

FLEXIBLE AND DEDICATED

Take responsibility for getting the job done completely and efficiently. Can work well on all levels - from budgetary needs, product knowledge, demographics, to planning marketing objectives for future quarters. Computer skills include Macintosh, WordPerfect and MicroSoft Word.

SKILLS ACQUIRED

Managerial Skills - Being Persistent and Not Giving Up! - Public Relations - Never Ending Search for Knowledge and Information

Note that no employment dates are included, nor are educational specifics. She can, of course, explain this in an interview......

Lots of skills mentioned

Submitted by: Gayle Bernstein, CPRW Indianapolis, Indiana

A BRIEF CAREFULLY WRITTEN RESUME
FOR AN EXPERIENCED MANAGER. AND
ON ONE PAGE!!

ROBERT W. WILSON
67 Ottawa Drive
Englishtown, New Jersey 07726
(908) 536-6420

PROFILE

Eighteen years of retail experience.......Proven track record as a team player with increasing responsibilities in multi-unit management......Strong organizational skills, articulate, with a constant focus on **customer service and profitability**. Approach responsibilities with a sense of urgency......work well under pressure and change .....excellent troubleshooter.

EXPERIENCE

MODELLS SPORTING GOODS   1978-Present

Responsibilities include six years of District Management, covering seven different markets in the Mideast and Northeast. Managed districts with up to 18 stores, over 250 employees and volumes to $45M. Accountable for P&L performance, operational integrity, recruiting, training, and merchandising standards.

Accomplishments:

• Developed new store opening manual for field operations, adopted company wide.

• Recruited high performance management, effectively reducing turnover, maintaining greater continuity of management teams.

• Developed market, district, and store communication systems which helped to improve efficiency and organization at each level.

• Successfully managed new store openings and closings. Supervised renovation projects up to $1M in 21,000 sq. foot units.

• Consistently maintained direct store expenses within targets.

• Utilized extensively by the company as a troubleshooter, taking on several district assignments managing one sixth of our company's 240 stores.

MITCHELL'S, SPORTS DIRECTIONS LTD.   1975-1978

Positions included: Buyer, Merchandise Coordinator, and Store Manager. Served as Buyer for one of the nations leading outdoor retailers. Involved in production of mail order catalog. Responsible for merchandise presentations, inventory levels, and product training in an eleven store chain. Managed the largest volume store in the chain, volume over $6m with over 30 employees.

EDUCATION

Two years study at Temple University, Philadelphia, PA.
Attended several management workshops including those by Career Track, Communispond, and Paul Hersey.

SUBMITTED BY: BEVERLY BASKIN, CPRW
MARLBORO, NEW JERSEY

A GOOD EXAMPLE OF USING JUST ONE PAGE TO PRESENT A LOT OF EXPERIENCE.

SAMUEL WEINSTEIN

1111 East Shaw Avenue
Fresno, California 93726

Residence: (209) 222-2222
Business: (209) 111-1111

EXPERTISE

Retail Management ▪ **Merchandising** ▪ **Marketing**

Seasoned executive with impressive track record with national retailer. Currently provide visionary leadership and management for operation with **$40+ million in sales**. Demonstrated aptitude for regional general merchandise management, as well as store operations, buying, assorting, and merchandising. Special talent for regionalized marketing, advertising, promotions. Career reflects consistent record of corporate recognition for contributions to operations, sales, and profit.

PROFESSIONAL EXPERIENCE

RETAILERS OF AMERICA

GOOD USE OF NUMBERS TO SUPPORT PERFORMANCE

Store Manager, Valencia, CA (1988-1993): Full profit and loss responsibility for high volume store staffed with 300. Direct and monitor management team of 25 in buying, assortment, presentation, marketing, advertising, housekeeping, and merchandising functions.

- **Increased volume from $30 to $40 million**, reversing trend from red to black P&L. Led store to rank in top 25 among 800 nationwide.
- Created and introduced innovative domestics line, generating $4+ million in sales; department has subsequently been launched in over 100 stores with profitable results.
- Envisioned regionalized marketing, advertising, and promotional strategies to tap large Hispanic market.
- Made substantial strides in affirmative action, creating staffing mix representative of the community.

Store Manager, Angus, CA (1984-1987): Hands-on management for $30 million unit with 200+ employees.

- **Doubled net profit**, with volume increase from $25 to $30 million.
- Directed $1.9 million remodel project (brought in on time and under budget, using store staff).
- Formed a cohesive staff using skills in recruitment, team building, empowerment, employee relations.

Regional General Merchandise Manager, Los Angeles, CA (1983-1984): Managed total store buying, assortment, and advertising for $400 million region with 27 locations throughout Nevada and California.

- **Boosted national ranking** of region from bottom 40 to top 15 for profitability.
- Was first in company to implement "flighting" advertising.
- Served as youngest General Merchandise Manager in the company.

"OLD" JOBS GET MUCH LESS MENTION

Store Manager, Stockton, CA (1982-1983): Was entrusted with large volume store in first store manager assignment; promoted within six months to Regional General Merchandise Manager.

Prior Experience:

Western States Territorial Staff General Merchandise Manager, Los Angeles, California (1981-1982)
Group Staff Merchandise Manager (Home Fashions/Home Improvement), Los Angeles, CA (1978-1980)
Soft Lines Merchandise Manager, Las Vegas, NV (1976-1977)
Hard Lines Merchandise Manager, Phoenix, AZ (1971-1976)

EDUCATION

B.S., Business Administration, California State University, Fresno

SUBMITTED BY: SUSAN BRITTON WHITCOMB, CPRW FRESNO, CALIFORNIA

INCORPORATES VARIOUS LAYOUTS IN SAME RESUME BUT DOES NOT LOOK "BUSY".

SELL M. MOORE
CENTERED

1515 Gogetem Crescent
Any City, USA   22222

Home: (808) 666-6666
Business: (808) 444-4444

FLUSH RIGHT

A VISUALLY EFFECTIVE WAY TO PRESENT A LOT OF SKILLS

RETAIL SALES / MANAGEMENT

Seeking position in retail sales where extensive experience can be utilized. Capabilities include:

← 3 COLUMNS

• Operations Management	• Store Design/Set Up	• Inventory Control
• Leasing Negotiations	• Cash Management	• Advertising / Media Buying
• Budget Control	• Personnel Management	• Forecasting
• Customer Relations	• Personnel Training	• Merchandising

RETAIL EXPERIENCE

FLUSH LEFT

Owner / Manager, The Great Store, Any City, VA   1986 - present

Developed and built business from ground floor level. Generated annual sales to a high of $2,100,000. Actively involved in all operations.

- Negotiated contracts for leasing of space and pricing from suppliers.
- Designed store lay-out and merchandise display.
- Supervised staff of 9 full-time employees and 8 - 12 part-time/seasonal employees.
- Handled all aspects of advertising including media buying, writing ad copy, and co-op advertising with suppliers.
- Full responsibility for sales projections, budgeting, and inventory control.

Vice President, The Best Possible Company, Any City, VA   1979 - 1985

Began as manager of one store with annual sales of $1.5 million. Within 3 years, advanced to supervisor of six stores. In 1983, promoted to Vice President with responsibility for twelve stores.

- Developed leases to open new stores.
- Coordinated store design with architects and contractors.
- Actively involved in set up and opening of all new stores.
- Monitored expense budgets/sales projections for each store.
- Supervised store managers. Wrote training manuals for use by managers.
- Handled all advertising including media buying, writing ad copy, generating co-op advertising dollars from suppliers.

Manager Trainee, World's Best Company, This City, VA   1977 - 1978

Completed 1 year management training program.

EDUCATION

Bachelor's Degree, The Greatest University, Any Town, USA

*SUBMITTED BY: SUSIE BRADY
VIRGINIA BEACH, VIRGINIA*

ROBERT BISCAY

2222 East Feldon Way
Fresno, California 93722
(209) 222-2222

OBJECTIVE

A GOOD OBJECTIVE AS IT INCLUDES A "PROFIT" LANGUAGE WHICH MAKES SENSE IN A SALES ENVIRONMENT.

Outside Sales ▪ Route Sales position with a company that will benefit from my proven ability to generate new business, service and develop existing accounts, and earn bottom-line profits.

PROFESSIONAL EXPERIENCE

COLORADO WATERS COMPANY, Phoenix, Arizona   1986-Present

Route Salesman, Bottled Water Division: Over six years' commission sales experience, managing business growth, account retention, and deliveries to Phoenix area customers. Developed new business through prospecting and referrals. Serviced over 800 commercial and residential accounts. Prepared daily activity reports to track sales, inventory, collections, and cash receipts. Accustomed to heavy work load and long hours. (1986-1992)

I LIKE HIS USE OF NUMBERS TO SUPPORT RESULTS

- Increased territory volume approx. 155% despite influx of new competition.
- Continually exceeded goals, generating sales to warrant territory division into three separate routes.
- Selected for Hall of Fame two years (top 10% for sales, add-on sales, and new customers).
- Collected cash on 37% of accounts, well above the company norm.
- Trained 10 new salesmen over tenure, many of whom are now top producers.

Route Salesman, Coffee Division: Presently managing coffee route for two territories, covering some 100 miles daily. Perform sales, sales recordkeeping, and training responsibilities similar to those listed above. (1992-Present)

- Built number of accounts from 90 to 150 in just one year.
- Demonstrated company loyalty and longevity throughout seven-year tenure (average employee turnover for industry is two years).

ARIZONA EQUIPMENT, Phoenix, Arizona   1985-1986

Machinist: Built drivelines for diesel trucks and automobiles using high-technology equipment.

OLDER JOBS DON'T NEED MUCH DESCRIPTION.

WATERSOFT, Flagstaff, Arizona   1984-1985

Route Driver: Scheduled and made deliveries of water softening tanks throughout the Central Valley.

BUSINESS MACHINES, INC., Flagstaff, Arizona   1980-1984

Driver/Repairman: Part-time employment concurrent with college.

EDUCATION

Accounting/General Education -- Flagstaff City College, Flagstaff, Arizona

References Upon Request

SUBMITTED BY: SUSAN BRITTON WHITCOMB, CPRW FRESNO, CALIFORNIA

A SKILLS RESUME FROM SOMEONE WITH A LONG-TERM JOB AND NOTHING TO HIDE. THE TWO-PAGE FORMAT ALLOWS FOR GOOD USE OF WHITE SPACE.

Diane Downs

1050 N Horner St	Yakima, WA 98901	[509]555-1599

SUMMARY OF QUALIFICATIONS:

- ❖ Extensive experience/expertise in retail fashion merchandising management....

- ❖ Managed upscale women's clothing store/boutique....women's/men's departments for major department store....

- ❖ Strong merchandiser....

- ❖ Doubled merchandise/increased sales 20% in first year....maintained profit margins....

- ❖ Handled all merchandise buying for specialty store....

- ❖ Developed successful advertising campaign which resulted in increased visibility/sales....

- ❖ Maintained awareness of current fashion/merchandise trends in marketplace....

- ❖ Trained/supervised sales staff....cultivated strong customer service attitude in staff members....taught how to counter buying objections....

- ❖ Established more sophisticated accounting procedures....initiated tracking of mark-downs for more accurate P & L....kept running inventory....

- ❖ Created/produced fashion shows for various organizations....wrote scripts/modeled/fitted clothing/coordinated models....

- ❖ Excellent communications skills....loyal....dedicated....able to establish quick rapport with customers....detail oriented....take pride in knowledge of products/customers....

AFFILIATIONS:

Soroptomist International - Assisted with Thrift Shop
DECCA - Acted as Judge
PEO - Served as Treasurer
Mesa Chamber of Commerce
Deacon of my church - coordinated home visitations for 15 deacons

professional profile

PROFESSIONAL HIGHLIGHTS:

Retail Merchandising/Management

AN UNUSUAL BUT EFFECTIVE PRESENTATION. NOTE HER EMPHASIS ON PROMOTIONS.

Began as part-time sales in hotel boutique....**promoted** to assistant manager....stocked merchandise....arranged store/window displays.... provided alterations necessary for fashion shows....**promoted** to Ladies Wear Manager after one year with major department store....**promoted** to assistant manager in larger Men's Sportswear Dept....one of youngest in management position....represented Dept. Manager at monthly sales meetings....shared information with sales staff at weekly meetings....**promoted** to Ladies Wear Manager at store with higher volume/merchandise....managed women's specialty store....hired/fired/trained sales staff....moderated staff meetings....presented "Dress for Success" program for both men/ women....increased visibility in community....assigned department classifications to merchandise in order to more efficiently track sales/mark- downs....dealt with local vendors....consistently maintained all sales quotas....

EMPLOYERS: CELIA'S FASHIONS   - Yakima, WA
                 Manager: 1984 to present.

NOTICE THAT NO DATES ARE INCLUDED

HANNY'S TRI-CITY STORES - Yakima, WA
  Department Manager:

TREASURE TROVE HOTEL BOUTIQUE - Selah, WA
  Assistant Manager:

SIMPLE BUT CLEAR
WAY TO PRESENT A
RANGE OF JOB
OBJECTIVES

JASON DEAN

(209) 222-2222 • 1255 West Shaw • Fresno, CA 93711

A SIMPLE GRAPHIC
ELEMENT SUCH
AS THIS IMPROVES
APPEARANCE.

EXPERTISE: Sales Management ... Marketing ... Account Management

SUMMARY OF QUALIFICATIONS:

Over 14 years' successful experience in sales management and sales. Consistently made significant contributions to corporate goals for business growth and profits. Created, implemented, and managed productive marketing programs for tangibles and intangibles.

INCLUDES
TWO KEY
SKILLS.

Customer-driven focus: Built strong business partnerships, maximized account retention, and improved customer loyalty. **Team-oriented:** Recruited, motivated, and managed productive sales and sales support teams.

PROFESSIONAL EXPERIENCE:

GENERAL SALES MANAGER -- Pacific Sales, Fresno, CA   4/92 - Present
                                                                          and 2/80 - 11/87

NOTE BULLETS
EMPHASIZING
KEY
ACCOMPLISHMENTS:

- Promoted from Sales Manager to General Sales Manager in less than one year.
- Directly accountable for sales management, marketing, promotions, and programming.
- Manage national accounts. Negotiate co-op advertising and sponsorship packages.
- Was recruited to **revitalize sales** -- accomplished this goal through restructuring sales force, conducting intensive sales training, and implementing successful incentive programs.
- Personally **generated significant new business.**

AGENT MARKETING COORDINATOR -- Western Sales, Fresno, CA   10/89 - 3/92

- Liaison between Western Sales and 30 retail outlets to coordinate indirect distribution channel for cable service.
- Motivated and trained sales force; created successful incentive programs.
- **One of 20 nationwide** to earn "Manager Achievement Award" (awarded for design of successful promotions and management of outside agencies in a highly regulated market).
- Selected to **"Circle of Excellence"** (awarded to one per market nationally for overall performance).
- Featured in national monthly newsletter for consistently exceeding monthly goals.
- Won numerous incentive awards (including trip to London) for quota achievement.

GENERAL SALES MANAGER -- Americom Leasing, Fresno, CA   11/87 - 2/89

- Managed and motivated sales team. Coordinated marketing strategies.
- Personally sold to and serviced regional accounts.
- Increased sales 500%; advanced from 15th to 3rd highest billing station in market among 30 stations.

EDUCATION:

DEGREE PROGRAM: A.S., Business Merchandising & Management, Sacramento City College

Sales and Sales Management Seminars:
- Jones & Associates: "Fundamentals of Consultant Sales," "Leading High Performance Sales Teams"
- IBM Training: "Selling Technology," "Selling Naturally," "Retail Sales Skills and Management"
- CareerTrack Seminars: "High Impact Communication Skills"

SUBMITTED BY: SUSAN BRITTON WHITCOMB, CPRW
FRESNO, CALIFORNIA

THIS IS A RESUME FOR A CAREER CHANGER OR RECENT GRADUATE

PAUL A. COLE

161 Nehoiden Street
Needham, MA 02192

(617)449-4838

OBJECTIVE

To obtain a position in a social service agency using extensive experience working with adults and adolescents and an excellent educational background.

SUMMARY

- Excellent communication and empathetic skills.
- Able to successfully handle multiple assignments and priorities.
- Strong organizational skills.
- Eager to learn and apply new information and skills.
- Capable of working effectively with very little supervision.
- Proven capacity to approach problems creatively and effectively.
- Demonstrated ability to exercise good judgment under pressure.

EDUCATION

BECAUSE THESE CREDENTIALS ARE RECENT, IT IS APPROPRIATE TO HIGHLIGHT THEM HERE AND TO PROVIDE COURSE DETAILS

Framingham State College   Framingham, MA
Master of Arts in Counseling. May, 1993.
Relevant Courses
- Theories of Psychotherapy
- Substance Abuse
- Case Study
- Social Science Research Methods
- Advanced Principles of Assessment
- Family Counseling
- Group Processes
- Counseling Lab
- Practicum
- Advanced Abnormal Psychology

Boston State College   Boston, MA
C.A.G.S., Instructional Media. 1981.
M.Ed., Secondary Education. 1968

Newton College of the Sacred Heart   Newton, MA
B.A., in Biology. 1968.

PRACTICUM

Fall 92 - Spring 93

HIS EDUCATION-RELATED EXPERIENCE GETS MORE COVERAGE HERE THEN HIS YEARS OF EXPERIENCE IN JOBS UNRELATED TO HIS CURRENT OBJECTIVE

Family Service of Dedham   Dedham, MA
- Conduct a therapy group for 7-8 year old children from families that are undergoing significant change.
- Run a girls group for 6th graders on enhancing self esteem.
- Work with a number of individual clients.
- Implemented a didactically based Parenting Communication Workshop.
- Delivering a Mother-Child program to a mother modeling communication and broad based parenting skills with her toddler.

OTHER EXPERIENCE

1980 - 1991

Creative Systems, Inc.   Newton, MA
Operations Manager
- Scheduled and supervised a staff of four. Computerized a number of units including accounts receivable, order entry and inventory control.

1968 - 1980

Boston Public Schools   Boston, MA
Science Teacher - High School
- Acting Department Head; Faculty Advisor to the Athenian Club.

SUBMITTED BY: STEVEN GREEN NORTHBORO, MASSACHUSETTS

O.K. THIS RESUME IS FOR A KITTY CAT. I'VE INCLUDED IT HERE AS ENTERTAINMENT AND TO SEE IF ANYONE NOTICES . . . .

SPOTSWOOD BRAVO

265 Charlotte Street
Asheville, NC 28801
704/254-7893

Office Cat

Seeking a career of challenge and service in professional environment. Documented competence and initiative; promotion to high visibility position on executive desk (in Out-Box) gained through merit and softness of fur. Highly unusual markings. Dedicated; often asleep.

EXPERIENCE

GATEHOUSE BUSINESS SERVICES, Asheville, NC
Supervisor/Mouse Patrol
- Initiated and implemented program of systematic reduction of staff in mouse department; 75% reduction in record time.
- Enthusiastic purring, adaptability, and open-door accessibility resulted in marked improvement in office morale.

JOHN JONES HOUSEHOLD, Asheville, NC
House Cat
- Consistently met mouse quota while maintaining appearance of complete ease.
- Liaison to dog, successfully representing 2 other much-older cats in difficult negotiations.
- Communications ability, far-sightedness (can see in the dark), combined with excellent climbing and decision-making skills, led to rapid promotion as Top Cat.

HUMANE SOCIETY, Asheville, NC
Kitten
- Instrumental in bringing record number of potential adopters to kitten section during open house.
- Outstanding good looks resulted in adoption of mother as well as siblings.

EDUCATION

Graduate, The Silent Miaow, Paul Gallico course on how to become an indispensable member of a human household.

REFERENCES

Excellent, perhaps overly enthusiastic references available on request.

SUBMITTED BY: DAYNA FEIST
ASHEVILLE, NORTH CAROLINA

A DIETICIAN — CHANGING CAREERS TO INCLUDE SOCIAL WORK, UPON GRADUATION FROM COLLEGE — MUCH OF HER PREVIOUS EXPERIENCE IS IN THE DIETETIC AREA.

Victoria A. Brown

2047 Nostrand Avenue, #1E   Brooklyn, N.Y. 11210   (212) 723-4782

DIETARY COUNSELOR

Skilled dietetic seeking a position that will allow me to **offer professional consultation** to meet the nutritional needs, and assist in advancing social needs of individuals and families in a community.

AN INTERESTING WAY TO PRESENT TWO RELATED AREAS OF SKILLS AND EXPERIENCE - AND IT DIRECTLY SUPPORTS HER JOB

SUMMARY OF QUALIFICATIONS *OBJECTIVE.*

Dietetic Concentration	*Social Work Concentration*

Responsible for overseeing the dietetic needs of more than **11,000 patients over 16 years.** Duties included training new employees, individual and family therapy, menu preparation for employee's cafeteria and doctor's dining room, mixing formulas, chef sheets, etc.

Experienced in child welfare, counseling unwed mothers, assisting terminally ill patients, opening day care centers, assisting handicapped children, advising criminal offenders, etc.

INCLUDING NUMBERS HELPS SUPPORT HER SKILLS

- Reported to Chief Dietitian.

- **Saved $10,000** by selecting high-quality, low-cost meals.

- Checked food trucks to insure proper food selections for over **11,000** patients.

- Visited patients and altered menus whenever possible.

- Planned hospital catering events for **over 500 employees.**

- Planned cafeteria menus.

- Coordinated diabetic patient's diet with doctor's prescription and advised patient and family members of proper nutritional diet.

- Tallied chef sheets.

- Worked all hospital shifts.

- Responsible for **opening 10 day care centers** for children (ages 3-5) including interaction with City, State, and Federal government officials; complying with Board of Health guidelines to obtain certificates; screening and interviewing prospective employees; planning trips for children and parents; selecting toys and equipment.

- Planned holiday parties and special occasion events for **more than 150 children bound in wheelchairs** and with other disabilities.

- Assisted in **counselling 30-40 male prisoners** on how to live peaceably in society. Inmates completed education, and avoided becoming "repeat offenders".

- Cared for **12 children** so unwed mothers could complete school and find employment. 11 women completed school - were employed by Board of Education, New York University, etc.

- Administered medication to cancer patients; took care of hygienic needs; transported patients to and from hospital.

SUBMITTED BY: MARGARET LAWSON NEW YORK, NEW YORK

Victoria A. Brown

Dietetic Concentration	*Social Work Concentration*
• Ordered daily, weekly, and monthly food supply.	• Written presentations expounding on the functions of Red Cross and the New York Philanthropic League, including organization chart, funding sources, who is serviced, and how choices of service are made.
• Taught 1st & 2nd cooks, pantry workers, and salad persons to comply with Board of Health guidelines.	
• Mixed formulas for ulcer and intravenous patients.	• **Directed 100 emergency building inspectors** to inspect heat, lack of hot water, and other complaints. Tenants were taught to organize rent strikes by depositing rent in escrow accounts.

WORK HISTORY

New York State Correction Officer
Correction Officer
New York, N.Y.

Project Rescue
Clerk-Supervisor of Shift
Brooklyn, N.Y.

Youth & Action Head Start
Assistant to Bishop's wife
Brooklyn, NY

NOTE THAT NO DATES ARE INCLUDED, PERHAPS TO "SOFTEN" HER BACKGROUND AS A DIETICIAN.

Jewish Chronic Disease
Dietician
Brooklyn, N.Y.

Interboro General Hospital
Assistant Chief Dietitian
Brooklyn, N.Y.

New York Infirmary Hospital
Dietician
New York, N.Y.

Horace Harding Hospital
Assistant Chief Dietitian
Queens, N.Y.

EDUCATION

Borough of Manhattan Community College
Major: Social Work
Expected date of graduation: June 1992

Institute of Dietetics
Certificate Awarded:
Food and Nutrition

AWARDS

CUNY Coalition of Disabled Students Award	1991
Outstanding Student Award	1989
Women's Forum Educational Award	1988

AFFILIATIONS

CUNY Wide Coalition of Students with Disabilities

THIS RESUME PRESENTS PREVIOUS MINISTERIAL EXPERIENCE IN A WAY TO HELP HIM MAKE A TRANSITION INTO THE CORPORATE WORLD. THE SKILLS FORMAT ALLOWS HIM TO PRESENT HIS EXPERIENCE IN THE BEST WAY POSSIBLE.

GEORGE A. WHITELEY

1111 East Tuolumne
Fresno, California 93700
(209) 111-1000

QUALIFICATIONS

Accomplished 17-year career encompassing strengths in:

♦ Administration/Management
♦ Resource Development/Fundraising
♦ Human Resources/Personnel

PROFESSIONAL EXPERIENCE

Administration/Management:

NOTE EMPHASIS ON BUSINESS AND "PEOPLE" SKILLS

- Planned and managed business operations for non-profit organizations, including finance, budgeting, facilities management, staffing, programming, and public relations.
- Prepared comprehensive business operating plan with short-range and long-range goals.
- Negotiated contractual agreements pertaining to purchase of property, rental of facilities valued at $2 million, refinancing, and construction/remodel projects.
- Balanced budget after long history of deficits.
- Supervised seven department directors and support staff.

Human Resources/Personnel:

- Managed all facets of Human Resource Department including start-up of new department.
- Experienced in recruiting, interviewing, placement, and evaluation of personnel (program managers, departmental supervisors, construction/trades, educators, and support staff).
- Conducted orientation and wrote curricula for training.
- Researched, presented for CEO approval, and administered employee benefits program.
- Wrote policy and procedures manual.
- Developed personnel forms.

Resource Development/Fundraising:

- Directed resource development programs for multi-state region.
- Targeted untapped cities through direct mail, generating $25,000 in revenue.
- Achieved $10,000 through direct mail alone, using segmented list with genesis series of letters.
- Developed prospect lists and data files for new donor acquisition.
- Took over planning for annual banquet and generated $25,000 (prior year's event lost money).
- Assisted in developing a deferred giving and financial counseling program.

EDUCATION

Master of Arts Degree, Regent University
Bachelor of Science Degree, Biola University

NOTE THAT THERE IS NO MENTION OF HIS MAJOR HERE, WHICH WAS RELIGION-ORIENTED

EMPLOYMENT HISTORY

Director of Personnel/Resource Development: His Ministries, Inc., Fresno, CA	1991-Pres.
Senior Administrative Pastor: Intercity Ministries, Norfolk, VA	1988-1991
Senior Administrative Pastor: Fellowship Alliance, Norfolk, VA	1981-1988

EVEN HIS MINISTERIAL JOBS HAVE BUSINESS-SOUNDING TITLES

SUBMITTED BY: SUSAN BRITTON WHITCOMB, CPRW FRESNO, CALIFORNIA

ANOTHER RESUME FOR A HIGH SCHOOL SENIOR SEEKING A COLLEGE ATHLETIC SCHOLARSHIP.

Terry Lantz

Vandalia High School
28382 Berry Street • Indianapolis, Indiana 46223 • (317) 234-8989

ACADEMIC GOAL

To attend a college or university focusing on Business, Engineering, Math, or Science. Long term goal is to attain a graduate degree in my chosen field.

ATHLETIC GOAL

To utilize my experience and strong background of 12 years to become a member of a college/university baseball team.

ACADEMIC ACHIEVEMENTS/ACTIVITIES

Vandalia High School, Indianapolis, Indiana
G.P.A.: 3.68   CLASS RANK: 59/727
National Honor Society
Key Club Member

ATHLETIC ACHIEVEMENTS

JUNIOR YEAR, 1991-1992
- **Varsity Baseball** (Marion County Championship Team; Semi-State Finalists)
  * Left Field (Lead Off Hitter)
  * Second Team All County
- **Varsity Soccer** (State Runner-Up 1991; State Champions, 1992)
  * Defense
  * Academic All-State

SOPHOMORE YEAR, 1990-1991
- **Reserve Baseball**
  * Left Field
  * Indiana Amateur Baseball Association All-Star Selection
- **Reserve Soccer**
  * Defense

FRESHMAN YEAR, 1989-1990
- **Baseball**
  * Left Field
  * Indiana Amateur Baseball Association All-Star Selection
- **Reserve Soccer**
  * Defense
- **Wrestling**
  * Record - 19/3

USING A CHART HERE IS AN EFFECTIVE WAY TO PRESENT THIS INFORMATION.

VARSITY STATISTICS/Junior Year/1992 Season

* Team Leader

	Avg.	Slg.	OB%	G	AB	Run	H	1B	2B	3B	HR
Spring	.289	.451	.513	30*	85	25*	24	14	6*	3*	1
Summer	.379	.539	.602	16	49	17*	18	11	5*	1	0
	RBI	TB	SC	OE	HP	BB	SO	SB	SA	SB%	
Spring	15	40	4	7	4	31*	20	7*	9*	.779	
Summer	8	26	2	3	0	17*	8	8*	10*	.817*	

SUBMITTED BY: GAYLE BERNSTEIN, CPRW INDIANAPOLIS, INDIANA

THIS PERSON WENT BACK TO SCHOOL TO PICK UP TRAINING TO ALLOW HER TO MOVE OUT OF THE DENTAL OFFICE JOBS SHE HAD AND INTO A LARGER BUSINESS

VALERIE FRANCIS

5211 Hallers Street
Bronx, NY   10475
(718) 235-8749

OBJECTIVE

- A position as a Word Processing Secretary which will utilize my computer knowledge, strong people skills, organizational abilities and business experience.

OVERVIEW

- Experienced, organized, take-charge office professional with demonstrated ability to successfully overhaul procedures, thereby increasing productivity.
- Ability coordinate multiple projects; can shift to cover a multitude of positions as needed.
- Detail oriented person with exceptional follow through abilities; able to oversee projects from concept to finished product.
- Able to work well with individuals on all levels.
- People person, sensitive and perceptive; extensive customer/client contact.
- Demonstrated ability to develop and maintain sound relationships with customers, anticipating their needs.

MOST OF CONTENT PRESENTS SKILLS RELATED TO CURRENT JOB OBJECTIVE

AREAS OF EFFECTIVENESS

Organizational Ability - Successfully revamped inventory/supply and purchasing systems which eliminated over-ordering by 31%. Received credit for returned supplies. Comparison shopped for best prices when purchasing thereby cutting monthly expenditures by 28%. Increased efficiency allowed for a greater number of clients to be serviced.

Finance - Attention to detail, communication with clients and contact with insurance companies generated an additional $3,000 per month in revenue while decreasing over-due payments by 8%.

EXPERIENCE
1989 - 1991

DR. PAUL S. TAXIN, New Rochelle, NY
Dental Assistant in a four-handed expanded dental practice.
- Oversaw scheduling and ordering of supplies.
- Provided training to office personnel.
- Coordinated patient care.

DEVOTES LITTLE SPACE TO PREVIOUS JOBS, EMPHASIZING BUSINESS SKILLS

1986 - 1989

DR. BARRY JASON, Mt. Vernon, NY
Office Manager in a practice with six locations plus a mobile unit.
- Scheduled appointments in multiple locations.
- Handled insurance, accounts payable, accounts receivable.
- Assisted dentist in direct patient care.

ADDITIONAL SKILLS

- Experience in mainstream Word Processing packages; knowledge of Display Write 4 and Multimate.
- Computer literate; hands-on experience in Lotus 1-2-3 with macros, using Allways to generate business graphics.
- Significant expertise in dBase III.
- Working knowledge of DOS.
- Familiarity with Word Perfect.

EDUCATION
1992 - Present

B.O.C.E.S. SOUTHERN WESTCHESTER, Valhalla, NY
Majoring in: Computerized Information Technologies

1978 - 1980

BRONX COMMUNITY COLLEGE, Bronx, NY
Major: Business Communications

REFERENCES

Available upon request.

SUBMITTED BY: MARK D BERKOWITZ, NCCC YORKTOWN HEIGHTS, NEW YORK

LYNN E. HIGGINS
622 Benner Road
Allentown, PA 18104
(213) 555-7272

OBJECTIVE

Seeking a challenging position as an Advertising Copywriter utilizing proficient research, sales and writing skills.

SKILL AREAS

THIS APPROACH ALLOWS HER TO PRESENT LOTS OF SKILLS IN A COMPACT FORMAT.

Writing
- Sales call scripts
- Presentation guidelines
- Procedure manuals
- Sales training programs
- Monthly reports
- Client correspondence

Research/Analytical
- Customer Surveys
- Individual business profiles
- Sales campaign planning
- Competitive market analysis
- Sales training research

Program Management
- Interviewing and hiring
- Establishing program goals
- Counseling/Advising
- Sales training

Sales
- Customer needs analysis
- Sales presentations
- Overcoming objections
- Post-sale follow-up

PROFESSIONAL EXPERIENCE

MATRIXX MARKETING, INC., Cincinnati, OH   1978-1992
Subsidiary of Cincinnati Bell, Inc.
Sales Program Manager, 1981-1992
- Directly supervised inside sales representatives assigned to client programs.
- Analyzed market information and developed program objectives with clients.
- Researched cross-section of sales training materials; designed and wrote two company training programs.
- Planned and conducted sales strategy meetings with sales representatives.
- Analyzed sales calls; adapted presentations for increased effectiveness.
- Planned and executed sales incentive programs.

Inside Sales Representative, 1978-1981
- Maintained on-going sales coverage of business customers generated from MATRIXX clients.
- Developed individual business profiles involving products used, buying patterns, deciding factors, business size, etc.
- Signed new products, upgrades and line extensions; switched customers from competitors.
- Provided quality customer service coverage.
- Earned two "Outstanding Sales Performance" awards.

EDUCATION

B.A., Political Science (Cum Laude), Miami University, Oxford, OH

REFERENCES AVAILABLE UPON REQUEST

SUBMITTED BY: JOHN A SUAREZ, CRW ST LOUIS, MISSOURI

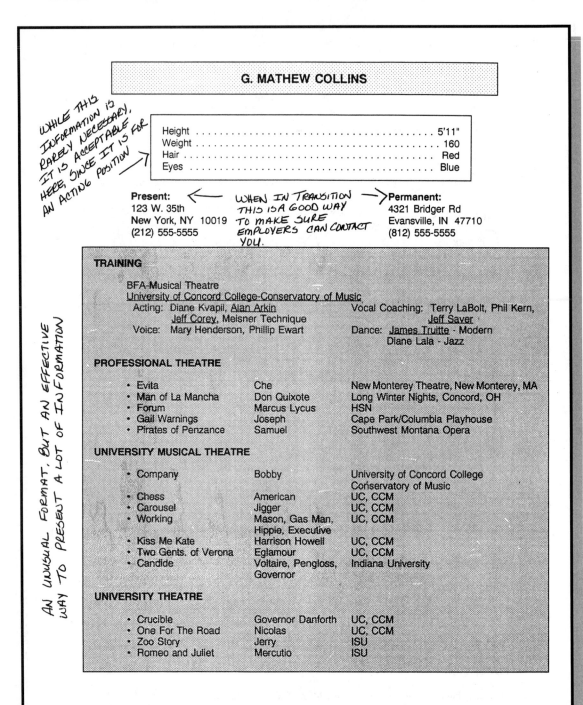

G. MATHEW COLLINS

WHILE THIS INFORMATION IS RARELY NECESSARY, IT IS ACCEPTABLE HERE, SINCE IT IS FOR AN ACTING POSITION →

Height	5'11"
Weight	160
Hair	Red
Eyes	Blue

Present: ← *WHEN IN TRANSITION THIS IS A GOOD WAY TO MAKE SURE EMPLOYERS CAN CONTACT YOU.* → **Permanent:**

Present:
123 W. 35th
New York, NY 10019
(212) 555-5555

Permanent:
4321 Bridger Rd
Evansville, IN 47710
(812) 555-5555

TRAINING

BFA-Musical Theatre
University of Concord College-Conservatory of Music

Acting: Diane Kvapil, Alan Arkin
Jeff Corey, Meisner Technique
Voice: Mary Henderson, Phillip Ewart

Vocal Coaching: Terry LaBolt, Phil Kern,
Jeff Saver
Dance: James Truitte - Modern
Diane Lala - Jazz

PROFESSIONAL THEATRE

• Evita	Che	New Monterey Theatre, New Monterey, MA
• Man of La Mancha	Don Quixote	Long Winter Nights, Concord, OH
• Forum	Marcus Lycus	HSN
• Gail Warnings	Joseph	Cape Park/Columbia Playhouse
• Pirates of Penzance	Samuel	Southwest Montana Opera

UNIVERSITY MUSICAL THEATRE

• Company	Bobby	University of Concord College Conservatory of Music
• Chess	American	UC, CCM
• Carousel	Jigger	UC, CCM
• Working	Mason, Gas Man, Hippie, Executive	UC, CCM
• Kiss Me Kate	Harrison Howell	UC, CCM
• Two Gents. of Verona	Eglamour	UC, CCM
• Candide	Voltaire, Pengloss, Governor	Indiana University

UNIVERSITY THEATRE

• Crucible	Governor Danforth	UC, CCM
• One For The Road	Nicolas	UC, CCM
• Zoo Story	Jerry	ISU
• Romeo and Juliet	Mercutio	ISU

SPECIAL SKILLS: Guitar • Football and Baseball • Historian • Cabaret • Studio Vocalist

SUBMITTED BY: TEREDA COLLINS, CPRW + ERICA HANSON
EVANSVILLE, INDIANA

AN UNUSUAL FORMAT, BUT AN EFFECTIVE WAY TO PRESENT A LOT OF INFORMATION

USES SMALL TYPE TO PACK IN DETAILS. BUT THE INFORMATION IS VERY GOOD.

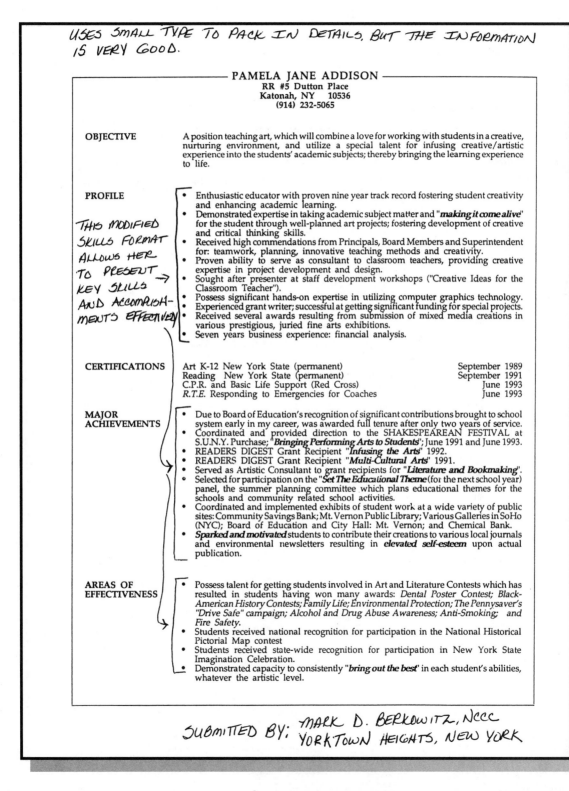

—— PAMELA JANE ADDISON ——
RR #5 Dutton Place
Katonah, NY   10536
(914) 232-5065

OBJECTIVE

A position teaching art, which will combine a love for working with students in a creative, nurturing environment, and utilize a special talent for infusing creative/artistic experience into the students' academic subjects; thereby bringing the learning experience to life.

PROFILE

THIS MODIFIED SKILLS FORMAT ALLOWS HER TO PRESENT → KEY SKILLS AND ACCOMPLISHMENTS EFFECTIVELY

- Enthusiastic educator with proven nine year track record fostering student creativity and enhancing academic learning.
- Demonstrated expertise in taking academic subject matter and "*making it come alive*" for the student through well-planned art projects; fostering development of creative and critical thinking skills.
- Received high commendations from Principals, Board Members and Superintendent for: teamwork, planning, innovative teaching methods and creativity.
- Proven ability to serve as consultant to classroom teachers, providing creative expertise in project development and design.
- Sought after presenter at staff development workshops ("Creative Ideas for the Classroom Teacher").
- Possess significant hands-on expertise in utilizing computer graphics technology.
- Experienced grant writer; successful at getting significant funding for special projects.
- Received several awards resulting from submission of mixed media creations in various prestigious, juried fine arts exhibitions.
- Seven years business experience: financial analysis.

CERTIFICATIONS

Art K-12 New York State (permanent)	September 1989
Reading New York State (permanent)	September 1991
C.P.R. and Basic Life Support (Red Cross)	June 1993
R.T.E. Responding to Emergencies for Coaches	June 1993

MAJOR ACHIEVEMENTS

- Due to Board of Education's recognition of significant contributions brought to school system early in my career, was awarded full tenure after only two years of service.
- Coordinated and provided direction to the SHAKESPEAREAN FESTIVAL at S.U.N.Y. Purchase; "*Bringing Performing Arts to Students*"; June 1991 and June 1993.
- READERS DIGEST Grant Recipient "*Infusing the Arts*" 1992.
- READERS DIGEST Grant Recipient "*Multi-Cultural Arts*" 1991.
- Served as Artistic Consultant to grant recipients for "*Literature and Bookmaking*".
- Selected for participation on the "*Set The Educational Theme* (for the next school year) panel, the summer planning committee which plans educational themes for the schools and community related school activities.
- Coordinated and implemented exhibits of student work at a wide variety of public sites: Community Savings Bank; Mt. Vernon Public Library; Various Galleries in SoHo (NYC); Board of Education and City Hall: Mt. Vernon; and Chemical Bank.
- *Sparked and motivated* students to contribute their creations to various local journals and environmental newsletters resulting in *elevated self-esteem* upon actual publication.

AREAS OF EFFECTIVENESS

- Possess talent for getting students involved in Art and Literature Contests which has resulted in students having won many awards: *Dental Poster Contest; Black-American History Contests; Family Life; Environmental Protection; The Pennysaver's "Drive Safe" campaign; Alcohol and Drug Abuse Awareness; Anti-Smoking; and Fire Safety.*
- Students received national recognition for participation in the National Historical Pictorial Map contest
- Students received state-wide recognition for participation in New York State Imagination Celebration.
- Demonstrated capacity to consistently "*bring out the best*" in each student's abilities, whatever the artistic level.

SUBMITTED BY: MARK D. BERKOWITZ, NCCC YORKTOWN HEIGHTS, NEW YORK

PAMELA JANE ADDISON   *page two*

PROFESSIONAL EXPERIENCE

1989 -
Present

THIS CHRONOLOGICAL LISTING SIMPLY SUPPORTS WHAT CAME BEFORE AND PROVIDES A FEW ADDITIONAL DETAILS.

WASHINGTON PERFORMING ARTS MAGNET SCHOOL, Mt. Vernon, NY
Teacher of Art: Grades 1 - 6
* Drafted the "blueprint" for the Arts Program.
* Developed curriculum; recognized for molding the direction that the program has taken.
* Provide art instruction for all levels including advanced sculpture and ceramics.
* Assist students in designing stage sets and large scale murals.
* Coordinate art projects and productions with Drama and Music teachers.
* Function as Art Program Director.
* Voluntarily conduct A.M Reading Readiness program for first grade students (1992 - 1993).

1987 -
1990

FRANKO MIDDLE SCHOOL (*formerly: Nichols Middle School*), Mt. Vernon, NY
Teacher of Art: Grades 7 and 8
* Infused Art program with American History and English.

1985 -
1987

DISTRICT WIDE HUMANITIES-ART PROGRAM
Coordinator: Fourth Grade Humanities Program
* Directed and coordinated program located at ten separate elementary schools which focused on: Art; Dance; and Social Studies.
* Developed and implemented the integration of art projects with Social Studies and Language Arts curricula which focused on the civilization/culture of Ancient Greece and Rome.

1984 -
1985

LONGFELLOW ELEMENTARY SCHOOL, Mt. Vernon, NY
Teacher of Arts and Crafts

1976 - 1984

MOTHER, HOUSEWIFE and STUDENT

BECAUSE THIS WAS A LONG TIME AGO, IT REQUIRES LITTLE DETAIL.

1969 -
1976

MOBIL OIL CORPORATION, New York, NY
Various analytical positions.

EDUCATION

HERBERT H. LEHMAN COLLEGE (C.U.N.Y.), Bronx, NY
M.S. Education: Reading   June 1989
B.A. Art/Art History *with Departmental Honors*   June 1983

FORDHAM UNIVERSITY, Bronx, NY
Major: Computer Science/Marketing   1968 - 1972

REFERENCES

And visual documentation available upon request.

AN UNUSUAL STATEMENT BUT IT MAKES SENSE FOR AN ARTIST!!

A Successful career change from manufacturing to social service.

Cathy H. Balwin
11 Wetfield Avenue
Southbridge, Massachusetts 01550
(508) 764-0856

QUALIFICATIONS SUMMARY

Eight years experience working with individuals/families in conflict. Highly developed **mediation, counseling, and crisis intervention skills** used in group and individual settings. After several years in the manufacturing environment, where attention to detail was prized, successfully made a transition to the service sector.

MEDIATION/ CONFLICT RESOLUTION SKILLS

* Mediate marital disputes, parent/child/couple relations, and neighbor or individual conflicts; resulting in visitations, property settlements, restitutions, enhanced relationships and less/no court involvement.
* Develop ground rules, clarify major issues, evaluate and summarize conflicting ideas, aid in agreement and contract structuring; in the Worcester and South Central Area.
* Performed mediation for Spencer District Court.
* Assisted courts by interviewing and assessing cases before being placed on court docket for possible diversion through mediation and conflict resolution.

ORGANIZATIONAL/ ADMINISTRATIVE/ INVESTIGATIVE SKILLS

* Recruited, placed, trained and provided supervision and support for the mediation volunteers on an on-going basis.
* Coordinated a site, a volunteer mediator, and the parties for resolution.
* Assisted in the organization and implementation of a new mediation program in Southern Worcester County.
* Developed conflict resolution teacher training at the Middle School level.
* Provide curriculum design for G.E.D. program coupled with job development.
* Presentation skills used for ME /YOU, Inc. in marketing programs for community awareness, Parents Anonymous, employer relations, workshops and trainings,
* Compiled program statistics and make yearly comparisons for program evaluation.
* Developed a conflict management program in the business community.

Submitted by: Myla Clark
Oxford, Massachusetts

THIS PACKS CONSIDERABLE DETAIL ON A ONE PAGE RESUME BY USING BULLETS AND CAREFULLY SELECTED WORDING.

Andrea M. Salter
1200 Mall Avenue
State College, Pennsylvania 21101
(215) 555-6239
(215) 555-7732 (messages)

CAREER OBJECTIVE
Director of Audio Visual Instructional Media

EMPLOYMENT HISTORY

August, 1992
to
Present

Pennsylvania State University
State College, Pennsylvania

Head, Department of Instructional Media
Supervise 15 employees, plus 40 students as part-time staff. Propose and control budget. Administer complete department, including microforms, films, videotapes, transparencies. Provide all media services to campus:
· Graphic arts and photography
· Circulation of audio-visual equipment
· Operator assistance and scheduling
· Production of slide programs
· Production of videotapes
· Minor repairs, troubleshooting, and general maintenance consultation on production topics to faculty & staff
Recommend and purchase hardware, software, supplies, rentals. Approve services and procedures. Recommend and supervise design, construction, and scheduling of all facilities. Develop, implement, and supervise all policies and guidelines for instructional media, including security and inventory control.

January, 1989
to
August, 1992

Kimball Broadcasting Corporation/KKBC
Las Vegas, Nevada

Assistant Engineer for Audio
Designed, updated, and upgraded complete radio broadcasting facility and studio. Contracted for and supervised erecting of tower. Recommended equipment; purchased complete studio. Installed and repaired equipment. Wrote operating policies and guidelines. Ensured compliance with FCC regulations. Recommended programming policies and changes to improve ratings. Handled all on-location broadcasts. Worked with on-air personalities. Trained employees.

EDUCATION

Master of Science Degree in Media, 1989
University of Wisconsin - Stout
Grade average: 3.85/4.0

Bachelor of Arts Degree in Business Administration
University of Southern Iowa, 1986
Rolland, Iowa

PROFESSIONAL AFFILIATIONS

"Who's Who in American Colleges and Universities," 1985-1986
Instructor in Media Techniques, University of Southern Iowa
Member, Business and Professional Media People

REFERENCES

Business, personal, and educational references will be furnished on request

FROM "THE RESUME SOLUTION" BY DAVID SWANSON

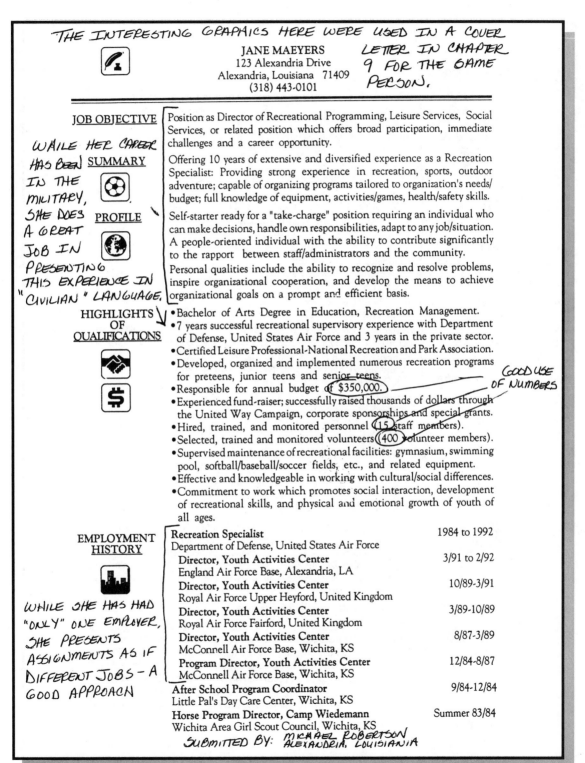

THE INTERESTING GRAPHICS HERE WERE USED IN A COVER LETTER IN CHAPTER 9 FOR THE SAME PERSON.

JANE MAEYERS
123 Alexandria Drive
Alexandria, Louisiana 71409
(318) 443-0101

JOB OBJECTIVE

Position as Director of Recreational Programming, Leisure Services, Social Services, or related position which offers broad participation, immediate challenges and a career opportunity.

WHILE HER CAREER HAS BEEN **SUMMARY** *IN THE MILITARY, SHE DOES* **PROFILE** *A GREAT JOB IN PRESENTING THIS EXPERIENCE IN "CIVILIAN" LANGUAGE.*

Offering 10 years of extensive and diversified experience as a Recreation Specialist: Providing strong experience in recreation, sports, outdoor adventure; capable of organizing programs tailored to organization's needs/budget; full knowledge of equipment, activities/games, health/safety skills.

Self-starter ready for a "take-charge" position requiring an individual who can make decisions, handle own responsibilities, adapt to any job/situation. A people-oriented individual with the ability to contribute significantly to the rapport between staff/administrators and the community.

Personal qualities include the ability to recognize and resolve problems, inspire organizational cooperation, and develop the means to achieve organizational goals on a prompt and efficient basis.

HIGHLIGHTS OF QUALIFICATIONS

- Bachelor of Arts Degree in Education, Recreation Management.
- 7 years successful recreational supervisory experience with Department of Defense, United States Air Force and 3 years in the private sector.
- Certified Leisure Professional-National Recreation and Park Association.
- Developed, organized and implemented numerous recreation programs for preteens, junior teens and senior teens.
- Responsible for annual budget of $350,000. *GOOD USE OF NUMBERS*
- Experienced fund-raiser; successfully raised thousands of dollars through the United Way Campaign, corporate sponsorships and special grants.
- Hired, trained, and monitored personnel (15 staff members).
- Selected, trained and monitored volunteers (400 volunteer members).
- Supervised maintenance of recreational facilities: gymnasium, swimming pool, softball/baseball/soccer fields, etc., and related equipment.
- Effective and knowledgeable in working with cultural/social differences.
- Commitment to work which promotes social interaction, development of recreational skills, and physical and emotional growth of youth of all ages.

EMPLOYMENT HISTORY

WHILE SHE HAS HAD "ONLY" ONE EMPLOYER, SHE PRESENTS ASSIGNMENTS AS IF DIFFERENT JOBS – A GOOD APPROACH

Recreation Specialist	1984 to 1992
Department of Defense, United States Air Force	
Director, Youth Activities Center	3/91 to 2/92
England Air Force Base, Alexandria, LA	
Director, Youth Activities Center	10/89-3/91
Royal Air Force Upper Heyford, United Kingdom	
Director, Youth Activities Center	3/89-10/89
Royal Air Force Fairford, United Kingdom	
Director, Youth Activities Center	8/87-3/89
McConnell Air Force Base, Wichita, KS	
Program Director, Youth Activities Center	12/84-8/87
McConnell Air Force Base, Wichita, KS	
After School Program Coordinator	9/84-12/84
Little Pal's Day Care Center, Wichita, KS	
Horse Program Director, Camp Wiedemann	Summer 83/84
Wichita Area Girl Scout Council, Wichita, KS	

SUBMITTED BY: MICHAEL ROBERTSON ALEXANDRIA, LOUISIANA

JANE MAEYERS
Page 2

EDUCATION & **SPECIALIZED** **TRAINING**	Bachelor of Arts Degree in Education	1985

Major: Recreation Management
WICHITA STATE UNIVERSITY, Wichita, KS
  Honors: • Graduated Cum Laude.
    • Dean's Honor Roll
    • Cumulative GPA: 3.26

Associate of Arts Degree in Education   1982
FORT SCOTT COMMUNITY COLLEGE, Fort Scott, KS
  Honors: • Graduated Sigma Cum Laude.
    • Dean's Honor Roll
    • Cumulative GPA: 3.65

Continuing Education Units   1985
"Volunteerism: Skills for the 80's"   9 CEU's
WICHITA STATE UNIVERSITY, Wichita, KS

Master Level Course Work in Management   88/89 term
WEBSTER UNIVERSITY, St. Louis, MO   6 credit hours GPA: 4.0

Master Level Course Work in Recreation   88/89 term
FLORIDA STATE UNIVERSITY, Tallahassee, FL 2 credit hours GPA: 4.0

• United States Air Force **Child Abuse,**   1985
  Child Sexual Abuse & Child Neglect Training Program
  McConnell Air Force Base, Wichita, KS   40 hour training course

• United States Air Force in Europe   1985
  Teen Outdoor Adventure Training Program
  Berchtesgaden, Germany   64 hour training course

• United States Air Force in Europe   1990
  Youth Directors' Training Conference
  Ramstein Air Base, Germany   40 hour training course

• United States Air Force **Morale, Welfare**   *1990 Honor Graduate*
  and Recreation Managers Training Course
  Keesler Air Force Base, Biloxi, MS   260 hour training course

CERTIFICATIONS	• Certified Leisure Professional-National Recreation & Park Association

• National Certified Softball Umpire-Amateur Softball Association
• High School Softball Official-National High School Scholastic Association
• High School Basketball Official-National High School Scholastic Association
• Lifetime Coach and Certified Clinition-National Youth Sports
  Coaches Association

MEMBERSHIPS • National Recreation and Park Association

HONORS & **AWARDS**

• Certificate of Achievement for Excellent Leadership and Management of
  Morale, Welfare & Recreation Programs for the United States Air Force 1986
• Program Excellence Award for Outstanding Programming of Morale, Welfare
  & Recreation Activities, United States Air Force   1986 and 1991
• Letter of Appreciation from Youth Activities Director, McConnell Air Force
  Base, KS, for superior program planning/management assistance; led to
  Outstanding rating from Military Inspection General Rating Team   1985

REFERENCES   Available upon request.

Handwritten note: WHILE THIS TAKES UP A LOT OF SPACE, SHE DOES PRESENT DETAILS OF ACHIEVEMENT, SUCH AS GOOD GRADES. SHE COULD HAVE CUT SOME DETAILS HERE OR PRESENTED THEM IN LESS SPACE, BUT IT WORKS WELL.

THIS IS AN EXAMPLE OF A RESUME "COVER". SINCE IT IS FOR A
POSITION IN THE TRAVEL INDUSTRY, THE GRAPHICS ARE APPROPRIATE,
THOUGH A MUCH SIMPLER DESIGN WOULD ALSO CREATE A GOOD
IMPRESSION FOR MORE
CONSERVATIVE POSITIONS

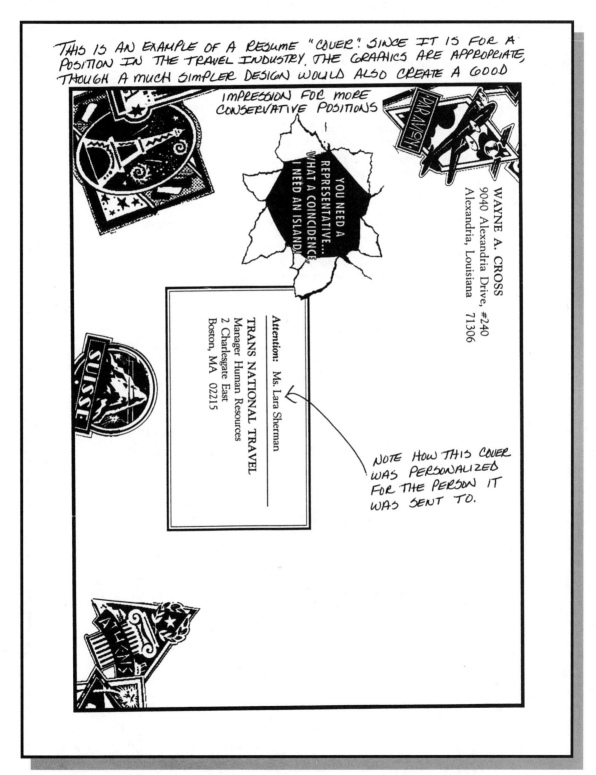

YOU NEED A
REPRESENTATIVE...
WHAT A COINCIDENCE,
I NEED AN ISLAND!

WAYNE A. CROSS
9040 Alexandria Drive, #240
Alexandria, Louisiana   71306

Attention: Ms. Lara Sherman

TRANS NATIONAL TRAVEL
Manager Human Resources
2 Charlesgate East
Boston, MA   02215

NOTE HOW THIS COVER
WAS PERSONALIZED
FOR THE PERSON IT
WAS SENT TO.

WHILE RECENT EXPERIENCE IS IN THE MILITARY, THIS RESUME DOES A NICE JOB IN PRESENTING SUMMER AND "OLDER" WORK EXPERIENCE TO SUPPORT HIS CURRENT JOB OBJECTIVE.

WAYNE A. CROSS
9040 Parliament Drive, #240
Alexandria, Louisiana 71306
(318) 441-9085

OBJECTIVE	Position as Island Representative/Tour Guide working directly with guests as their activity coordinator.
SUMMARY	Well-traveled, people-oriented individual with the ability to plan and supervise events for large groups of people. Strong background of participation in outdoor activities as events coordinator, guide and outdoor enthusiast.
HIGHLIGHTS OF QUALIFICATIONS	•Firsthand experience with worldwide range of cultures •Relate easily and openly with all ages and types •Honest and reliable in keeping commitments •Outstanding leadership and organization skills •Successful work experience as tour guide

RELATED EXPERIENCE

6/22-29/90-91	•**THE LIBERTY TRAIL CYCLE TOUR** - France, Luxembourg, Belgium Stateside Representative/Participant 1000-mile cycling tour across France, Luxembourg and Belgium, commemorating sacrifices of Allied Forces and French citizens in the Liberation of France.
7/91	•**3 WEEK CYCLING TOUR of ENGLAND-WALES-SCOTLAND**
12/88-3/89	•**YANKEE FLEET FISHING TOUR** - Key West, Florida Ship Mate/Deck Hand Assisted on fishing tours (up to 40 passengers) on Yankee Fleet-115' boat.
Summer 1988	•**VERMONT COUNTRY CYCLERS,** Waterbury, Vermont Tour Guide Lead bicycle tours with Vermont Country Cyclers, the nation's leading bicycle touring company, offering gourmet food and deluxe accommodations.
Summer 1981	•Completed **Outward Bound,** Ely, Minnesota 25-Day, Wilderness Survival School

WORK EXPERIENCE

Vehicle Maintenance Officer, Lieutenant, United States Air Force

England Air Force Base, Alexandria, Louisiana	1/91-Present
Sheppard Air Force Base, Wichita Falls, Texas	9/90-12/90
Comiso Air Station, Sicily - Italy	11/89-8/90
Davis Monthan Air Force Base, Tucson, Arizona	5/89-11/89

Responsibilities include:
  •Administration/maintenance control of all government vehicles on base
  •Diagnostic and quality assurance of the all vehicle maintenance shops
  •Supervision of up to 45 mechanics
  •Manage and maintenance of department budget over $600,000.

EDUCATION	**Bachelor of Science in Business Administration** - Managing & Marketing **Norwich University,** Northfield, Vermont, 1988.

SUBMITTED BY: MICHAEL ROBERTSON
ALEXANDRIA, LOUISIANA

RECENT GRAD USES A CHRONOLOGICAL FORMAT TO PRESENT HIS MILITARY EXPERIENCE AS SEPARATE JOBS.

JOHN ROBERT BURNS, JR.

0 Academy Cove • Oxford, Mississippi 38655 • (601) 555-1615   Hermland Plantation • Gibson, Mississippi 39150 • (601) 555-5595

OBJECTIVE:	Obtain an administrative or managerial position with a technical firm utilizing my leadership, technical, and business skills.
EDUCATION:	**Master of Business Administration** University of Mississippi, Oxford, Mississippi Completion: December 1992
	Bachelor of Engineering University of Mississippi, Oxford, Mississippi Emphases: Telecommunications and Business Completion: December 1991

WORK EXPERIENCE:

November 1989 - Present

Communications NCOIC
Mississippi Army National Guard, Jackson, Mississippi
- Responsible for 21 subordinates, 3 vehicles and all communications equipment

December 1988 -
October 1989

DMZ Sincgars Trainer
United States Army, Camp Howze, South Korea
- Taught DMZ battalion the characteristics, use and maintenance of Sincgars
- Responsible for $1.5 million in secret radio inventories

December 1988 -
October 1989

Communication Security Custodian
United States Army, Camp Howze, South Korea
- Responsible for security, destruction, and dissemination of materials to subordinate units

July 1888 - December 1988

Radio Section Sergeant
United States Army, Camp Howze, South Korea
- Responsible for all communications equipment, 15 radios, 4 vehicles, and 12 people

July 1986 - April 1988

Radio Team Chief
United States Army, Fort Bragg, North Carolina
- In charge of Radio/Teletype team, 3 people, equipment, vehicle, and generator

April 1984 - April 1985

Maintenance Manager
Southwest Supply Company, Laurel, Mississippi
- Maintained efficient warehouse
- Operated heavy transportation equipment

May 1981 - December 1982
Summers 1980 & 1983

Skilled Labor
Arrow Contractors, Venice, Louisiana
- Served as lead-off hand on maintenance crew, crane operator, and pipe fitter
- Responsible for tools, equipment, and crane

HONORS & ACTIVITIES:
Academic
- Chancellor's Honor Roll
- Dean's List

Military
- United States Paratrooper
- 2 Army Achievement Medals
- 2 Army Commendation Medals
- Honors Graduate of Primary Leadership Development Course
- Honors Graduate of Basic Non-Commissioned Officer Course

SUBMITTED BY: LEO J. LAZARUS
OXFORD, MISSISSIPPI

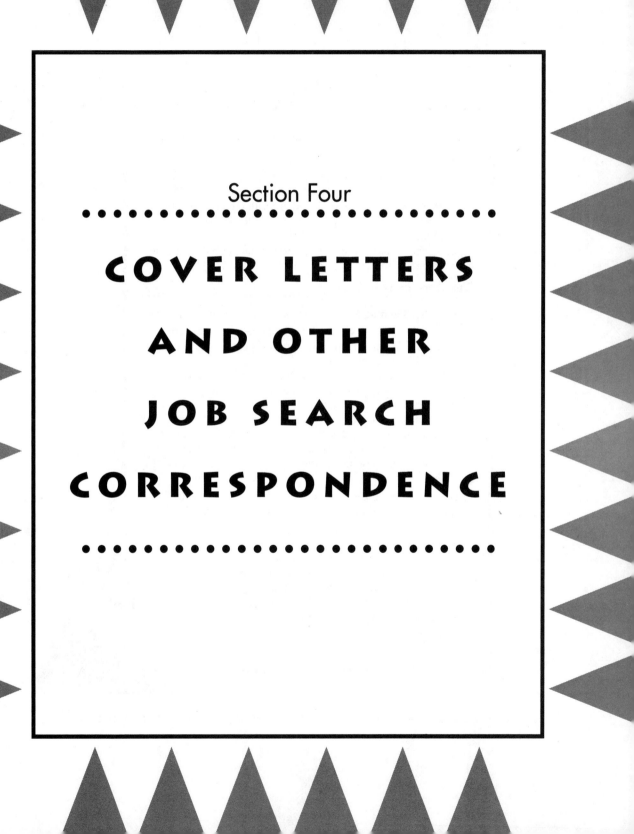

Section Four

COVER LETTERS AND OTHER JOB SEARCH CORRESPONDENCE

Introduction

During the course of an active job search, you will probably send out a variety of correspondence. Resumes are often sent along with a "cover" letter. These will be discussed in Chapter 9. But there are also a variety of other written communications that are used during a job search that are often overlooked in most resume books. Thank-you notes, for example, can make a big difference if used well. These and similar forms of written communication are the focus of Chapter 10.

Chapters in This Section:

Chapter 9: When and How to Write a Good Cover Letter

You typically send a resume with a separate letter that "covers" the resume. This same letter often provides details that may not be included in the resume.

As with resumes, a big mistake with cover letters is to use them as part of a passive job search campaign that sends out lots of unsolicited resumes. I feel that cover letters are best used *after* you have made some personal contact with a potential employer by phone or in person rather than as a replacement for direct contact. This chapter presents the basics of how to write cover letters that are appropriate for most situations and gives specific examples.

Chapter 10: Other Correspondence, Including Thank-You Notes—A Powerful and Often Overlooked Job Search Tool

Thank-you notes make a difference, yet they are rarely mentioned in job search or resume books. If used well, they can help you be remembered fondly following interviews and in many other situations throughout your job search. Believe it or not, that can make a big difference in getting or not getting job offers. This chapter also covers a variety of other miscellaneous correspondence that can be used in your search for a job, including letters of reference, follow-up letters, and others.

WHEN AND HOW TO WRITE A GOOD COVER LETTER

Quick Tip

This chapter provides advice on writing cover letters and includes various samples. I've tried to keep this simple, with an emphasis on letters that are sent after you have made some sort of personal contact with an employer. Letters, after all, won't get you a job offer—just like a resume...

It is not appropriate to send a resume to someone without some explanation as to why you are sending it. The traditional way to do this is to provide a letter *along with* your resume—a cover letter. Depending on the circumstances, the letter would explain your situation and would ask the recipient for some specific action, consideration, or response.

There are entire books written on the art of writing a cover letter. Some of the authors of these books go into great detail on how to construct a "powerful" cover letter. Some suggest that a cover letter can actually be used to replace the resume by providing similar information but targeting the content specifically to the person who is receiving it. While there are merits to these ideas, my objective here is to provide you with a simple and quick review of cover letter basics that will meet most needs.

THE ONLY TWO GROUPS OF PEOPLE WHO WILL GET YOUR COVER LETTERS

If you think about it, there are only two different groups of people to whom you send a resume and cover letter. They are:

1. People you know

2. People you don't know

While I realize that this sounds too simple, it's true. And this observation makes it easier to understand how you might structure your letters to each of these groups. But before I demonstrate some useful and effective cover letters, let's first review some basics regarding writing cover letters in general.

Quick Tip

While many situations require writing a formal letter, there are also many instances where a simple note will do (for example, when you know the person you are writing to). Additional information on informal notes will be provided later in this chapter.

TIPS FOR SUPERIOR COVER LETTERS

No matter who you are writing to, virtually every good cover letter should follow these guidelines:

☑ WRITE TO SOMEONE IN PARTICULAR

NEVER send a cover letter "To whom it may concern" or use some other impersonal opening. We all get enough junk mail and if you don't send your letter to someone by name, it *will* be treated like junk mail.

Quick Alert

☑ MAKE ABSOLUTELY NO ERRORS

One way to offend people quickly is to misspell their name or use an incorrect title. If there is any question, call and verify the correct spelling of the name and other details before you send the letter. Also review your letters carefully to be sure that they do not contain any typographical, grammatical, or other errors.

☑ PERSONALIZE YOUR CONTENT

I've never been impressed by form letters of any kind and you should not use them. Those computer-generated letters that automatically insert your name never fool anyone and I find cover letters done this way a bit offensive. While I know some resume and cover letter books recommend that you send out lots of these "broadcast letters" to people you don't know, I suggest that doing so is a waste of time and money. If you can't personalize your letter in some way, don't send it.

☑ PRESENT A GOOD APPEARANCE

Your contacts with prospective employers should always be professional. Buy good quality stationery and matching envelopes. The standard 8 1/2-by-11-inch paper size is typically used but you can also use the smaller "Monarch" size paper with matching envelopes, too. Use only good quality paper—I prefer a white, ivory, or light beige-colored paper. A typewriter with excellent type quality or a word processor with letter quality or laser output (not poor quality dot-matrix) is a must in most cases.

☑ USE AN APPROPRIATE FORMAT

Any standard business correspondence format is acceptable. Look at the sample cover letters at the end of this chapter for ideas.

☑ PROVIDE A FRIENDLY OPENING

Begin your letter with a reminder of any prior contacts and the reason for your correspondence now. The examples will give you some ideas on how this can be handled.

☑ TARGET YOUR SKILLS AND EXPERIENCES

To do this well, you must know something about the organization or person with whom you are dealing. Present any relevant background that may be of particular interest to the person you are writing.

☑ DEFINE THE NEXT STEP

Don't close your letter without clearly identifying what you will do next. I do not recommend that you simply leave it up to the employer to contact you, since that really doesn't guarantee you a response. Close on a positive note and let them know you desire further contact with them and their organization.

Quick Tip

Using a few simple techniques, it is possible to make the acquaintance of all sorts of people. That's why I say that it is a waste of time and money to send your resume or cover letter to strangers—it is relatively easy to make direct contact. Section 5 provides additional details on how to make contact with people you don't already know and I recommend that you learn more about this.

WRITING COVER LETTERS TO SOMEONE YOU KNOW

It is always best if you have are already known to the person you are writing. As I have said elsewhere, any written correspondence is less effective than personal contact, and the ideal circumstance is to send a resume and cover letter after already having spoken with the person directly.

For example, it is far more effective to first call someone who has advertised in the paper than to simply send a letter and resume. There are also the *Yellow Pages*, personal referrals, and many other ways of coming to know someone. So, I'll assume you have made some sort of personal contact before sending your resume. Within this assumption there are hundreds of variations, but I will review the most important ones and let you adapt them to your own situation.

THE FOUR TYPES OF COVER LETTERS TO PEOPLE YOU KNOW

There are four basic situations you can consider when sending out a cover letter and each one requires a different approach. The situations are presented below, along with an explanation of each.

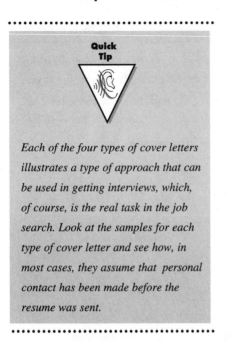

Quick Tip

Each of the four types of cover letters illustrates a type of approach that can be used in getting interviews, which, of course, is the real task in the job search. Look at the samples for each type of cover letter and see how, in most cases, they assume that personal contact has been made before the resume was sent.

1. **An interview is scheduled and there is a specific job opening that may interest you.** In this case, you have already arranged an interview for a job opening that interests you and the cover letter should provide details of your experience that relate to that specific job.

2. **An interview is scheduled, but no specific job is available.** I will explain in more detail, in Section 5, why this situation is such a good one for you to set up. In essence, this is a letter you will send for an interview with an employer who does not have a specific opening for you now but who might in the future. This is fertile ground for finding job leads where no one else may be looking.

3. **After an interview takes place.** Many people overlook the importance of sending a letter after an interview. This is a time to say that you want the job (if that is the case, say so) and to add any details on why you think you can do the job well.

4. **No interview is scheduled, yet.** There are situations where you just can't arrange an interview before you send in a resume and cover letter. For example, you may be responding to a newspaper want ad that only provides a box number for your response. Or you may be trying to see a person whose name was given to you by a friend, but that person is on vacation. In these cases, sending a good cover letter and resume will allow any later contacts to be more effective.

SAMPLE COVER LETTERS ADDRESSED TO PEOPLE YOU KNOW

The following are sample cover letters for each of the four situations above. Note that they use different formats and styles in an effort to show you the range of styles that are appropriate. Each addresses a different situation and each incorporates all of the cover letter writing guidelines presented earlier in this chapter.

SAMPLE COVER LETTER: PRE-INTERVIEW, FOR A SPECIFIC JOB OPENING

Comments: This writer called first and arranged an interview, the best approach of all. Note how this new graduate included a specific example of how he saved money for a business by changing its procedures. Though it is not clear, his experience with lots of people was gained by working as a waiter. Note also how he included skills such as "hard worker" and "deadline pressure" that I reviewed in Chapter 4 of this book.

Quick
Reference

Richard Swanson
113 South Meridian Street
Greenwich, Connecticut 11721

March 10, 19XX

Mr. William Hines
New England Power and Light Company
604 Waterway Blvd.
Parien, Connecticut 11716

Mr. Hines,

    I am following up on the brief chat we had today by phone. After getting the details on the position you have open, I am certain that it is the kind of job I have been looking for. A copy of my resume is enclosed providing more details of my background. I hope you have a chance to review it before we meet next week.

    My special interest has long been in the large-volume order processing systems that your organization has developed so well. While in school, I researched the flow of order processing work for a large corporation as part of a class assignment. With some simple and inexpensive procedural changes I recommended, check-processing time was reduced by an average of three days. For the number of checks and dollars involved, this one change resulted in an estimated increase in interest revenues of over $35,000 per year.

    While I have recently graduated from business school, I do have considerable experience for a person of my age. I have worked in a variety of jobs dealing with large numbers of people and deadline pressures. My studies have also been far more "hands-on" and practical than those of most schools, so I have a good working knowledge of current business systems and procedures. This includes a good understanding of various computer spreadsheet and applications programs, the use of automation, and experience with cutting costs and increasing profits. I am also a hard worker and realize I will need to apply myself to get established in my career.

    I am most interested in the position you have available and am excited about the potential it offers. I look forward to seeing you next week.

Sincerely,

Richard Swanson

Comments: This letter indicates that the writer first called and set up an interview as the result of someone else's tip. The writer explains why she is moving to the city and asks for help in making contacts there. While there is no job opening here, she is wise in assuming that there might be one in the future. Even if this is not the case, she asks the employer to think of others who might have a position for someone with her skills. Assuming that the interview goes well and the employer gives her names of others to call, she can then follow up with them.

ANNE MARIE ROAD
616 Kings Way • Minneapolis, MN 54312

February 10, 19XX

Ms. Francine Cook
Park-Halsey Corporation
5413 Armstrong Drive
Minneapolis, Minnesota 54317

Dear Ms. Cook,

When Steve Marks suggested I call you, I had no idea you would be so helpful. I've already followed up with several of the suggestions you made and am now looking forward to meeting with you next Tuesday. The resume I've enclosed is to give you a better sense of my qualifications. Perhaps it will help you think of other organizations who may be interested in my background.

The resume does not say why I've moved to Minneapolis and you may find that of interest. My spouse and I visited the city several years ago and thought it a good place to live. He has obtained a very good position here and, based on that, we decided it was time to commit ourselves to a move.

As you can see from my work experience, I tend to stay on and move up in jobs, so I now want to research the job opportunities here more carefully before making a commitment. Your help in this task is greatly appreciated.

Feel free to contact me if you have any questions, otherwise, I look forward to meeting with you next Tuesday.

Sincerely,

Anne Marie Road

Comments: This letter shows you how you might follow up after an interview and make a pitch for solving a problem—even when no job formally exists. In this example, the writer suggests that she can use her skills to solve a specific problem that she uncovered during her conversation with the employer. While it never occurs to many job seekers to set up an interview where there appears to be no job opening, many jobs are *created* as a result of such an interview. (I have done it myself, just to make room for a good person.)

Quick
Reference

SANDRA A. ZAREMBA
115 South Hawthorn Drive
Port Charlotte, Florida 81641

April 10, 19XX

Christine Massey
Import Distributors, Inc.
417 East Main Street
Atlanta, Georgia 21649

Dear Ms. Massey,

I know you have a busy schedule so I was pleasantly surprised when you arranged a time for me to see you. While you don't have a position open now, your organization is just the sort of place I would like to work. As we discussed, I like to be busy with a variety of duties and the active pace I saw at your company is what I seek.

Your ideas on increasing business sound creative. I've thought about the customer service problem and would like to discuss a possible solution. It would involve the use of a simple system of color-coded files that would prioritize correspondence to give older requests priority status. The handling of complaints could also be speeded up through the use of simple form letters similar to those you mentioned. I have some thoughts on how this might be done too, and I will work out a draft of procedures and sample letters if you are interested. It can be done on the computers your staff already uses and would not require any additional cost to implement.

Whether or not you have a position for me in the future, I appreciate the time you have given me. An extra copy of my resume is enclosed for your files—or to pass on to someone else.

Let me know if you want to discuss the ideas I presented earlier in this letter. I will call you next week, as you suggested, to keep you informed of my progress.

Sincerely,

Sandra A. Zaremba

Comments: This letter explains why the person is looking for a job as well as presents additional information that would not normally be included in a resume. Note that the writer had obtained the employer's name from the membership list of a professional organization, one excellent source of job leads. Also note that the writer stated that he would call again to arrange an appointment. While this letter is assertive and *might turn off* some employers, many others would be impressed with his assertiveness and willing to see him when he finally reaches them. Samples of the "JIST Card" mentioned in this letter can be found at the end of Chapter 3 and are covered briefly in Chapter 11.

JUSTIN MOORE

Quick Reference

January 5, 19XX

Doris Michaelmann
Michaelmann Clothing
8661 Parkway Blvd.
Phoenix, AZ 27312

Ms. Michaelmann:

As you may know, I phoned you several times over the past week while you were in meetings. I hope that you received the messages. Since I did not want to delay contacting you, I decided to write.

I got your name from the American Retail Clothing Association membership list. I am a member of this group and wanted to contact local members to ask their help in locating a suitable position. I realize that you probably don't have an available position for someone with my skills but I ask you to do two things on my behalf.

First, I ask that you consider seeing me at your convenience within the next few weeks. Though you may not have a position available for me, you may be able to assist me in other ways. And, of course, I would appreciate any consideration for future openings. Second, you may know of others who have job openings now or might possibly have them in the future.

While I realize that this is an unusual request and that you are quite busy, I do plan on staying in the retail clothing business in this area for some time and would appreciate any assistance you can give me in my search for a new job.

My resume is attached for your information along with a "JIST Card" that summarizes my background. As you probably know, Allied Tailoring has closed and I stayed on to shut things down in an orderly way. In spite of their regrettable business failure, I was one of those who was responsible for Allied's enormous sales increases over the past decade and have substantial experience to bring to any growing retail clothing concern, such as I hear yours is.

I will contact you next week and arrange a time that is good for us both. Please feel free to contact me at any time regarding this matter.

Sincerely,

Justin Moore

8661 Bay Drive • Temple, AZ 27317 • 727-483-3643

Quick Fact

COVER LETTERS TO SOMEONE YOU DON'T KNOW

If it is not practical to directly contact a prospective employer by phone or some other method, it is acceptable to send a resume and cover letter. This approach makes sense in some situations such as if you are moving to a distant location, or responding to a "blind" ad offering only a post office box number.

The approach of sending out "To Whom It May Concern" letters by the basketful has been discussed elsewhere in this book. I do not recommend it. However, there are ways to modify this "shotgun" approach to be more effective. Try to find something you have in common with the person you are contacting. By mentioning this link, your letter then becomes a very personal request for assistance. Look at the two letters that follow for ideas.

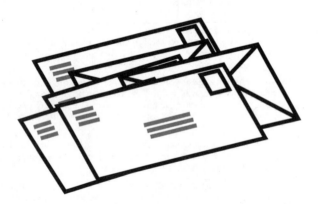

Comment: Responding to a want ad puts you in direct competition with the many others who will read the same ad, so the odds are not good that this letter would get a response at all. The fact that the writer does not yet live in the area is another negative. Still, I do believe that you should follow up on any legitimate lead you find. In this case, the position will likely be filled by someone who is available to interview right away but there is always the chance that, with good follow-up, another position will become available. Or, the employer might be able to give the writer the names of others to contact.

Quick Reference

John Andrews
12 Lake Street
Chicago, Illinois 60631

January 17, 19XX

The Morning Sun
Box N4317
2 Early Drive
Toronto, Ontario R5C 1S3

re: Receptionist/Bookkeeper Position

As I plan on relocating to Toronto, your advertisement for a Receptionist/Bookkeeper caught my attention. Your ad stated yours is a small office and that is precisely what I am looking for. I like dealing with people, and in a previous position, had over 5,000 customer contacts a month. With that experience, I have learned to handle things quickly and pleasantly.

The varied activities in a position combining bookkeeping and reception sound very interesting. I have received formal training in accounting methods and am familiar with accounts receivable, accounts payable, and general ledger posting. I am familiar with several computerized accounting programs and can quickly learn any others that you may be using.

My resume is enclosed for your consideration. Note that I went to school in Toronto and I plan on returning there soon to establish my career. Several members of my family also live there and I have provided their local phone numbers, should you wish to contact me. Please contact that number as soon as possible, since I plan on being in Toronto in the near future and would like to speak with you about this or future positions with your company. I will call you in the next few weeks to set up an appointment should I not hear from you before then.

Thank you in advance for your consideration in this matter.

Sincerely,

John Andrews

245

Comments: This is another example of a person conducting a long distance job search using names obtained from a professional association. This one also explains why he is leaving his old job and includes positive information regarding his references and skills that would not normally be found in a resume. This one also asks for an interview even though there may not be any jobs open now. Mr. Goode also asks for names of others to contact.

John B. Goode
321 Smokie Way
Nashville, Tennessee 31201

Quick
Reference

July 10, 19XX

Paul Resley
Operations Manager
Rollem Trucking Co.
I-70 Freeway Drive
Kansas City, Missouri 78401

Mr. Resley,

I obtained your name from the membership directory of the Affiliated Trucking Association. I have been a member for over 10 years and I am very active in the Southeast Region. The reason I am writing is to ask for your help. The firm I had been employed with has been bought by a larger corporation. The operations here have been disbanded, leaving me unemployed.

While I like where I live, I know that finding a position at the level of responsibility I seek may require a move. As a center of the transportation business, your city is one of those I have targeted for special attention. A copy of my resume is enclosed for your use. I'd like you to review it and consider where a person with my background would get a good reception in Kansas City. Perhaps you could think of a specific person for me to contact?

I have specialized in fast-growing organizations or ones that have experienced rapid change. My particular strength is in bringing things under control, then increasing profits. While my resume does not state this, I have excellent references from my former employer and would have stayed if a similar position existed at their new location.

As a member of the association, I hoped that you would provide some special attention to my request for assistance. Please call my answering service collect if you have any immediate leads. I plan on coming to Kansas City on a job-hunting trip within the next six weeks. Prior to my trip I will call you for advice on who I might contact for interviews. Even if they have no jobs open for me now, perhaps they will know of someone else who does!

Thanks in advance for your help on this.

Sincerely,

John B. Goode
Treasurer, Southeast Region
Affiliated Trucking Association

246

**Quick
Reference**

ADDITIONAL SAMPLE COVER LETTERS

I have included additional cover letters that cover a variety of situations. Most of those that do not include graphics were formatted in letter templates provided with a well-known word processing program. While the formats are not fancy, they show formats produced according to a predetermined design.

The letters from Patricia Dugan and Douglas Parker came from Dave Swanson's book, *The Resume Solution*. I've also included letters by John Harris, Marquita Lipscomb, John Trost, and Richard Peterson that feature interesting design elements and formats. These letters were provided by Rafael Santiago in Papillion, Nebraska. Jane Maeyers' letter was provided by Michael Robertson in Alexandria, Virginia. Both are professional resume writers whose addresses are in Appendix B of this book. The remaining letters came from various books I have written in the past. These designs will give you a glimpse of what can be done today by many word processing and desktop design computer programs.

I hope that these samples, along with the rest of the chapter, give you ideas on writing your own cover letters. Just keep in mind that the best cover letter is one that follows your having set up an interview following a direct contact. Anything else is just second best, at best. . .

947 Cherry Street
Middleville, Ohio 01234
October 1, 19XX

Mr. Alfred E. Newman, President
Alnew Consolidated Stores, Inc.
1 Newman Place
New City, OK 03033

Dear Mr. Newman:

I am interested in the position of national sales director, which you recently advertised in the *Retail Sales and Marketing* newsletter.

I am very familiar with your company's innovative marketing techniques as well as your enlightened policy in promoting and selling environmentally sound merchandise nationwide. I have been active for some time now in environmental protection projects, both as a representative of my current employer and on my own. I recently successfully introduced a new line of kitchen products that exceeds federal standards, is environmentally safe, and is selling well.

The enclosed resume outlines my experience and skills in both sales and marketing in the retail field. I would like to meet with you to discuss how my skills would benefit Alnew Consolidated Stores. I will contact you soon to request an interview for current or future positions and may be reached at (513) 987-6543.

Thank you for your time and consideration.

Sincerely,

Robin Redding

LISA MARIE FARKEL

3321 East Haverford Road
Baldwin, North Carolina 122934

April 20, 1994

Mr. Howard Duty
WXLC TV
10212 North Oxford Avenue
Halstead, South Carolina 124567

Dear Mr. Halstead,

Thank you for agreeing to meet with me at 3:00 p.m. on March 23rd to talk about job opportunities for broadcast technicians. Although I understand that you have no openings right now, I'm enclosing my resume to give you some information about my training and background.

You will see that I have worked on both up-to-date and as well as older equipment. Working part-time for a small station, I've learned to monitor, adjust and repair a variety of equipment including both the newer automated and computerized items as well as the older ones. Keeping a mix of older and newer equipment working smoothly has required me to learn many things and has been an invaluable experience. At Halstead Junior College, I have become the person to call if their new, state-of-the-art audio and video equipment does not perform as it should.

I look forward to graduating and devoting all my time and energy to my career. Your help is greatly appreciated, particularly your invitation to spend more time observing field operations during your live election coverage.

Sincerely,

Lisa Marie Farkel

Enclosure: resume

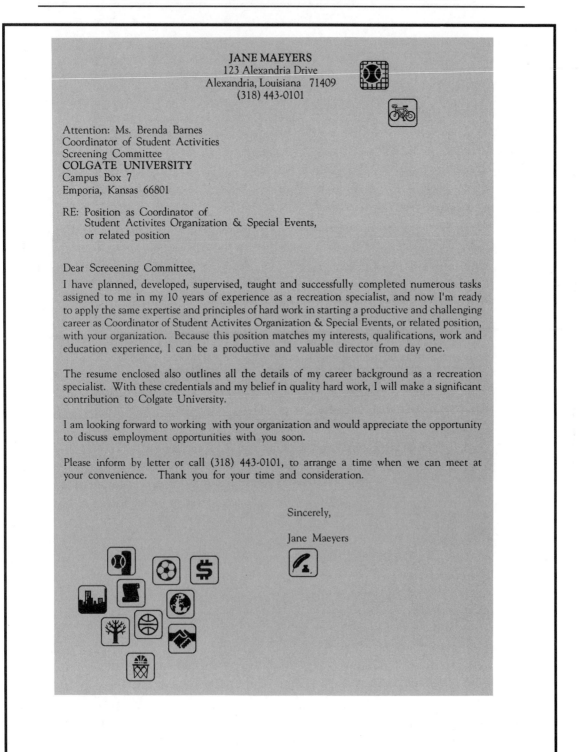

JANE MAEYERS
123 Alexandria Drive
Alexandria, Louisiana 71409
(318) 443-0101

Attention: Ms. Brenda Barnes
Coordinator of Student Activities
Screening Committee
COLGATE UNIVERSITY
Campus Box 7
Emporia, Kansas 66801

RE: Position as Coordinator of
Student Activites Organization & Special Events,
or related position

Dear Screeening Committee,

I have planned, developed, supervised, taught and successfully completed numerous tasks assigned to me in my 10 years of experience as a recreation specialist, and now I'm ready to apply the same expertise and principles of hard work in starting a productive and challenging career as Coordinator of Student Activites Organization & Special Events, or related position, with your organization. Because this position matches my interests, qualifications, work and education experience, I can be a productive and valuable director from day one.

The resume enclosed also outlines all the details of my career background as a recreation specialist. With these credentials and my belief in quality hard work, I will make a significant contribution to Colgate University.

I am looking forward to working with your organization and would appreciate the opportunity to discuss employment opportunities with you soon.

Please inform by letter or call (318) 443-0101, to arrange a time when we can meet at your convenience. Thank you for your time and consideration.

Sincerely,

Jane Maeyers

6345 Highland Boulevard
Minneapolis, Minnesota

August 11, 19XX

Mr. James A. Blackwell
Vice President, Engineering
Acme Revolving Door Company
New Brunswick, Pennsylvania 21990

Dear Mr. Blackwell:

    I graduated from the University of Minnesota this spring with a 3.66 grade average and a Bachelor of Science Degree in Mechanical Engineering.

    Your company has been highly recommended to me by my uncle, John Blair, the Pennsylvania District Governor for Rotary, International. He has appreciated your friendship and business relationship over the years and has advised me to forward my resume. My own reading in business publications has kept me aware of the new products which Acme has marketed.

    My objective is to design mechanical parts for a privately owned company which enjoys an excellent reputation and which conducts business internationally.

    I hope that I may take the liberty of calling your office to see if we might meet to discuss possible opportunities with Acme. I plan to be in Pennsylvania toward the end of next month, and this might provide a convenient time to meet, if your schedule permits.

Sincerely,

Patricia Dugan
(612) 555-3445

1768 S. Carrollton Street
Nashville, TN 96050
May 26, 1995

Ms. Karen Miller
Office Manager
Lendon, Lendon, and Sears
Suite 101, Landmark Building
Summit, NJ 11736

Dear Ms. Miller:

Enclosed is a copy of my resume which describes my work experience as a legal assistant. I hope this information will be helpful as background for our interview next Monday at 4 o'clock.

I appreciate your taking time to describe your requirements so fully. This sounds like a position that could develop into a satisfying career. And my training in accounting -- along with experience using a variety of computer programs -- seems to match your needs.

Lendon, Lendon, and Sears is a highly respected name in New Jersey. I am excited about this opportunity and I look forward to meeting with you.

Sincerely,

Richard Wittenberg

YALE BUSINESS SERVICES
Alexander Bell, Director of Human Resources
1005 Denver Street, Suite 1
Bellevue, Nebraska 68005-4145

B

ALBAROSA
BARTON

12603 S. 33rd St

Omaha, NE 68123

Tel: (402)292-9052

Fax: (913)752-8956

Dear Mr. Bell,

I am enclosing a copy of my resume for your consideration, and would like to call your attention to the areas of skill and achievement in my background that are most relevant.

I am an achiever, with four years of experience as a highly successful administrator. I've always set high standards and consistently achieved my goals. I've served in the United States Air Force since February 1989 as an Administrative Specialist/Assistant. I acquired my training through the excellent programs the Air Force provides. I am highly motivated and would be a dynamic administrator for whatever company I represent.

I am confident in my administrative abilities, and have already proven myself in the areas of office administration and customer relations.

I look forward to hearing from you soon and having the opportunity to discuss your needs.

Cordially,

ALBAROSA BARTON

4550 Parrier Street
Espinosa, California 4478

September 11, 19XX

Mr. Craig Schmidt
District Manager
Desert Chicken Shops
Post Office Box 6230
Los Angeles, California 98865

Dear Mr. Schmidt,

My resume (enclosed) outlines my four years of successful experience as a fast food manager with a nationwide network of restaurants. I graduated from a Restaurant Management curriculum at Harman University with a 3.75 GPA in 1985.

I have been impressed with the rapid growth and exceptional quality of product and service for which Desert Chicken has become well known. This is the kind of organization I hope to work for.

My experience includes positions as cook, night manager, assistant manager, and as manager for my current employer.

I will call your office in a few days to see if we might schedule a convenient time to meet and discuss some areas of mutual interest.

Thanks very much for your consideration.

Sincerely,

Douglas Parker

Enclosure

ARE YOU UNDERSTAFFED?

MEET MARQUITA! "A SECRETARY IF I EVER MET ONE!"

MARQUITA IS:

Creative
Intelligent
Honest
Quick to learn
Willing to learn
Resourceful

QUALIFIED...STRONG PEOPLE BACKGROUND AND PEOPLE SKILLS IN:

Knowing When and How to ask Questions
Handling Complaints
Motivating Others
Knowing When to Listen

I AM LOOKING FOR FULL-TIME SECRETARIAL WORK AND WILL PROVIDE YOU WITH TOP-NOTCH, QUALITY SERVICE. IF YOU ARE LOOKING FOR THE BEST, WHY NOT GIVE ME A CALL?

Marquita M. Lipscomb

1005 Denver Street · Bellevue, Nebraska 68005 · Tel: (402) 733-0200

255

Apartment A35
4085 Larchmont Road
Seattle, WA 97033
September 1, 1995

The Seattle News
Box N9142
1414 East New York Street
Seattle, WA 97002

Your advertisement for an Administrative Secretary could have been written with me in mind. I have had three years experience in a busy office where time management, communication skills and ability to deal with all kinds of people are vital.

Directing junior secretarial staff, writing customer service letters, and preparing monthly, quarterly, and yearly sales reports are my responsibilities. I regularly use computer software packages to track and maintain our sales revenues and customer mailing lists. I am also proficient in word processing and spreadsheet software on both Mac and PC based computers. My communication skills are excellent and I can work on multiple tasks and still meet deadlines.

For your consideration, I have enclosed a resume that more completely describes my education and experience. I look forward to meeting with you soon.

Sincerely,

Susan Deming

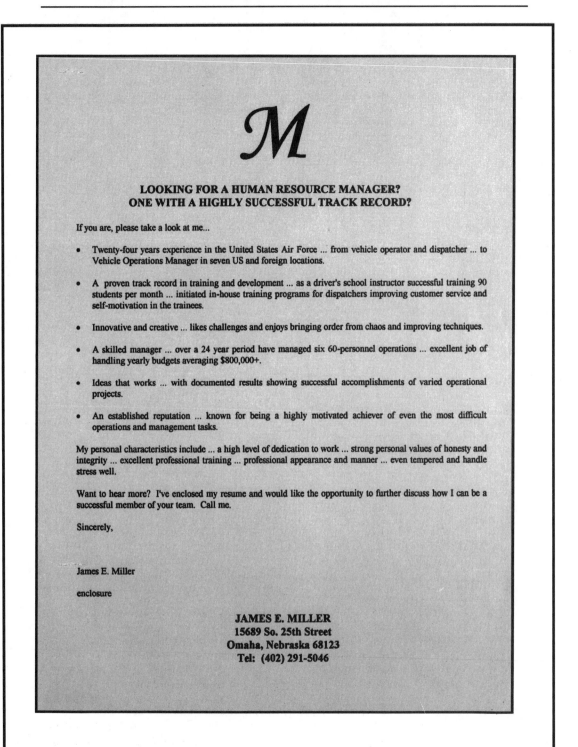

M

LOOKING FOR A HUMAN RESOURCE MANAGER?
ONE WITH A HIGHLY SUCCESSFUL TRACK RECORD?

If you are, please take a look at me...

- Twenty-four years experience in the United States Air Force ... from vehicle operator and dispatcher ... to Vehicle Operations Manager in seven US and foreign locations.

- A proven track record in training and development ... as a driver's school instructor successful training 90 students per month ... initiated in-house training programs for dispatchers improving customer service and self-motivation in the trainees.

- Innovative and creative ... likes challenges and enjoys bringing order from chaos and improving techniques.

- A skilled manager ... over a 24 year period have managed six 60-personnel operations ... excellent job of handling yearly budgets averaging $800,000+.

- Ideas that works ... with documented results showing successful accomplishments of varied operational projects.

- An established reputation ... known for being a highly motivated achiever of even the most difficult operations and management tasks.

My personal characteristics include ... a high level of dedication to work ... strong personal values of honesty and integrity ... excellent professional training ... professional appearance and manner ... even tempered and handle stress well.

Want to hear more? I've enclosed my resume and would like the opportunity to further discuss how I can be a successful member of your team. Call me.

Sincerely,

James E. Miller

enclosure

JAMES E. MILLER
15689 So. 25th Street
Omaha, Nebraska 68123
Tel: (402) 291-5046

C H A P T E R

10

OTHER CORRESPONDENCE, INCLUDING THANK-YOU NOTES—A POWERFUL AND OFTEN OVERLOOKED JOB SEARCH TOOL

Quick Tip

The information in this chapter is often overlooked in "resume books." That is too bad, since in my experience thank-you notes are a very effective tool—far more effective than sending out unsolicited resumes, for example. So do pay attention to this chapter's content. It is short, but important.

While resumes and cover letters get the attention, thank-you notes often get results. That's right, sending thank-you notes makes both good manners and good job search sense. When used properly, they can help you make a positive impression with employers that more formal correspondence often can't.

So, in just a few pages, here are the basics of writing and using thank-you notes, an often overlooked but surprisingly effective job search tool.

SOME TIPS ON WHEN TO SEND THANK-YOU NOTES—AND WHY

Quick Fact

Thank-you notes get results. They have a social tradition that is more intimate and friendly than more formal and manipulative business correspondence. I think that is one of the reasons they work so well—people respond to those who show good manners and say thank you. Here are some situations when you should use them, along with some sample notes.

☑ BEFORE AN INTERVIEW

There are some situations when you can send a less formal note before an interview. In some cases, you can simply thank someone for being willing to see you. Enclosing a resume in this situation strikes me as a bit inappropriate (remember, this is supposed to be a sincere thanks for their help and not an assertive business situation).

SAMPLE THANK-YOU NOTE #1

Quick Reference

April 8, 19XX

Cynthia Kijek,

Thanks so much for your willingness to see me next Wednesday at 9:00 a.m. I know that I am one of many who is interested in working with your organization and appreciate the opportunity to meet you and learn more about the position.

I've enclosed a JIST Card that presents the basics of my skills for this job and will bring a copy of my resume to the interview. Please call me if you have any questions at all.

Sincerely,

Bruce Vernon

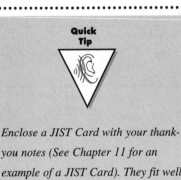

Enclose a JIST Card with your thank-you notes (See Chapter 11 for an example of a JIST Card). *They fit well into a thank-you note sized envelope and they provide key information (such as a phone number) that an employer can use to contact you. JIST Cards also provide key skills and other credentials that will help you create a good impression. And, of course, the employer could always forward the card to someone else who might have a job opening for you.*

☑ AFTER AN INTERVIEW

One of the best times to send a thank-you note is right after an interview. There are several reasons for this, in my opinion:

1. It creates a positive impression that you have good follow-up skills—to say nothing of good manners.

2. It creates yet another opportunity for you to remain in the employer's consciousness at an important time.

3. Should they have buried, passed along, or otherwise lost your resume and previous correspondence, sending a thank-you note and a corresponding JIST Card provides one more chance for them to find your number and call you.

For these reasons, I suggest that you send a thank-you note right after the inteview and certainly within 24 hours. The following is an example of such a note.

SAMPLE THANK-YOU NOTE #2

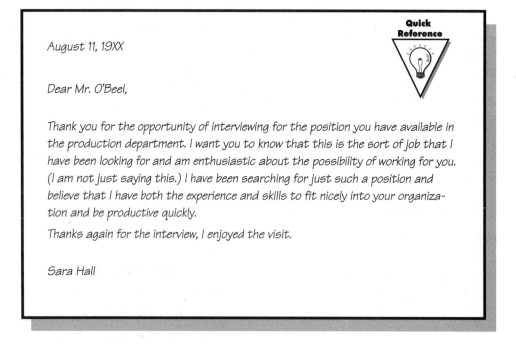

Quick
Reference

August 11, 19XX

Dear Mr. O'Beel,

Thank you for the opportunity of interviewing for the position you have available in the production department. I want you to know that this is the sort of job that I have been looking for and am enthusiastic about the possibility of working for you. (I am not just saying this.) I have been searching for just such a position and believe that I have both the experience and skills to fit nicely into your organization and be productive quickly.

Thanks again for the interview, I enjoyed the visit.

Sara Hall

Quick
Tip

Send a thank-you note as soon as possible after an interview or meeting. This is when you are freshest in the mind of the person who receives it and are most likely to create a good impression.

WHENEVER ANYONE HELPS YOU IN YOUR JOB SEARCH

Send a thank-you note to anyone who helps you during your job search. This includes those who give you referrals, people who provide advice, or simply those who are supportive of you during your search for a new job. I suggest you routinely enclose one or more JIST Cards in these notes since the recipient can then give them to others who may be in a better position to help you.

SAMPLE THANK-YOU NOTE #3

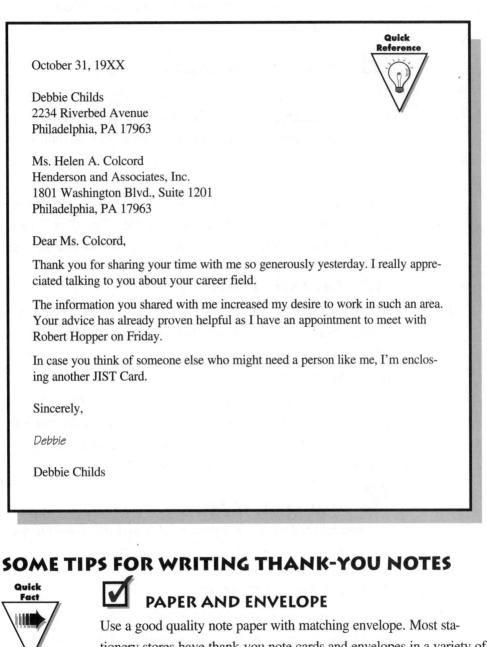

October 31, 19XX

Debbie Childs
2234 Riverbed Avenue
Philadelphia, PA 17963

Ms. Helen A. Colcord
Henderson and Associates, Inc.
1801 Washington Blvd., Suite 1201
Philadelphia, PA 17963

Dear Ms. Colcord,

Thank you for sharing your time with me so generously yesterday. I really appreciated talking to you about your career field.

The information you shared with me increased my desire to work in such an area. Your advice has already proven helpful as I have an appointment to meet with Robert Hopper on Friday.

In case you think of someone else who might need a person like me, I'm enclosing another JIST Card.

Sincerely,

Debbie

Debbie Childs

SOME TIPS FOR WRITING THANK-YOU NOTES

☑ PAPER AND ENVELOPE

Use a good quality note paper with matching envelope. Most stationery stores have thank-you note cards and envelopes in a variety of styles. Select a note that is simple and professional—avoid cute graphics and sayings. A simple "Thank You" on the front will do.

I suggest off-white and buff colors. You also can use simple but excellent quality stationery with matching envelopes, although I prefer the printed cards.

☑ TYPED VERSUS HANDWRITTEN

The tradition with thank-you notes is that they are handwritten. If your handwriting is good, it is perfectly acceptable to write them. If not, they can be typed, but avoid making them appear too formal.

☑ SALUTATION

Unless you already know the person you are thanking, don't use their first name. Write "Dear Ms. Pam Smith," or "Ms. Smith," or "Dear Ms. Smith," rather than the less formal "Dear Pam." Include the date.

☑ THE NOTE ITSELF

Keep it short and friendly. This is not the place to write "The reason you should hire me is . . ." Remember, the note is a thank-you for what *they* did, not a hard-sell pitch for what *you* want. As appropriate, be specific about when you will next contact them. If you plan to meet with them soon, still send a note saying you look forward to the meeting and thanking them for the appointment. And make sure that you include something to remind them of who you are as your name alone may not be enough for them to recollect you.

☑ YOUR SIGNATURE

Use your first and last name. Avoid initials and make your signature legible.

☑ WHEN TO SEND IT

Write and send your note no later than 24 hours after you make your contact. Ideally, you should write it immediately after the contact while the details are still fresh in your mind. Always send a note after an interview, even if things did not go well. It can't hurt.

☑ **ENCLOSE A JIST CARD**

Depending on the situation, a JIST Card is often the ideal enclosure to include with a thank-you note. It's small, soft-sell, and provides your phone number, should the employer wish to reach you. It is both a reminder of you, should any jobs open up, and a tool to pass along to someone else. Make sure your thank-you notes and envelopes are big enough to enclose an unfolded JIST Card.

MORE SAMPLE THANK-YOU NOTES

Here are a few more samples of thank-you notes and letters. They cover a variety of situations and will give you ideas on how to structure your own. Notice that they are all short, friendly, and typically mention that the writer will follow up again in the future—a key element of a successful job search campaign. Also note that several are following up on interviews where there was no specific job opening, yet. As I've mentioned elsewhere in this book, getting interviews before there is a job opening is a very smart thing to do. All of these examples came from David Swanson's book titled *The Resume Solution* and are used with permission.

Quick Reference

April 22, 19XX

Dear Mr. Nelson,

Thanks so much for seeing me while I was in town last week. I appreciate your kindness, the interview, and all the information you gave me.

I will call you once again in a few weeks to see if any openings have developed in your marketing research department's planned expansion.

Appreciatively,

Phil Simons

Answering machine: (633) 299-3634

September 17, 19XX

Mr. Bill Kenner
Sales Manager
WRTV
Rochester, Minnesota 87236

Dear Mr. Kenner:

Thank you very much for the interview and the market information you gave me yesterday. I was most impressed with the city, your station, and with everyone I met.

As you requested, I am enclosing a resume and have requested that my ex-manager call you on Tuesday, the 27th, at 10:00 a.m.

Working at WRTV with you and your team would be both interesting and exciting for me. I look forward to your reply and the possibility of helping you set new records next year.

Sincerely,

Anne Bently
1434 River Drive
Polo, Washington 99656

October 14, 19XX

Dear Bill,

I really appreciate your recommending me to Alan Stevens at Wexler Cadillac. We met yesterday for almost an hour and we're having lunch again on Friday. If this develops into a job offer, as you think it may, I will be most grateful.

Enclosed is a copy of a reference letter by my summer employer. I thought you might find this helpful.

You're a good friend, and I appreciate your thinking of me.

Sincerely,

Dave

July 26, 19XX

Dear Ms. Bailey,

Thank you for the interview for the auditor's job last week.
I appreciate the information you gave me and the opportunity to interview with John Peters. He asked me for a transcript, which I am forwarding today.

Working in my field of finance in a respected firm such as Barry Productions appeals to me greatly.

I appreciate your consideration and look forward to hearing from you.

Sincerely,

Dan Rehling

Quick Reference

May 21, 19XX

Quick Reference

Mrs. Sandra Waller
Yellow Side Stores
778 Northwest Boulevard
Seattle, Washington 99659

Dear Ms. Waller:

Thank you so much for the interview you gave me last Friday for the Retail Management Training Program. I learned a great deal and know now that retailing is my first choice for a career.

I look forward to interviewing with Mr. Daniel and Ms. Sobczak next week. For that meeting, I will bring two copies of my resume and a transcript, as you suggested.

Enclosed is a copy of a reference letter written by my summer employer. I thought you might find it helpful.

Sincerely,

Elizabeth Duncan

March 22, 19XX

Dear Ms. Samson:

Thanks for talking with me by phone today. You made me feel at ease!

I appreciate your granting me an interview appointment and will look forward to meeting you in your office at 10:00 a.m. on Tuesday, March 29.

I will bring my design portfolio with me. Thanks again.

Sincerely,

Bradley Kurtz

Quick Reference

OTHER JOB SEARCH CORRESPONDENCE

Quick Fact

There are a variety of miscellaneous things you can send to people during the course of your job search. Following are some brief comments about some of them.

☑ FOLLOW-UP LETTERS

After an interview, to solve a problem, or to present a proposal, you might wish to send some follow-up correspondence. I have already shown you some examples of letters and notes that were sent following an interview. In some cases, a longer or more detailed letter would be appropriate. The objective here would be either to provide additional information or to present a proposal. The sample letter from Sandra Zaremba in Chapter 9 is an example of a follow-up letter that suggests a specific proposal. In some cases, you could submit a much more comprehensive proposal that would essentially justify your job. If there were already a job opening available, you could submit an outline of what you would do if hired. If there were no available job, you could submit a proposal that would create a job, and state what you would do to make it pay off.

In writing such a proposal, it is essential that you be specific in telling them what you would do and what results these actions would bring. For example, if you felt that you could increase sales, how would you do it and how much might they increase? It is not that unusual for a job to be created as a result of this approach.

☑ ENCLOSURES

In some cases, you may want to include something along with the correspondence, such as a sample of your writing. This can be appropriate, although I advise against sending too much material unless it is requested by the employer. Never send originals of anything unless you are willing to lose it. Assume, in all cases, that what you send will be kept.

☑ POST-IT™: NOTES

You have surely seen and used those little notes that stick to papers, walls, and other things. These can be useful when used to call attention to specific points on attachments, to provide additional details, or simply to indicate who the materials are coming from. However, use one or two of these notes at the most. Avoid making your correspondence look like a patchwork quilt.

☑ TO PEOPLE WHO HELP YOU "NETWORK"

As I mentioned in the thank-you note section, you should consider sending notes or letters to anyone who helps you in your job search. This includes those who simply give you the name of someone else to contact or who spoke with you on the phone. Besides showing good manners, it provides you with an opportunity to do two other things:

1. Give them additional information about you via an enclosed resume and JIST Card (which they can pass along to others)

2. Help to keep your needs in their consciousness

While this list of advantages should look suspiciously like the one I presented in the chapter on cover letters, it's worth repeating here.

Anyone can become part of your network and can help you during your job search. Staying in touch—and giving them tools such as a JIST Card—allows them to help you in ways that are difficult to know in advance.

☑ A LIST OF REFERENCES

Once an employer begins to get serious, they may want to contact your references as part of their final screening process. To make this easier for them, I suggest that you prepare a list of people to contact. This list should include the complete name, title, organization, address, and phone number for each person. You should also include information about how each person knows you. For example, indicate that Mr. Rivera was your immediate supervisor for two years.

Be sure to inform those on your list that they may be contacted and asked to provide references. In some cases, you should take the time to prepare them by sending them information on the types of jobs that you now seek, a current resume, and other details. If there is any question whether they would provide you with a positive reference, discuss this in advance so that you know what they are likely to say about you. If it is not positive, consider dropping them from your list.

☑ LETTERS OF REFERENCE

Many organizations fear lawsuits as the result of giving out negative information regarding an ex-employee. For this reason, it can often be difficult for a caller to get any meaningful information over the phone. This is one reason that I recommend that you request previous employers and other references to write you a letter that you can submit to others if asked to do so. If the letters are positive, the advantages should be clear. Even if the letter is negative, at least you now know that there is a problem with this reference. Depending on the situation, you might contact this previous employer and negotiate what they will tell those who contact them. Of course, you should not volunteer a negative letter of reference.

Quick
Fact

UNSOLICITED LETTERS REQUESTING AN INTERVIEW OR OTHER ASSISTANCE

Once more, I want to discourage you from doing this as a primary technique. Even though many resume books recommend sending out lots of unsolicited letters and resumes, the evidence is overwhelming that this method does not work for most people. The rare exception is if your skills are very much in demand. In most cases, you would be far better off to simply pick up the phone and ask for an interview.

I do think that sending a letter to people with whom you share a common bond—such as alumni or members of a professional group—can be reasonably effective. This is particularly so if you are looking for a job in another city or region and you send a letter asking someone to help you by providing names of contacts. Several of the sample cover letters provide examples of this very technique and it can work, particularly if you follow up by phone.

HOW TO GET A GOOD JOB IN LESS TIME

Introduction

How to Get a Good Job in Less Time

This is the last, but not least, section of this book. It is designed to provide you with an overview of career planning and job seeking skills.

While a resume is a tool to help you get a job, few resume books provide much good advice on job seeking. In fact, many resume books provide bad advice. For example, they will often tell you that you need to send out lots of resumes and get them into the stacks on employers' desks. Then, if your resume and/or cover letter is good enough, they will pick yours out of the pile and ask you in for an interview. This is, in my opinion, an old fashioned concept. It puts you at the mercy of some employer whose mindset is to screen people out. It encourages you to be passive and wait for them to call you. And, worst of all, it assumes that the job search is limited to talking to employers who have a job opening now and excludes all those who do not—but who might soon.

So I think that the traditional advice on resumes and job seeking is (to put it kindly) not good. There are techniques that you can use that are far more effective than the traditional ones. I've been working on this for over 20 years now, and the best techniques are based on common sense. They encourage you to be clear about what you want and then to go out and actively look for it. It does take some nerve, but people who use the techniques that are presented in this section have proven that they do work. They tend to help you find better jobs in less time. And that is what it should be all about, isn't it?

While this chapter is short, it does present the basic job search methods that I have developed and found to be most effective. If you do what I suggest, you can cut the amount of time it takes to find a job by quite a bit.

The material in this chapter is based on a small book I wrote titled *The Quick Job Search*, published by JIST. I have adapted it for use here. If you are planning your career or need to know more about finding a job, I strongly encourage you to learn and do more. A book that I wrote titled *The Very Quick Job Search*, also published by JIST, covers the techniques in this chapter in much greater depth and provides lots of other information as well. It is available through most bookstores and libraries.

And that is the end of this commercial message, other than to wish you well in your career planning and job search now and in the future.

11

SEVEN STEPS FOR GETTING THE JOB YOU WANT

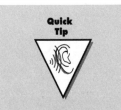

Quick Tip

This is a chapter that you should have jumped to after finishing one of the basic resumes I suggested in Section 1 of this book. I hope that is the case, because a resume's value is only in what it will help you accomplish—which is getting a job. While this is a short chapter, it provides you the basic "how-to" information for getting a good job in less time.

CHANGING JOBS AND CAREERS IS OFTEN HEALTHY

Most of us were told from an early age that each career move must be up, involving more money, responsibility, and prestige. However, research indicates people change careers for many other reasons as well.

In a survey conducted by the Gallup Organization for the National Occupational Information Coordinating Committee, 44 percent of the working adults surveyed expected to be in a different job within three years. This is a very high turnover rate, yet only 41 percent had a definite plan to follow in mapping out their careers.

Logical, ordered careers are found more often with increasing levels of education. For example, while 25 percent of the high school dropouts took the only job available, this was true for only 8 percent of those with at least some college. But you should not assume this means that such occupational stability is healthy. Many adult developmental psychologists believe occupational change is not only normal but may even be necessary for sound adult growth and development. It is common, even normal, to reconsider occupational roles during your twenties, thirties, and forties, even in the absence of economic pressure to do so.

One viewpoint is that a healthy occupational change is one that allows some previously undeveloped aspect of the self to emerge. The change may be as natural as from clerk to supervisor; or as drastic as from professional musician to airline pilot. Although risk is always a factor when change is involved, reasonable risks are healthy and can raise self-esteem.

> **"**The techniques in this chapter are based on years of experience in helping people find good jobs.**"**

NOT JUST ANY JOB WILL DO—OR ANY JOB SEARCH

Whether you are seeking similar work in another setting or changing careers, you need a workable plan to find the right job. The rest of this chapter gives you the information you need to help you find a good job quickly. While the techniques in this chapter are presented briefly, they are based on my years of experience in helping people find good jobs (not just any job) and find jobs in less time. The job-seeking skills that are presented are ones that have been proven to reduce the amount of time required to find a good job.

Of course, complete books have been written on job-seeking techniques and you may want to look into buying one or more of the better ones to obtain additional information. But, short as this chapter is, it *does* present you with the basic skills to find a good job in less time. The techniques work.

SEVEN STEPS FOR A SUCCESSFUL JOB SEARCH

You can't just read about getting a job. The best way to get a job is to go out there and get interviews! And the best way to get interviews is to make a job out of getting a job. That's what this chapter will help you do.

Here are the seven basic steps of a quick and successful job search:

1. **KNOW YOUR SKILLS.**
2. **HAVE A CLEAR JOB OBJECTIVE.**
3. **KNOW WHERE AND HOW TO LOOK.**
4. **SPEND AT LEAST 25 HOURS A WEEK LOOKING.**
5. **GET TWO INTERVIEWS A DAY.**
6. **DO WELL IN INTERVIEWS.**
7. **FOLLOW UP ON ALL CONTACTS.**

STEP 1: KNOW YOUR SKILLS

Quick Reference

An effective career plan requires that you know your skills. Chapter 4 reviews the basics of how to identify your key skills and I won't repeat that material here. If you have not spent time on this issue, I strongly suggest you do so, since it is a very important one for both planning your career and throughout the job search.

A survey of employers found that 90 percent of the people they interviewed could not explain their skills. They could not answer the question, "Why should I hire you?" The consequence of not being able to answer that question, as you might guess, is that your chances of getting a job offer are greatly reduced. Knowing your skills, therefore, offers you a distinct advantage in the job search as well as helps you write a more effective resume.

If you have not done the skills identification activities in Chapter 4— or are not able to identify your key skills—I strongly suggest that you review that chapter before you go on with your search for a job.

STEP 2: HAVE A CLEAR JOB OBJECTIVE

Quick Reference

Having a good job objective is not just an issue for your resume. While I realize how difficult it can be to figure it out, it is essential that you do so. Even if you don't know exactly what you want to do long term, you at least have to decide what you want to do next.

☑ TRADITIONAL JOB-SEARCH METHODS

Help Wanted Ads: Everyone who reads the paper knows about these job openings. So competition for these jobs is fierce. Still, some people do get jobs this way, so go ahead and apply. Just be sure to spend most of your time using more effective methods.

The State Employment Service: Often called the "*Un*employment Office," they offer free job leads and other services in addition to the unemployment compensation checks for the unemployed. Each state has a network of these offices. Only about 5 percent of all job seekers get their jobs here. This service usually knows of only one-tenth (or fewer) of the available jobs in your area. Still, it is worth a weekly visit. If you ask for the same counselor, you might impress the person enough to remember you and refer you to the better openings.

Private Employment Agencies: Recent studies have found that private agencies work reasonably well for those who use them. But there are cautions to consider. For one thing, these agencies work best for entry-level positions or for those with specialized skills that are in demand. Most people who use a private agency find jobs using some other source, which makes the success rate for an agency quite modest. Private agencies also charge a fee to either you (as high as 20 percent of your annual salary!) or the employer. Most of them call employers asking if they have any openings—something you could do yourself. Unless you have skills that are highly in demand, you may do better on your own (and save some money). At the least, you should use a private agency as just one of your techniques and not rely on them too heavily.

Temporary Agencies: These agencies can be a source of quick but temporary jobs. This can bring in some income as well as give you experience in a variety of settings—something that can help you land a full-time job later. More and more employers are also using them as a way to evaluate workers for permanent jobs. So consider using

Chapter 6 reviews the basics for researching a job objective, and other chapters provide you with details and examples of how to write a job objective for your resume. If, after completing that chapter, you are still not sure about what sort of job you want, you should at least settle on something that is reasonably acceptable to you—and that you can convince someone else you are able to do. Later, you should spend more time making a good decision regarding your long-term career plans.

STEP 3: KNOW WHERE AND HOW TO LOOK

Quick Reference

One survey found that 85 percent of all employers don't advertise at all. They hire people they already know, people who find out about the job through word of mouth, or people who simply happen to be at the right place at the right time. This is sometimes just luck, but this book will teach you ways to increase your "luck" in finding job openings.

The chart below shows that fewer than 15 percent of all job seekers get jobs from reading the want ads. Let's take a quick look at want ads and other traditional job search methods.

TRADITIONAL VS. INFORMAL JOB SEARCH METHODS

INFORMAL JOB-SEEKING METHODS 63.4%
- Direct contact with employers
- Networking

WANT ADS 13.9%

AGENCIES 12.2%

OTHER 10.5%

these agencies if it makes sense to do so, but make certain that you continue an active search for a full time job while you do.

Sending Out Resumes: As you have surely gathered from reading this book, I don't think that your resume alone is a particularly effective tool for getting interviews. *One survey found that you would have to mail more than 500 unsolicited resumes to get one interview!* A much better approach is to phone the person who might hire you to set up an interview directly, then send a resume. If you insist on sending out unsolicited resumes, do this on weekends—save your "prime time" for more effective job search techniques.

Filling Out Applications: Most applications are used to screen you out. Larger organizations may require them, but remember that your task is to get an interview, not fill out an application. If you do complete them, make them neat, error free, and do not include anything that could get you screened out. If necessary, leave a problem section blank. It can always be explained after you get an offer.

Personnel Departments: Hardly anyone gets hired by someone in a personnel department. Their job is to screen you and refer the "best" applicants to the person who would actually supervise you. You may need to cooperate with them, but it is often better to go directly to the person who is most likely to supervise you, even if there is no job opening just now. And remember that most organizations don't even have personnel offices!

☑ INFORMAL JOB SEARCH METHODS

Two-thirds of all people get their jobs using informal methods. These jobs are often not advertised and are part of the "hidden" job market. How do you find them?

There are two basic informal job search methods: networking with people you know (I call these "warm contacts") and making direct contacts with an employer. They are both based on the most important job search rule of all:

Quick Reminder

Don't Wait Until the Job Is Open! Most jobs are filled by someone the employer meets before a job is formally "open." So the trick is to meet people who can hire you *before* a job is available! Instead of saying "Do you have any jobs open?" say "I realize you may not have any openings now, but I would still like to talk to you about the possibility of future openings."

> **"***Developing new contacts from people you know is called networking.***"**

Quick Reference

Develop a Network of "Warm Contacts" Among People You Know: One study found that 40 percent of all people found their jobs through a lead provided by a friend, a relative, or an acquaintance. Since you already know these people, I call them Warm Contacts, and they are the most important (though often overlooked) group of people in your job search. If you are organized in asking them to help you, they can provide you with many job leads that you will not find in any other way. They can also lead you to other people they know. Developing new contacts from people you know is called "networking" and it works as follows.

Make Lists of People You Know: Develop a list of anyone you are friendly with, then make a separate list for all your relatives. These two lists alone often add up to 25 to 100 people or more. Then think of other groups of people with whom you have something in common, such as people you used to work with, people who went to your school, people in your social or sports groups, members of your professional association, former employers, and members of your religious group. You may not know many of these people personally, but most will help you if you ask them.

Quick Reference

Contact Them in a Systematic Way: Each of these people is a contact for you. Obviously, some lists and some people on those lists will be more helpful than others, but almost any one of them could help you find a job lead.

Start with your friends and relatives. Call them up and tell them you are looking for a job and need their help. Be as clear as possible about what you are looking for and what skills and qualifications you have. Look at the sample JIST Card and phone script later in this chapter for presentation ideas.

Develop a system for contacting these people. Keep track of who was very helpful and which leads they provided. You will need this information later when sending your thank-you notes. Remember, good manners never hurt and you may need the assistance of these contacts again someday.

Ask Them for Leads: It is possible that they will know of a job opening just right for you. If so, get the details and get right on it! More likely, however, they will not, so here are three questions you should ask.

When you get in touch with these leads, ask them the same questions. For each original contact, you can extend your network of acquain-

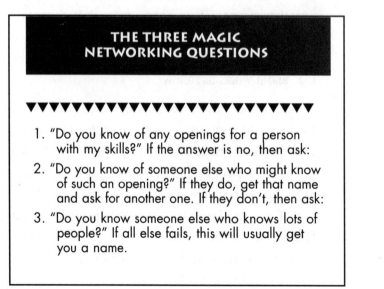

THE THREE MAGIC NETWORKING QUESTIONS

▼▼▼▼▼▼▼▼▼▼▼▼▼▼▼▼▼▼▼▼▼▼▼▼

1. "Do you know of any openings for a person with my skills?" If the answer is no, then ask:

2. "Do you know of someone else who might know of such an opening?" If they do, get that name and ask for another one. If they don't, then ask:

3. "Do you know someone else who knows lots of people?" If all else fails, this will usually get you a name.

● ●

NETWORKING:

ONE PERSON REFERS YOU TO TWO OTHERS

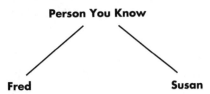

Person You Know

Fred   **Susan**

By the tenth level of contact, you will have been put in touch with over 1,000 people.

● ●

Quick Reference

tances by hundreds of people. Eventually, one of these people will hire you—or refer you to someone who will!

Use "Cold Contacts"—Contact Employers Directly: It takes more courage and perseverance, but contacting an employer directly is a very effective job-search technique. Next to getting leads from people you know, direct contacts with employers account for about 30 percent of how all people find jobs, which makes this technique the second most effective source of job leads.

There are two basic techniques for contacting employers directly:

1. **Call them:** Use the *Yellow Pages* to identify types of organizations that could use a person with your skills. Then call the organizations listed and ask to speak to the person who is most likely to hire you. There is a sample telephone script later in this chapter to give you ideas about what to say.

2. **Drop in:** You can also just walk in and ask to speak to the person in charge. This is particularly effective in small businesses, but it works surprisingly well in larger ones, too. Remember, you want an interview even if there are no openings now. If your timing is inconvenient, ask for a better time to come back for an interview. This being a resume book, you might also think that sending a resume to an employer would also count as a direct contact technique. I don't include it in this category because it is not a direct contact at all, but an indirect one. That is why sending out resumes was mentioned among the traditional— and more passive—techniques covered earlier.

Quick
Fact

☑ WHERE THE JOBS ARE—SMALL BUSINESS!

About two-thirds of all new jobs are now created by small businesses. While the largest corporations have reduced the number of employees,

• •

WHERE PEOPLE WORK

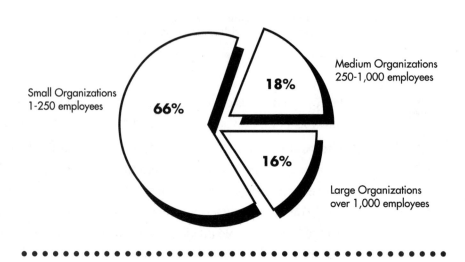

Small Organizations
1-250 employees

66%

18%

Medium Organizations
250-1,000 employees

16%

Large Organizations
over 1,000 employees

• •

small businesses have been creating as many as 80 percent of the new jobs. There are many opportunities to obtain training and advance in smaller organizations, too. Many do not even have a personnel department, so non-traditional job search techniques are particularly effective.

☑ JIST CARDS—AN EFFECTIVE MINI RESUME

JIST Cards are a job search tool that get results. They have been mentioned several times throughout this book and I've included a few samples in other chapters, but they are helpful enough to warrant a full explanation here.

Typed, printed, or even neatly written on a 3-by-5 inch card, a JIST Card contains the essential information most employers want to know. Look at the sample cards that follow:

Sandy Zaremba   Home: (512) 232-7608
Message: (512) 234-7465

Position: General Office/Clerical

Over two years' work experience plus one year of training in office practices. Type 55 wpm, trained in word processing operations, post general ledger, interpersonal skills and get along with most people. Can meet deadlines and handle pressure well.

Willing to work any hours

Organized, honest, reliable, and hardworking

Joyce Hua   Home: (214) 173-1659
Message: (214) 274-1436

Position: Programming/Systems Analyst

Over 10 years combined education and experience in data processing & related fields. Competent in programming in COBOL, FORTRAN, RPG II, BASIC PLUS, and database management on DEC and Prime computers. Extensive PC network applications experience. Have supervised a staff as large as seven on special projects and have a record of meeting deadlines. Operations background in management, sales, and accounting.

Desire career-oriented position, will relocate

Dedicated, self-starter, creative problem solver

Paul Thomas

Home: (301) 681-3922

Message: (301) 681-6966

Position: Research Chemist, Research Management in a small-to-medium-sized company

Ph.D. in Biochemistry plus over 15 years of work experience. Developed and patented various processes having current commercial applications worth many millions of dollars. Experienced with all phases of lab work with an emphasis on chromatography, isolation and purification of organic and biochemical compounds. Specialized in practical pharmaceutical and agricultural applications of chemical research. Have teaching, supervision, and project management experience.

Married over 15 years, stable work history, results and task oriented, ambitious, and willing to relocate

---

Richard Straightarrow

Home: (602) 253-9678

Message: (602) 257-6643

Objective: Electronics installation, maintenance & sales

Four years' work experience plus two year A.A. degree in Electronics Engineering Technology. Managed a $300,000/yr. business while going to school full time, with grades in the top 25%. Familiar with all major electronics diagnostic and repair equipment. Hands-on experience with medical, consumer, communication, and industrial electronics equipment and applications. Good problem-solving and communication skills. Customer service oriented.

Willing to do what it takes to get the job done

Self-motivated, dependable, learn quickly

Juanita Rodriquez

Home: (639) 247-1643

Message: (639) 361-1754

Position: Warehouse Management

Six years' experience plus two years of formal business coursework. Have supervised a staff as large as 16 people and warehousing operations covering over two acres and valued at over $14,000,000. Automated inventory operations resulting in a 30% increase in turnover and estimated annual savings over $250,000. Working knowledge of accounting, computer systems, time & motion studies, and advanced inventory management systems.

Will work any hours

Responsible, hardworking, and can solve problems

Deborah Levy   Home: (213) 432-8064
                                   Message: (213) 888-7365

Position: Hotel Management
Four years' experience in sales, catering, and accounting in a 300-room hotel. Associate's degree in Hotel Management plus one year with the Boileau Culinary Institute. Doubled revenues from meetings and conferences. Increased dining room and bar revenues by 44%. Have been commended for improving staff productivity and courtesy. I approach my work with industry, imagination, and creative problem-solving skills.

Enthusiastic, well-organized, detail-oriented

Jonathan Michael   Home: (614) 788-2434
                                    Message: (614) 355-0068

Objective: Management
Over 7 years of management experience plus a B.S. degree in business. Managed budgets as large as $10 million. Experienced in cost control and reduction, cutting over 20% of overhead while business increased over 30%. Good organizer and problem solver. Excellent communication skills.

Prefer responsible position in a medium to large business

Cope well with deadline pressure, seek challenge, flexible

JIST Cards are an effective job-search tool! Give them to friends and network contacts. Attach one to a resume. Enclose them in your thank-you notes before or after an interview. Leave it with an employer as a business card. Use them in many creative ways. They can be typed or even handwritten, but it is best to have 100 or more printed so you can put lots of them into circulation. Thousands of job seekers have used them and they get results!

Quick Reference

☑ USE A SCRIPT TO MAKE TELEPHONE CONTACTS

Once you have your JIST Card, it is easy to create a telephone contact "script" based on it. Adapt the basic script to call people you know or your *Yellow Pages* leads. Just pick out *Yellow Page* index categories that might be able to utilize a person with your skills. Then ask for the person who is most likely to supervise you and present your phone script.

While it doesn't work all the time, with practice, most people can get one or more interviews in an hour by making these cold calls. Here is a phone script based on another JIST card:

"Hello, my name is Richard Lee. I am interested in a position in hotel management. I have four years' experience in sales, catering, and accounting with a 300-room hotel. I also have an Associate Degree in Hotel Management plus one year with the Bradey Culinary Institute. During my employment, I helped double revenue from meetings and conferences and increase bar revenues by 46 percent. I have good problem-solving skills and am good with people. I am also well-organized, hard working, and detail-oriented. When can I come in for an interview?"

STEP 4: SPEND AT LEAST 25 HOURS A WEEK LOOKING

On average, most job seekers spend about five hours weekly actually looking for work. They are also unemployed an average of three or more months! People who follow my advice spend much more time on their job search each week. They also get jobs in less than half the average time. Time management is the key.

Decide how many hours per week you plan to look for a job. I suggest at least 25 hours per week if you are unemployed and are looking for a full-time job. The most important thing is to decide how many hours you can commit to your job search, and stay with it.

Decide on which days you will look for work. How many hours will you look each day? At what time will you begin and end your job search on each of these days? Look at the sample job search schedule that follows to see how one person planned her time. Create your own schedule on a sheet of paper or, better yet, set up your schedule in advance on a daily planner. You can buy a daily/weekly/monthly planner at many department or stationery stores.

SAMPLE WEEKLY JOB SEARCH SCHEDULE

Here is a simple schedule showing you how one person planned to organize her week into major blocks of time spent on her job search. You should use a similar form for planning your own job search schedule.

Schedule your time each day. This is very important since most job seekers find it hard to stay productive each day. You already know which job search methods are most effective and you should plan on spending more of your time using these methods. The sample daily schedule that follows has been very effective for people who have used it, and will give you ideas for your own schedule.

STEP 5: GET TWO INTERVIEWS A DAY

The average job seeker gets about five interviews a month—fewer than two interviews a week. Yet many job seekers using the job search techniques I suggest find it easy to get two interviews a day! To do this, you must redefine what an interview is.

● ●

SAMPLE DAILY SCHEDULE

7:00 to 8:00	Get up, shower, dress, eat breakfast.
8:00 to 8:15	Organize work space, review schedule for interviews or follow ups, update schedule.
8:15 to 9:00	Review old leads for follow up, develop new leads (want ads, *Yellow Pages*, networking lists, etc.).
9:00 to 10:00	Make phone calls, set up interviews.
10:00 to 10:15	Take a break!
10:15 to 11:00	Make more calls.
11:00 to noon	Make follow-up calls as needed.
noon to 1:00	Lunch break.
1:00 to 5:00	Go on interviews, make cold contacts in the field, research at the library.

● ●

A NEW DEFINITION OF AN INTERVIEW

> *An interview is face-to-face contact with anyone who has the authority to hire or supervise a person with your skills. This person may or may not have a job opening at the time you interview with them.*

Quick Fact

With this definition, it is *much* easier to get interviews. You can now interview with all kinds of potential employers, not just those who have a job opening. Many job seekers use the *Yellow Pages* to get two interviews after just an hour of calling by using the telephone contact script discussed earlier! Others simply drop in on potential employers and ask for an unscheduled interview—and they get them. Not always, of course, but often enough.

Getting two interviews a day equals 10 a week—over 40 a month. That's 800 percent more interviews than the average job seeker gets. Who do you think will get a job offer quicker?

> **"***A study indicates that 40 percent of those who made it to interviews created a bad first impression.***"**

STEP 6: YOU MUST DO WELL IN THE INTERVIEW

Quick Reminder

No matter how you get an interview, once you are there, you will have to create a good impression.

Even if your resume is one of the ten best ever written.

Even if you have the best of credentials.

Even if you really want the job.

Quick Fact

One study indicated that, of those who made it as far as the interview (many others were screened out before then), about 40 percent created a bad first impression, mostly based on their dress and grooming. First impressions *do* count and if you make a bad one, you will never get a chance to recover and your chances of getting a job offer rapidly decrease to about zero.

While there is more to making a good first impression than your dress and grooming, this is fortunately something that you can change readily. So, for this reason, I have created the following rule (and, I point out, this is one of the very few rules you will see in this book):

Quick Reference

FARR'S DRESS AND GROOMING RULE

> *Dress the way you think the boss is most likely to dress—only neater.*

Dress for success! If necessary, get help selecting an interview outfit from someone who dresses well. Pay close attention to your grooming, too. Incidently, written things like correspondence and resumes must be neat and error-free as well, since they also create a first impression.

Quick Fact

THE IMPORTANCE OF ANSWERING PROBLEM QUESTIONS

Many job seekers fail to answer one or more problem questions in their interviews. According to employers, this happens about 80 percent of the time, so this is a *big* problem! If you leave the interview without having answered one or more problem questions, your odds of getting a job offer are greatly decreased.

To help you do better than most, I have put together a list of interview questions that I think will prepare you for most of those that are likely to be asked.

The Ten Most Asked Problem Interview Questions:

1. Why don't you tell me about yourself?
2. Why should I hire you?
3. What are your major strengths?
4. What are your major weaknesses?
5. What sort of pay do you expect to receive?
6. How does your previous experience relate to the jobs we have here?
7. What are your plans for the future?
8. What will your former employer (or references) say about you?
9. Why are you looking for this type of position and why here?
10. Why don't you tell me about your personal situation?

We don't have the space here to give thorough answers to all of these questions and there are potentially hundreds more. But I *will* present you with a technique for answering these and most other interview questions.

Quick Reference

THE THREE-STEP PROCESS FOR ANSWERING INTERVIEW QUESTIONS

STEP 1: UNDERSTAND WHAT IS REALLY BEING ASKED.

Most questions are really asking about your adaptive skills and personality. Are you easy to get along with? Are you a good worker? These skills and traits were covered in Chapter 4 of this book and by now you realize how important they are to employers as well as to you. While they are rarely this blunt, the employer's *real* questions are more along these lines:

Can I depend on you?

Are you easy to get along with?

Are you a good worker?

Do you have the experience and training to do the job
if we hire you?

STEP 2: ANSWER THE QUESTION BRIEFLY, IN A NON-DAMAGING WAY.

Acknowledge the facts, but present them as an advantage, not a disadvantage.

STEP 3: ANSWER THE REAL CONCERN BY PRESENTING YOUR RELATED SKILLS.

- Base your answer on your key skills which you identified in Chapter 4 of this book.
- Give examples to support your skills statements.

For example, an employer might say, "We were looking for someone with more experience in this field. Why should we consider you?" Here is one possible answer: *I'm sure there are people who have more experience, but I do have over six years of work experience including three years of advanced training and hands-on experience using the latest methods and techniques. Because my training is recent, I am open to new ideas and am used to working hard and learning quickly."*

Whatever your situation, learn to use it to your advantage! Use "The Three-Step Process for Answering Interview Questions" to practice your interview responses. Rehearse your answers until they come easily and naturally. It works!

STEP 7: FOLLOW UP ON ALL CONTACTS

Quick Fact

People who follow up with potential employers and with others in their network get jobs faster than those who do not. It is as simple as that. Here are three guidelines to follow to get the best results from the contacts in your network:

1. Send a thank-you note to every person who helps you in your job search.

2. Send the thank-you note within 24 hours after you've spoken to someone.

3. Develop a system to continually follow up on all good contacts.

SEND LOTS OF THANK-YOU NOTES

I've already covered the basics of thank-you notes in Chapter 10. There is no need to review them here other than to emphasize that sending thank-you notes is one of the best things you can do in your job search. Send out lots of them.

USE JOB LEAD CARDS TO ORGANIZE YOUR CONTACTS

If you do as I suggest and make lots of contacts, you soon will begin to forget just who is who (or who gave you which name). For this reason, you need to have a simple system to organize your many contacts. You could use a computer to do this but you can also use a simple 3-by-5 inch card to log essential information about each person in your network. Buy a 3-by-5 inch card file box and tabs for each day of the month. File the cards under the date you want to contact the person, and the rest is easy. I've found that staying in touch with a good contact every other week can pay off. Here's a sample card to give you ideas on creating your own:

Organization: _Mutual Health Insurance_

Contact Person: _Anna Tomey_   **Phone:** _(317) 355-0216_

Source of Lead: _Steve Wiley_

Notes: _4/10-called. Anna on vacation. Call back 4/15._

4/15-Interview on 4/20 at 1:30. 4/20 Anna showed

me around. They use the same computer we used in

school! Friendly people. Sent thank-you note & JIST

card. Call back 5/1-2nd interview on 5/8 at 9 am.

THE QUICK JOB SEARCH REVIEW

To wrap up this chapter, here are a few of its most important points:

• •

☞ Tackle your job search as if it were a job itself.

☞ Get organized and spend at least 25 hours per week actively looking for a job.

☞ Know your skills and have a clear job objective.

☞ Believe in yourself and ask people to help you.

☞ If you want to get a good job quickly, get lots of interviews!

☞ Pay attention to all the details, then be yourself in the interview. Remember that employers are people, too. They will hire someone they feel will do the job well, who will be reliable, and who will fit easily into their work environment.

☞ Be able to answer the ultimate interview question: "Why should I hire you?"

☞ When you want the job, tell the employer why they should hire you. Tell them you want the job and why.

☞ Follow up on all the leads you generate and send thank-you notes.

☞ Keep following up and don't quit!

• •

It's that simple. I wish you well in your job search and your life.

APPENDICES

A

SAMPLE JOB DESCRIPTION FROM THE

OCCUPATIONAL OUTLOOK HANDBOOK

As mentioned in several places in this book, the *Occupational Outlook Handbook* (*OOH*) is an important source of information about many jobs. Updated every two years by the U.S. Department of Labor, it provides helpful descriptions for about 250 jobs. These jobs are the most popular ones in our economy and about 85 percent of all people work in one of them.

I have included here the content from one job listed in the *OOH* as an example. I selected the description for secretaries since I felt that most people would be familiar with this job. As you read the description for secretaries, understand that one or more similar descriptions are in the *OOH* for jobs that will interest you.

The *OOH* descriptions can be very helpful to you in a variety of ways. For example, as you read the description you can circle key skills the job requires. This will help you to know which skills you should emphasize in your resume and in interviews. If you are interviewing for a job, reviewing the description in advance can allow you to do a much better job in the interview.

Another way to use these descriptions is to look up those jobs you have had in the past to identify skills you needed for them. In many cases, those same or similar skills will be needed in the job you want now. You can cite your previous jobs to support your having the skills needed in the new job. For example, you will find that a secretary needs to be well organized, a skill that is required in many other jobs.

As you review the sample description that follows, note that it provides lots of other important information such as salary ranges, education or training required, related jobs, and other details that can help you in making career decisions as well as in looking for a job.

With a few exceptions, the sample description includes all the information found in the *OOH*. While the descriptions don't change much between editions, data on salaries and growth projections are typically several years old before they are published, so look for the most recent edition of the book.

I feel strongly about the value of the *OOH* and encourage you to use it routinely throughout your job search. The book is available in most libraries and a bookstore version, titled *America's Top 300 Jobs*, can also be obtained directly through the publisher via the order form at the back of this book.

SAMPLE OOH JOB DESCRIPTION

SECRETARIES (D.O.T. 201)

NATURE OF THE WORK

Most organizations employ secretaries to perform and coordinate office activities and to ensure that information gets disseminated in a timely fashion to staff and clients. Managers, professionals, and other support staff rely on them to keep administrative operations under control. Their specific duties depend upon their level of responsibility and the type of firm in which they are employed.

Secretaries are responsible for a variety of administrative and clerical duties that are necessary to run and maintain organizations efficiently. They schedule appointments, give information to callers, organize and maintain files, fill out forms, and take dictation. They may also type letters, make travel arrangements, or contact clients. Secretaries also operate office equipment like facsimile machines, photocopiers, and telephones with voice mail capabilities.

In today's automated offices, secretaries increasingly use personal computers to run spreadsheet, word processing, database management, desktop publishing, and graphics programs—tasks previously handled by managers and professionals. Secretaries sometimes work in clusters of three or four so that they can help each other. Because they are relieved from dictation and typing, for example, they can support several members of the professional staff.

Executive secretaries or administrative assistants perform fewer clerical tasks than lower level secretaries. As well as receiving visitors, arranging conference calls, and answering letters, they may handle more complex responsibilities such as doing research, preparing statistical reports, and supervising and training other clerical staff.

In addition to general administrative duties, some secretaries do highly specialized work. Knowledge of technical terminology and procedures is required for these positions. Further specialization in various types of law is common among legal secretaries. They prepare correspondence and legal papers such as summonses, complaints, motions, and subpoenas under the supervision of an attorney. They also may review legal journals and assist in other ways with legal research. Medical secretaries transcribe dictation, prepare correspondence, and assist physicians or medical scientists with reports, speeches, articles,

and conference proceedings. They record simple medical histories, arrange for patients to be hospitalized, or order supplies. They may also need to know insurance rules, billing practices, and be familiar with hospital or laboratory procedures. Other technical secretaries assist engineers or scientists. They may prepare much of the correspondence, maintain the technical library, and gather and edit materials for scientific papers.

WORKING CONDITIONS

Secretaries usually work in offices with other professionals or in schools, hospitals, or doctors' offices. Their jobs often involve sitting for long periods. If they spend a lot of time typing, particularly at a video display terminal, they may encounter problems of eyestrain, stress, and repetitive motion problems such as carpal tunnel syndrome.

Secretaries generally work a standard 40-hour week. In some cities, especially in the Northeast, the scheduled workweek is 37 hours or less.

Office work lends itself to alternative or flexible working arrangements, like telecommuting, and 1 secretary in 6 works part time. In addition, a significant number of secretaries work as temporaries. A few participate in job-sharing arrangements in which two people divide responsibility for a single job.

EMPLOYMENT

Secretaries held 3,576,000 jobs in [the early 1990's], making this one of the largest occupations in the U.S. economy. The following tabulation shows the distribution of employment by secretarial specialty:

Legal secretaries	280,000
Medical secretaries	232,000
All other secretaries	3,064,000

Secretaries are employed in organizations of every description. About one-half of all secretaries are employed in firms providing services, ranging from education and health to legal and business services. Others work for firms that engage in manufacturing, construction, wholesale and retail trade, transportation, and communications. Banks, insurance companies, investment firms, and real estate firms are important employers, as are federal, state, and local government agencies.

TRAINING, OTHER QUALIFICATIONS, AND ADVANCEMENT

High school graduates may qualify for secretarial positions provided they have basic office skills. Today, however, knowledge of word processing, spreadsheet, and database management programs is increasingly important and most employers require it. Secretaries must be proficient in keyboarding and good at spelling, punctuation, grammar, and oral communication. Shorthand is necessary for some positions.

The skills needed for a secretarial job can be acquired in various ways. Formal training, especially for computer skills, may lead to higher paying jobs. Secretarial training ranges from high school vocational education programs that teach office practices, shorthand, and keyboarding skills to 1- to 2-year programs in secretarial science offered by business schools, vocational-technical institutes, and community colleges. Specialized training programs also are available for students planning to become medical or legal secretaries or office automation specialists.

Employers also look for communication and interpersonal skills, since secretaries must be tactful in their dealings with many different people. Discretion, judgment, organizational ability, and initiative are important for higher level secretarial positions. As office automation continues to evolve, retraining and continuing education will remain an integral part of many jobs. Continuing changes in the office environment, for instance, have increased the demand for secretaries who are adaptable and versatile. Secretaries may have to attend classes to learn to operate new office equipment such as word processing equipment, information storage systems, personal computers, or new updated software packages.

The majority of openings for secretaries are filled by people who have not been working. Although some of these entrants have been in school or between jobs, many have been full-time homemakers, and some transfer from another clerical job. The majority of entrants are between 25 and 54 years of age. Many positions are filled by persons who have completed some college coursework.

Testing and certification for entry-level office skills is available through the Office Proficiency Assessment and Certification (OPAC) program offered by Professional Secretaries International (PSI). As secretaries gain experience, they can earn the designation Certified Professional Secretary (CPS) by passing a series of examinations given by the Institute for Certifying Secretaries, a department of PSI. This designation is recognized by a growing number of employers as the mark of excellence for senior-level office professionals. Similarly, those without experience who want to be certified as a legal support professional may be certified as an Accredited Legal Secretary (ALS) by the Certifying Board of the National Association of Legal Secretaries. They also administer an examination to certify a legal secretary with 3 years' experience as a Professional Legal Secretary (PLS).

Advancement for secretaries generally comes about by promotion to a more responsible secretarial position. Qualified secretaries who broaden their knowledge of their company's operations may be promoted to other positions such as senior or executive secretary, clerical supervisor, or office manager.

Secretaries with word processing experience can advance to jobs as word processing trainers, supervisors, or managers within their own firms or in a secretarial or word processing service bureau. They also can get jobs with manufacturers of word processing or computer equipment in positions such as instructor or sales representative.

JOB OUTLOOK

Employment of secretaries is expected to grow about as fast as the average for all occupations through the year 2005 in line with the general growth of the economy. Despite productivity gains made possible by office automation, there will continue to be strong demand for secretaries. Many employers currently complain of a shortage of first-rate secretaries. As a result, well-qualified and experienced secretaries will continue to be in great demand and should find many job opportunities. In addition to job openings resulting from growth in demand for secretaries, an exceptionally large number of job openings will arise due to replacement needs. Every year several hundred thousand secretaries transfer to other occupations or leave the labor force. In this occupation, as in most, replacement needs are the main source of jobs.

Demand for secretaries will rise as the labor force grows and as more workers are employed in offices. The trend toward having secretaries assume more responsibilities traditionally reserved for managers and professionals also will stimulate demand.

Productivity, gained with the use of new office technologies, will moderate employment growth, however. In firms that have invested in electronic typewriters, word processors, or personal computers, secretaries can turn out significantly more work than when they used electric or manual typewriters. New office technologies such as electronic mail, facsimile machines, and voice message systems are used in a growing number of organizations. These and other sophisticated computer software capabilities are expected to be used more widely in the years ahead and may limit demand for secretaries.Widespread use of automated equipment is already changing the workflow in many offices. Administrative duties are being reassigned and the functions of entire departments are being restructured. Large firms are experimenting with different methods of staffing their administrative support operations. In some cases, such traditional secretarial duties as typing or keyboarding, filing, copying, and accounting are being assigned to workers in other units or departments. In some law offices and physicians' offices, paralegals and medical assistants are taking over some tasks formerly done by secretaries. Professionals and managers increasingly do their own word processing rather than submit the work to secretaries and other support staff, as they did previously. In addition, there is a trend in many offices for groups of professionals and managers to "share" secretaries, as opposed to the traditional practice of having one secretary work for only one professional or manager.

Developments in office technology are certain to continue, and they will bring about further changes in the secretary's work environment. However, many of a secretary's job duties are of a personal interactive nature—such as scheduling conferences, receiving clients, and transmitting staff instructions—and hence not easily automated. Because automated equipment cannot substitute for the personal skills that are essential to the job, the need for secretaries will continue to grow.

EARNINGS

The average annual salary for all secretaries is $24,100. Salaries vary a great deal, however, reflecting differences in skill, experience, and level of responsibility, ranging from $20,500 to $32,900.

Salaries in different parts of the country also vary; earnings generally are lowest in southern cities and highest in northern and western cities. In 1990, for example, secretaries averaged $25,400 a year in the Northeast, $23,700 in the Midwest, $25,000 in the West, and $22,000 in the South.

In addition, salaries vary by industry. Salaries of secretaries tend to be highest in transportation, legal services, and public utilities and lowest in retail trade and finance, insurance, and real estate.

The starting salary for inexperienced secretaries in the Federal Government was $15,200 a year in 1991. Secretaries employed by the Federal Government in 1990 averaged about $20,500.

RELATED OCCUPATIONS

A number of other workers type, record information, and process paperwork. Among these are bookkeepers, receptionists, stenographers, personnel clerks, typists, legal assistants, medical assistants, and medical record technicians.

SOURCE OF ADDITIONAL INFORMATION

For career information, contact:

Professional Secretaries International
10502 NW Ambassador Dr.
Kansas City, MO 64195-0404.
(Phone: 1-816-891-6600.)

Persons interested in careers as legal secretaries can request information from:

National Association of Legal Secretaries
(International)
2250 East 73rd St.
Suite 550
Tulsa, OK 74136.

State employment offices can provide information about job openings for secretaries.

B

LIST OF CONTRIBUTORS

The following persons are the contributors of the resumes and cover letters in this book. They are all professional resume writers. All but one are current or former members of The Professional Association of Resume Writers. I acknowledge with appreciation their voluntary submissions.

ALABAMA

Enterprise

Penny J. Rotolo
Laser Pages, Inc.
806 Boll Weevil Cir.
Enterprise, AL 36330
Phone: (205) 347-7468
Fax: (205) 347-7468

ALASKA

Kodiak

Jacqueline K. Herter, CPS
Professional Word Processing
P.O. Box 3629
Kodiak, AK 99615
Phone: (907) 486-6221
Fax: (907) 486-6267

ARIZONA

Phoenix

Bernard Stopfer
Resumes Plus
2855 W. Cactus Rd., #28
Phoenix, AZ 85029
Phone: (602) 789-1200
Fax: (602) 789-6014

Tempe

Fran Holsinger
Career Profiles
1726 E. Southern, Ste. 8
Tempe, AZ 85282
Phone: (602) 413-9383
Fax: (602) 345-9202

CALIFORNIA

Boulder Creek

Elaine Jackson
Sincerely Yours, Business Services
13140 Highway 9
Boulder Creek, CA 95006
Phone: (408) 338-3000
Fax: (408) 338-3666

Fresno

Susan Britton Whitcomb, CPRW
Alpha Omega Services
1255 W. Shaw, #101
Fresno, CA 93711
Phone: (209) 222-7474

Palo Alto

Ted Bache
Kingston-Bache Resumes
3130 Alpine Rd., Ste. 200-B
Portola Valley, CA 94028
Phone: (415) 854-8594

FLORIDA

Tampa

Diane McGoldrick
Business Services of Tampa Bay
10014 N. Dale Mabry Hwy. #101
Tampa, FL 33618
Phone: (813) 968-3131
Fax: (813) 960-9558

ILLINOIS

Flossmoor

Jennie R. Dowden
Jenn's Resume Service
Flossmoor, IL 60422
Phone: (708) 957-5976

Springfield

Laura G. Lichtenstein
**Lasting Impressions
    Resume & Writing
    Service**
Springfield, IL 62701
Phone: (217) 528-5782
Fax: (217) 528-5579

INDIANA

Evansville

Teresa Collins, CPRW
Erica Hanson
Quality Résumé
600 North Weinbach,
    Suite 810
Evansville, IN 47711
Phone: (812) 479-8380
Fax: (812) 473-4892

Indianapolis

Carole Pefley, CPRW
TESS, Inc.
6314 Morenci Trail,
    Suite 200
Indianapolis, IN 46268
Phone: (317) 291-3574
Fax: (317) 291-3640

Gayle Bernstein, CPRW
Typing PLUS
2710 East 62nd Street,
    Suite 1
Indianapolis, IN 46220
Phone: (317) 257-6789
Fax: (317) 479-3103

Lafayette

Alan D. Ferrell
The Wabash Group
1001 Salem Street
Lafayette, IN 47904
Phone: (317) 423-2311

IOWA

Iowa City

Elizabeth J. Axnix, CPRW
**QUALITY WORD
    PROCESSING**
329 East Court Street
Iowa City, IA 52240-4914
Phone: (800) 359-7822
Fax: (319) 354-7822

LOUISIANA

Alexandria

Michael Robertson
**Michael Robertson Resume
    Service**
P.O. Box 5025
Alexandria, LA 71307-5025
Phone: (318) 443-3366

MAINE

Auburn

Rolande L. LaPointe, CPRW
RO-LAN ASSOCIATES, INC.
86 Main Street
Auburn, ME 04210
Phone: (207) 784-1010
Fax: (207) 782-3446

MASSACHUSETTS

Northboro

Steven Green, CPRW
CareerPath
242 Brewer Street
Northboro, MA 01532
Phone: (508) 393-5548

MICHIGAN

Fremont

Patricia L. Nieboer, CPS,
    CPRW
The Office
25 W. Main St. B
Fremont, MI 49412-1135
Phone: (616) 924-6600
Fax: (616) 924-6694

MISSISSIPPI

Oxford

Leo J. Lazarus
**Mid-South Student
    Services**
Oxford, MS 38655
Phone: (601) 234-6077

MISSOURI

St. Louis

John A. Suarez, CPRW
The Impact Group
7935A Clayton Road
St. Louis, MO 63117-1373
Phone: (314) 721-3900
Fax: (314) 721-5805

NEBRASKA

Omaha

Rafael Santiago
FIRST IMPRESSIONS INC.
1257 Golden Gate Drive, Ste. 10
Papillion, NE 68046
Phone: (402) 331-2112
Fax: (402) 733-0200

NEW JERSEY

Marlboro

Beverly Baskin, CPRW
Executive Director
Baskin Business and Career Services
Offices in Marlboro, Princeton, and Woodbridge, NJ
Phone: 1 (800) 300-4079
Fax: 1 (800) 300-5056

West Paterson

Melanie Noonan, CPS
Peripheral Pro
West Paterson, NJ
Business: Little Falls, NJ
Phone: (201) 785-3011
Fax: (201) 785-3071

NEW YORK

Flushing

James Voketaitis
Resume Center of New York
39-15 Main Street, Suite 501
Flushing, NY 11354
Phone: (718) 445-1956
Fax: (718) 445-1291

New York

Margaret Lawson
Consultant
Career & Educational Trends
New York, NY
Phone: (212) 862-4874

Yorktown Heights

Mark D. Berkowitz, N.C.C.C.
Career Development Resources
1312 Walter Rd.
Yorktown Heights, NY 10598
Phone: (914) 962-1548

NORTH CAROLINA

Asheville

Dayna Feist, CPRW
Gatehouse Business Services
265 Charlotte Street
Asheville, NC 28801
Phone: (704) 254-7893
Fax: (704) 245-7894

TENNESSEE

Athens

Adelia Wyner - Owner
Secretarial Office Services
314 N. White Street
Athens, TN 37303
Phone: (615) 745-4513

VIRGINIA

Virginia Beach

Susie Brady
Letter Perfect
291 Independence Blvd., Ste. 442
Virginia Beach, VA 23462
Phone: (804) 473-0432
Fax: (804) 473-0709

WISCONSIN

Milwaukee

David Swanson
Career Seminars
1033 North Mayfair Rd. Ste. 200
Milwaukee, WI 53219
Phone: (414) 259-0265

THE COMPLETE GUIDE FOR OCCUPATIONAL EXPLORATION

By JIST Editorial Staff

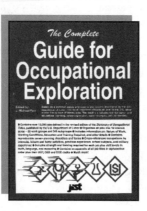

First revision since 1984! Based on the new *Dictionary of Occupational Titles*, *The Complete Guide* contains up-to-date information on today's occupations, many of which have been created or greatly changed by technology. More than 12,000 occupations are organized into: 12 major interests areas, 66 work groups, and 348 subgroups of related jobs.

- **A must book for career counselors, professionals, and school personnel**
- **The only book of its kind with up-to-date information**
- **One of the three major reference books used by job placement counselors**
- **Includes an alphabetical appendix listing almost 30,000 jobs.**

Career Reference
8-1/2 x 22, Paper, 936 pp.
ISBN 1-56370-052-2 • $34.95
8-1/2 x 22, Hardback, 936 pp.
ISBN 1-56370-100-6 • $44.95

OCCUPATIONAL OUTLOOK HANDBOOK, 1998-1999 Edition

By the U.S. Department of Labor

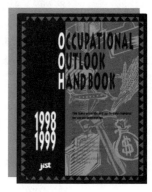

The best-selling job information book of all time!

The best source of information on growth projections salaries, education and training required, the nature of work—and more—for the jobs that 85 percent of Americans hold.

- **JIST's best-selling title**
- **A highly successful book for more than 50 years**
- **Updated every two years—an incredible resource!**
- **Explains education and training needed for every job**
- **Valuable salary information**

COMING IN SPRING OF 1998

Career Reference
8-1/2 x 22, Paper, 505 pp.
ISBN 1-56370-464-1 • $16.95
8-1/2 x 22, Hardback, 936 pp.
ISBN 1-56370-475-7 • $24.95

THE VERY QUICK JOB SEARCH,

2nd Edition

Get a Better Job in Half the Time!

By J. Michael Farr

"I gave a copy of this to my daughter, and she got a job. It lays everything out, exactly what you need to do. My daughter said, 'It's the best thing since sliced bread!' "
—Dr. Pat Schwallie-Giddis, Assistant Executive Director, American Vocational Association

How effective is the advice presented by Mike Farr, one of the founders of the self-directed job search movement, in this classic book? In a demonstration program in a city with an unemployment rate over 24 percent, 96 percent of the job seekers found jobs in an average of 2.4 weeks using these techniques!

- ■ **Proven, effective advice for students, job changers, job seekers, employers, educators, and counselors**
- ■ **Author's career books have sold more than 1.5 million copies**
- ■ **The latest information on market trends and results-oriented job search techniques**
- ■ **Includes a special annotated bibliography listing many additional resources**
- ■ **Author is a popular guest on radio talk shows**

Careers/Job Search

7.5 x 9.5, Paper, 501 pp.

1-56370-181-2 • $14.95

THE QUICK INTERVIEW & SALARY NEGOTIATION BOOK

Dramatically Improve Your Interviewing Skills in Just a Few Hours!

By J. Michael Farr

"In short punchy style, this book lives up to its claim that it will 'dramatically improve your interviewing skills in just a few hours.'"
—Orange County Register

This book could literally be worth thousands of dollars in salary increases! America's leading author of job search books shares simple, fast, effective techniques for improving interviewing skills, handling unusual and difficult interview situations, negotiating salaries and pay increases, and much more.

- ■ **Great advice for students, job changers, displaced professionals, and others**
- ■ **Graphic icons make information immediate and easy to follow**
- ■ **Includes average earnings information for hundreds of jobs**
- ■ **Tips on job seeking, resumes, and preparing for interviews**
- ■ **Author's books have sold more than 1.5 million copies**
- ■ **Author is a popular guest on radio talk-shows**

Careers

7.5 x 9.5, Paper, 379 pp.

1-56370-162-6 • $12.95

GALLERY OF BEST RESUMES

A Collection of Quality Resumes by Professional Resume Writers

By David F. Noble, Ph.D.

A one-of-a-kind "idea book" of exceptional resumes for all job seekers

"This book is superior in both its content and presentation. In my opinion, it is a highly valuable source for direction, instruction, and reference for any level or profession of employment seeker."
—Barbara A. Aversalo, CEO, Business Assistance Associate

" ... an impressive survey for any who wants a comprehensive volume."
—Midwest Book Review

Editor and business communications professor David Noble invited members of the Professional Association of Resume Writers to submit their best designs for review. This book is the result—a "best of the best" collection of 200 top resumes, plus invaluable resume writing and job search tips from the experts.

- ■ **Perfect idea-starter for all job seekers, regardless of age or employment experience**
- ■ **Includes selection of resumes printed on special paper to enhance eye appeal**
- ■ **A wide selection of resumes in many occupational categories, plus expert writing and design tips**
- ■ **Also includes 25 top cover letters**

Resumes

8.5 x 11, Paper, 400 pp.

1-56370-144-8 • $16.95

GALLERY OF BEST RESUMES FOR TWO-YEAR DEGREE GRADUATES

A Special Collection of Quality Resumes by Professional Resume Writers

By David F. Noble, Ph.D.

The finest resume book for two-year degree graduates

More students are enrolled in two-year degree programs than in traditional four-year degree programs. This unique resume guide helps two-year degree graduates present their special training in an effective and professional manner.

- ■ **Great advice on resume writing, layout, and design**
- ■ **Contains more than 200 sample resumes written by professional resume writers—the best by the best!**
- ■ **Bookstore seminars and signings**
- ■ **There are more than 5.5 million sutdents enrolled in two-year degree programs in public and private colleges**

Resumes

8.5 x 11, Paper, 392 pp.

1-56370-239-8 • $14.95

JIST Customer Information

JIST specializes in publishing the very best results-oriented career and self-directed job search methods. For sixteen years we have been a leading publisher in career assessment devices, books, videos, and software. We continue to strive to make our materials the best there are so that people can stay abreast of what's happening in the labor market, and so they can clarify and articulate their skills and experiences for themselves as well as for prospective employers. **Our products are widely available through your local bookstores, wholesalers, and distributors.**

The World Wide Web

For more occupational or book information, get on-line and see our web site at **http://www.jist.com/jist**. Advance information about new products, services, and training events is continually updated.

Quantity Discounts Available!

Quantity discounts are available for businesses, schools and other organizations.

The JIST Guarantee

We want you to be happy with everything you buy from JIST. If you aren't satisfied with a product, return it to us within 30 days of purchase along with the reason for the return. Please include a copy of the packing list or invoice to guarantee quick credit to your order.

How to Order

For your convenience, the last page of this book contains an order form.

24-Hour Consumer Order Line:
Call toll free 1-800-547-8872

Please have your credit card (VISA, MC or AMEX) information ready!

Mail: Mail your order to the address listed on the order form:

JIST Works, 720 North Park Avenue Indianapolis, IN 46202-3490

Fax: Toll free 1-800-547-8329

JIST Order Form

Please copy this form if you need more lines for your order.

Purchase Order #: _____

Billing Information

Organization Name: _____
Accounting Contact: _____
Street Address: _____
_____
_____
City, State, Zip: _____
Phone Number: ( ) _____

Phone: 1-800-547-8872
1-800-JIST-USA
Fax: 1-800-547-8329

Shipping Information (if different from above)

Organization Name: _____
Contact: _____
Street Address: (we canNOT ship to P.O. boxes) _____
_____
_____
City, State, Zip: _____
Phone Number: ( ) _____

Credit Card Purchases: VISA_____ MC_____ AMEX_____
Card Number: _____
Exp. date: _____
Name as on card: _____
Signature: _____

Quantity	Product Code	Product Title	Unit Price	Total
			Subtotal	
			+Sales Tax *Indiana residents add 5% sales tax.*	
			+Shipping / Handling *Add $3.00 for the first item and an additional $.50 for each item thereafter.*	
			TOTAL	

JIST Works, Inc.
720 North Park Avenue
Indianapolis, IN 46202

JIST thanks you for your order!